Tasmania

Portrait of an Island

Best wishes
2007

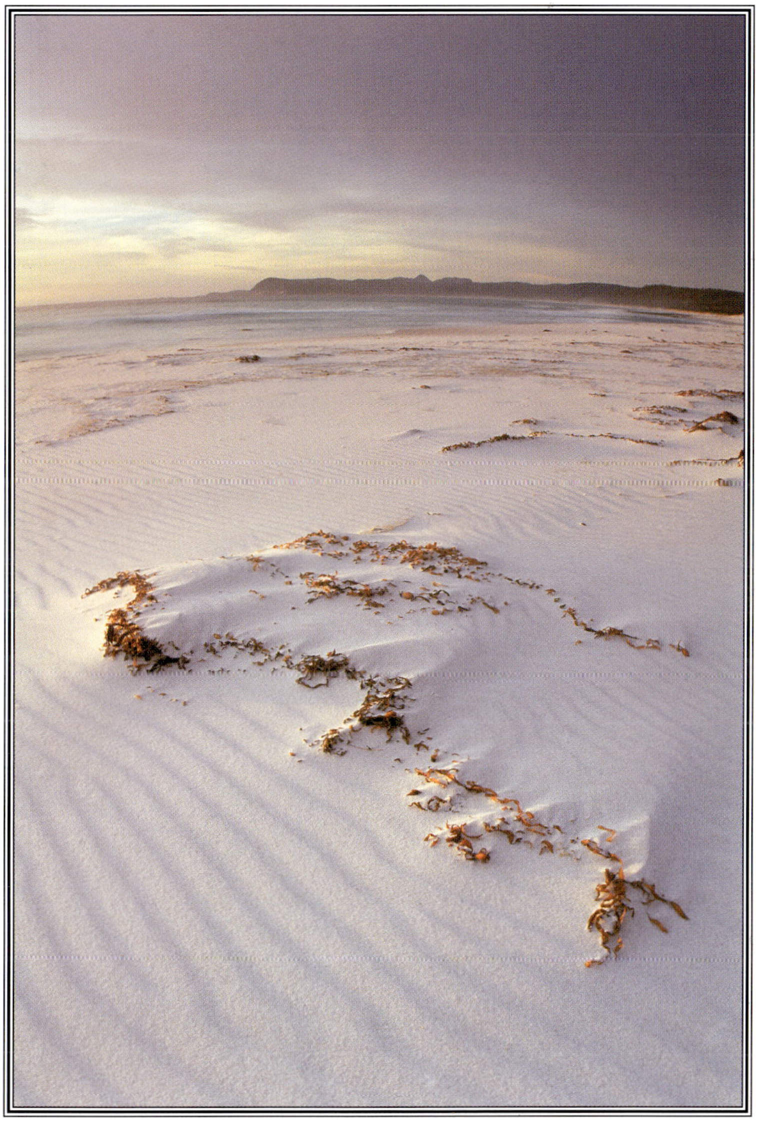

Front cover photograph:
Morning waves washing over seashells on Seven Mile Beach
Previous page:
Seaweed shapes in the dunes of Friendly Beaches

Published by
Ian Wallace
Alinda Images
PO Box 437
Rosny Park
Tasmania
Australia 7018
Phone: 0438 694 947
Email: ian@alindaimages.com.au
Web: www.alindaimages.com.au

National Library of Australia
Cataloguing-in-Publication data:
Wallace, Ian 1972- .
Tasmania : Portrait of an Island.

Includes index.
ISBN 0 9752454 0 6.

1. Landscape photography - Tasmania. 2. Tasmania - Pictorial works. I. Title.

919.46

Printed in China by Everbest Printing Co. Ltd.

Acknowledgements

I feel privileged to be able to use my skills and equipment to take photographs in some of the most peaceful and beautiful places on earth. Although the 'getting there' can often be challenging, labour intensive and sometimes dangerous, the serenity of just sitting and watching the light dancing over a spectacular landscape is always a pleasure. Perhaps these captured moments of time can never be repeated, but they can be appreciated and enjoyed forever in the form of a photograph.

I am indebted to many people over the years, who in many ways, have helped me pursue and achieve my goals both in photography and in life. My passion for photography was forged during my many years membership of the 'Knox Photographic Society' in Victoria, Australia. I would also like to acknowledge and thank my family, Jean, David, Barbara and Billy for their limitless support and assistance over the years. For her endless help and encouragement with this book, my career as a photographer and just about everything else in my life I must thank my partner Nina. After all, it was her idea to move to Australia's Island State, Tasmania. I would also like to thank the thousands of people I have met and talked to at the Salamanca Market in Hobart and the 'Ian Wallace Gallery' in Richmond, who have all contributed to my success in Tasmania. Finally and on a personal level, I thank Loïc Le Guilly and Doug Thost for their friendship.

Well - for all those people, my friends and family - here is my first book;
Tasmania - Portrait of an Island.

I hope you enjoy these photographs as much as I enjoyed taking them.

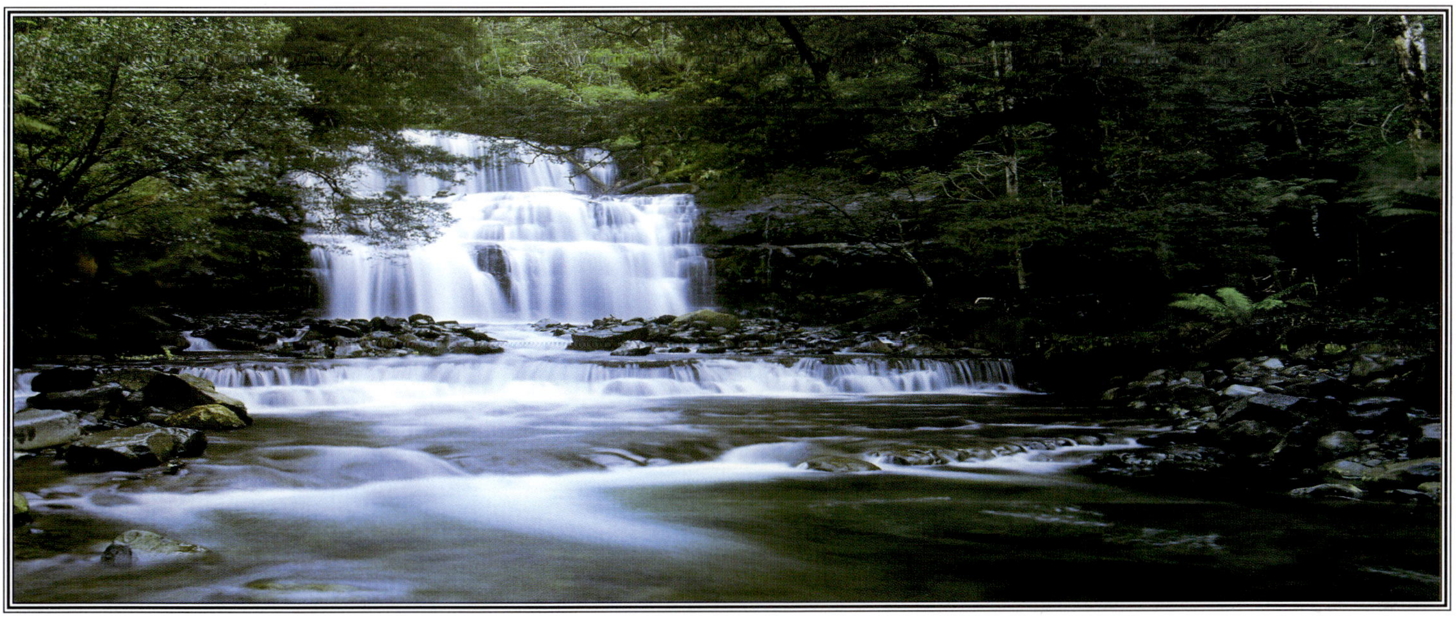

The lower cascade of Liffey Falls

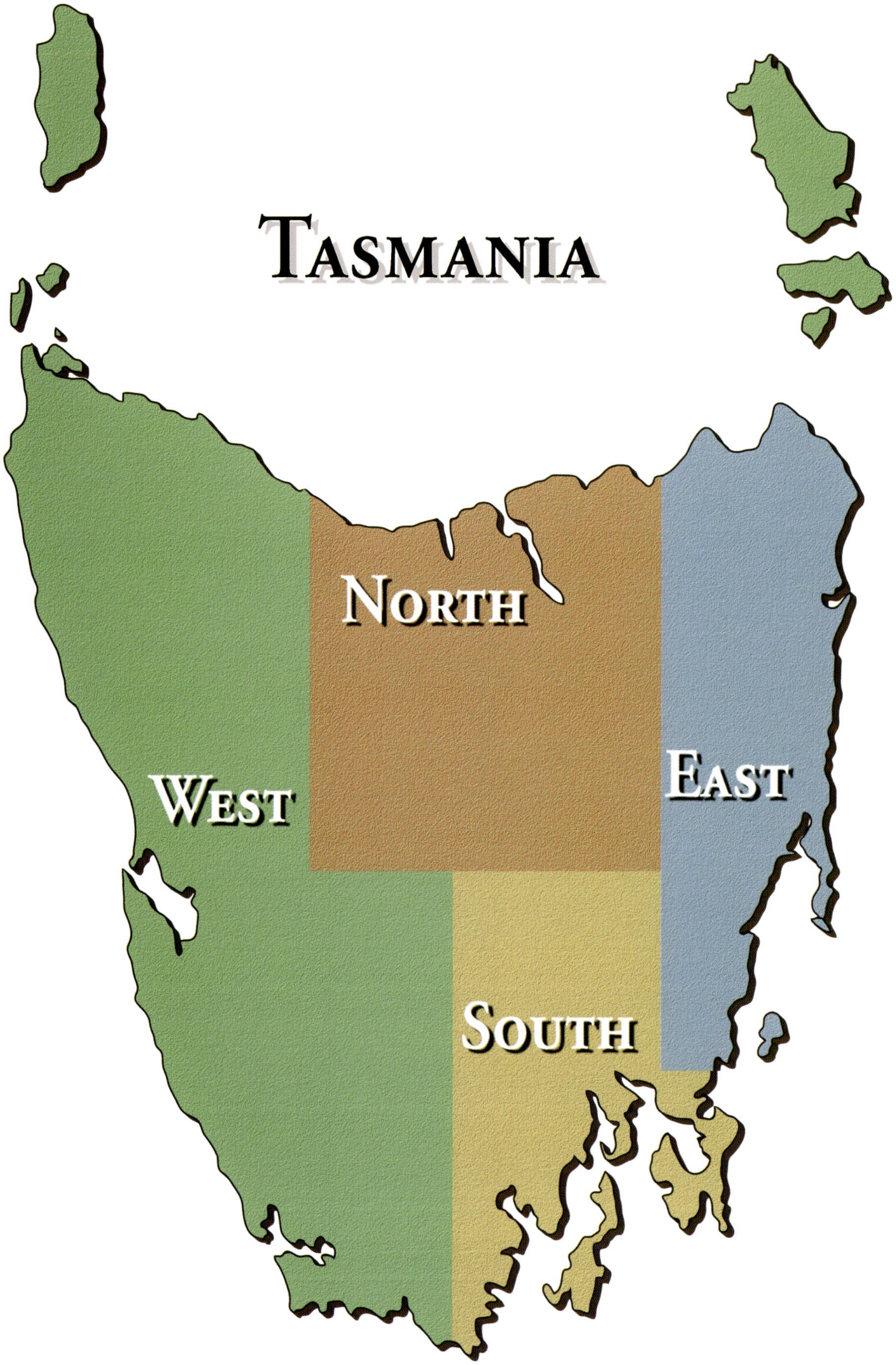
Tasmania
North
West
East
South

Contents

The North .... Page 2

Cataract Gorge Reserve
Cuckoo Falls
The Devils Gullet
Mt. Barrow
The Great Lake
Liffey Falls
The Midlands

The South........................... Page 14

Hobart
Mt. Wellington
Seven Mile Beach
Richmond
Port Arthur
The Tasman Peninsula
Cockle Creek

The East .... Page 34

Spiky Beach
Friendly Beaches
The Freycinet Peninsula
Binalong Bay

The West .... Page 52

Mt. Field National Park
The Tarn Shelf
Mt. Wedge
Hogarth Falls
Ocean Beach
Montezuma Falls
Cradle Mountain
Cox Bight
Melaleuca

Tasmania's North

Extending from the northern ports of Launceston, Devonport and Burnie to the historic townships of Ross, Campbell Town and Oatlands, Tasmania's north is an expanse of green rolling fields and lush forests shadowed by huge mountain ranges within which lay countless freshwater highland lakes.

Cloudless blue skies in summer, crisp frosts and snow in winter, weather patterns in the north can be as varied as its diverse landscapes, resulting in a region that offers plenty for visitors during all seasons.

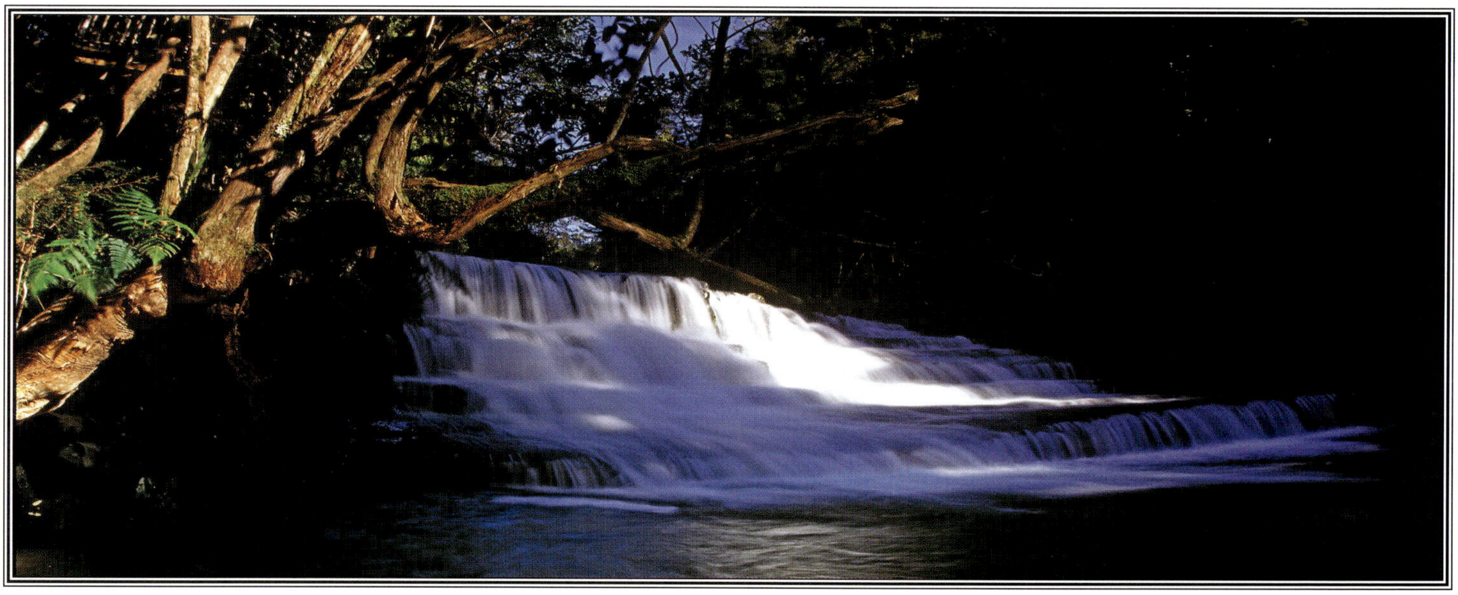

Early morning light on the first cascade of Liffey Falls

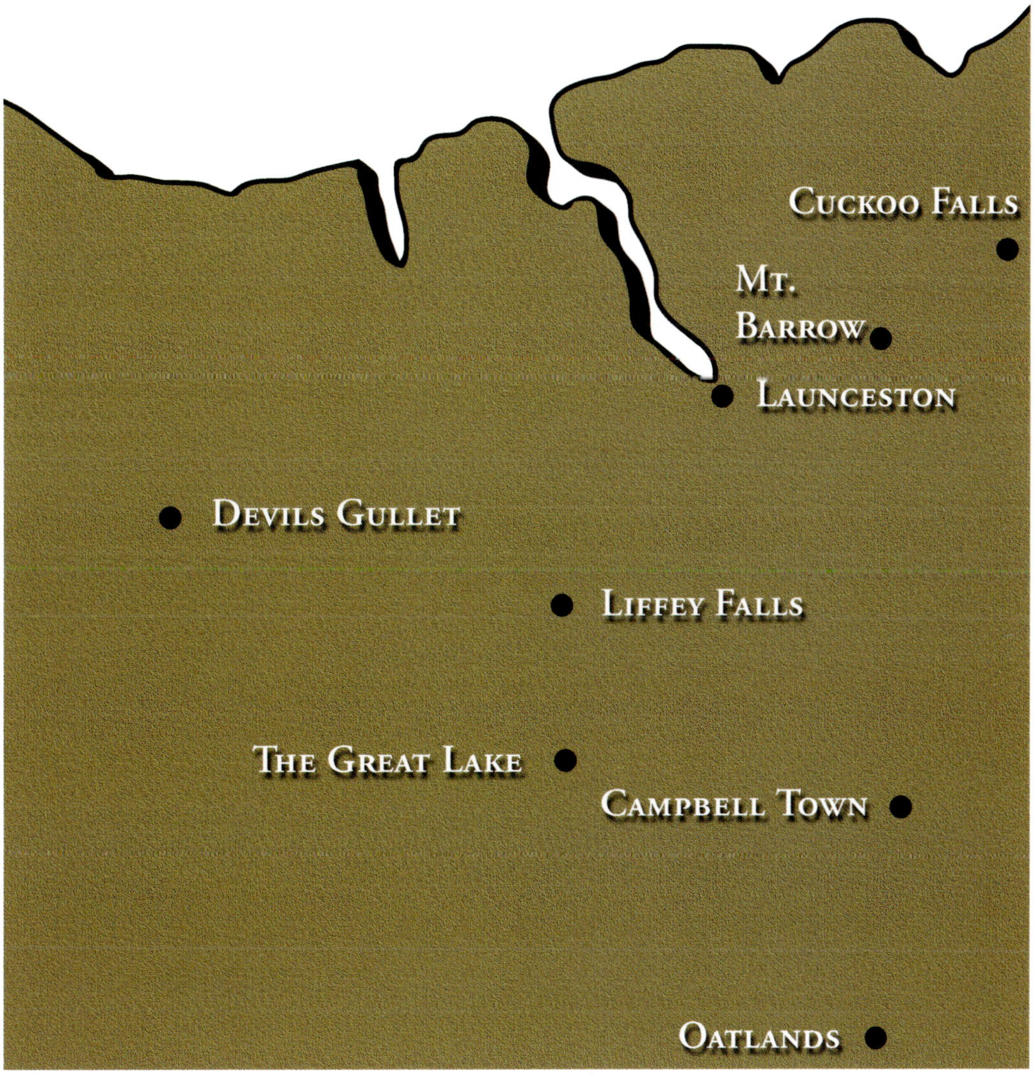
Cuckoo Falls
Mt. Barrow
Launceston
Devils Gullet
Liffey Falls
The Great Lake
Campbell Town
Oatlands

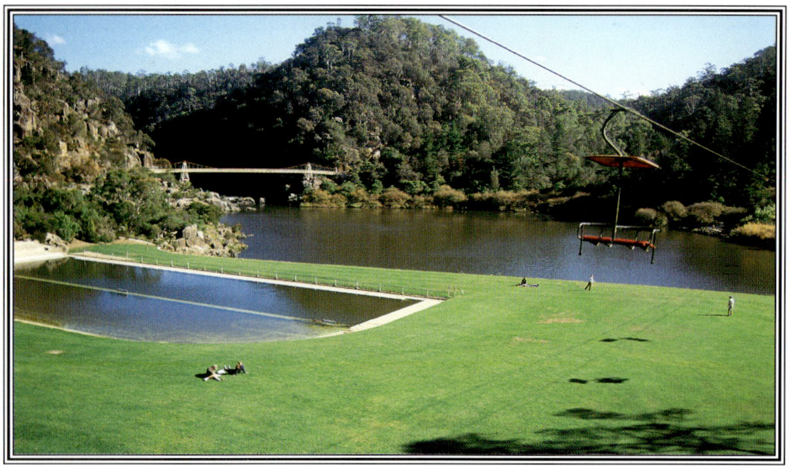

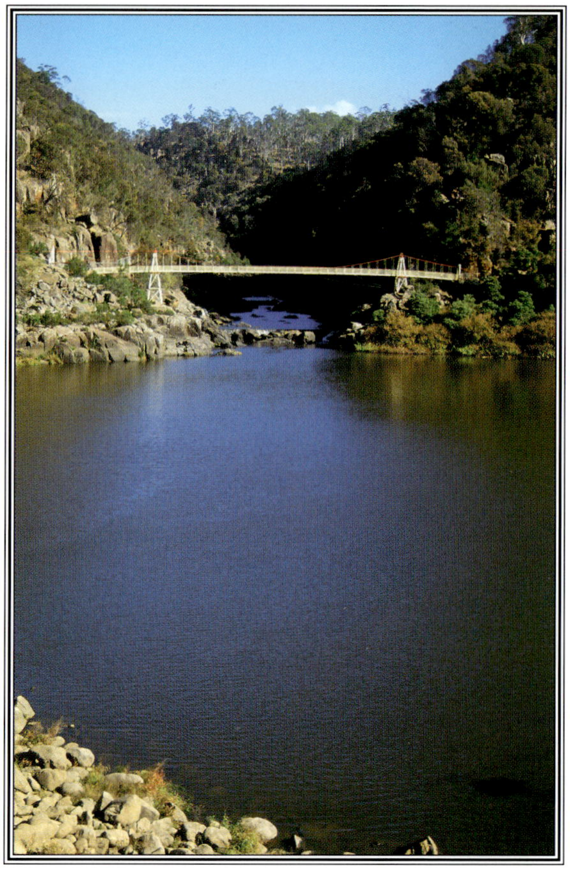

Cataract Gorge Reserve

Situated within Launceston is the Cataract Gorge Reserve. Visitors can enjoy the peace and tranquillity of a well-maintained expanse of public gardens.

Gaze down at spectacular gardens from the chair lift, explore the Alexandra Suspension Bridge, or simply follow the twisting tracks along rocky shelves, out to the Tamar river.

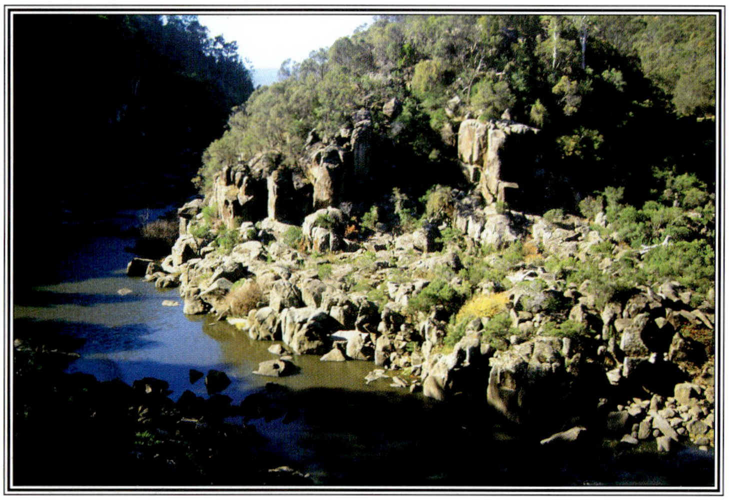

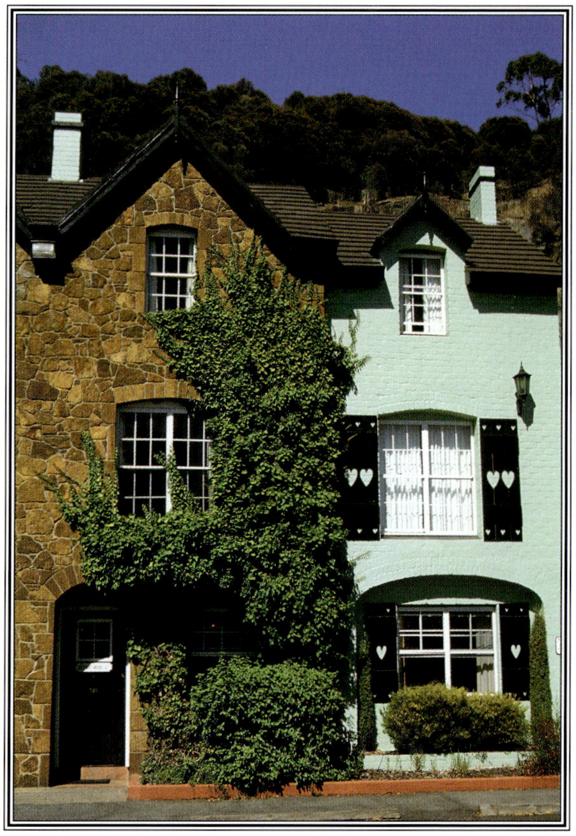

***Top**: Cataract Gorge Reserve*
***Bottom left**: The twisting gorge*
***Bottom right**: Ivy covered cottages at Penny Royal*

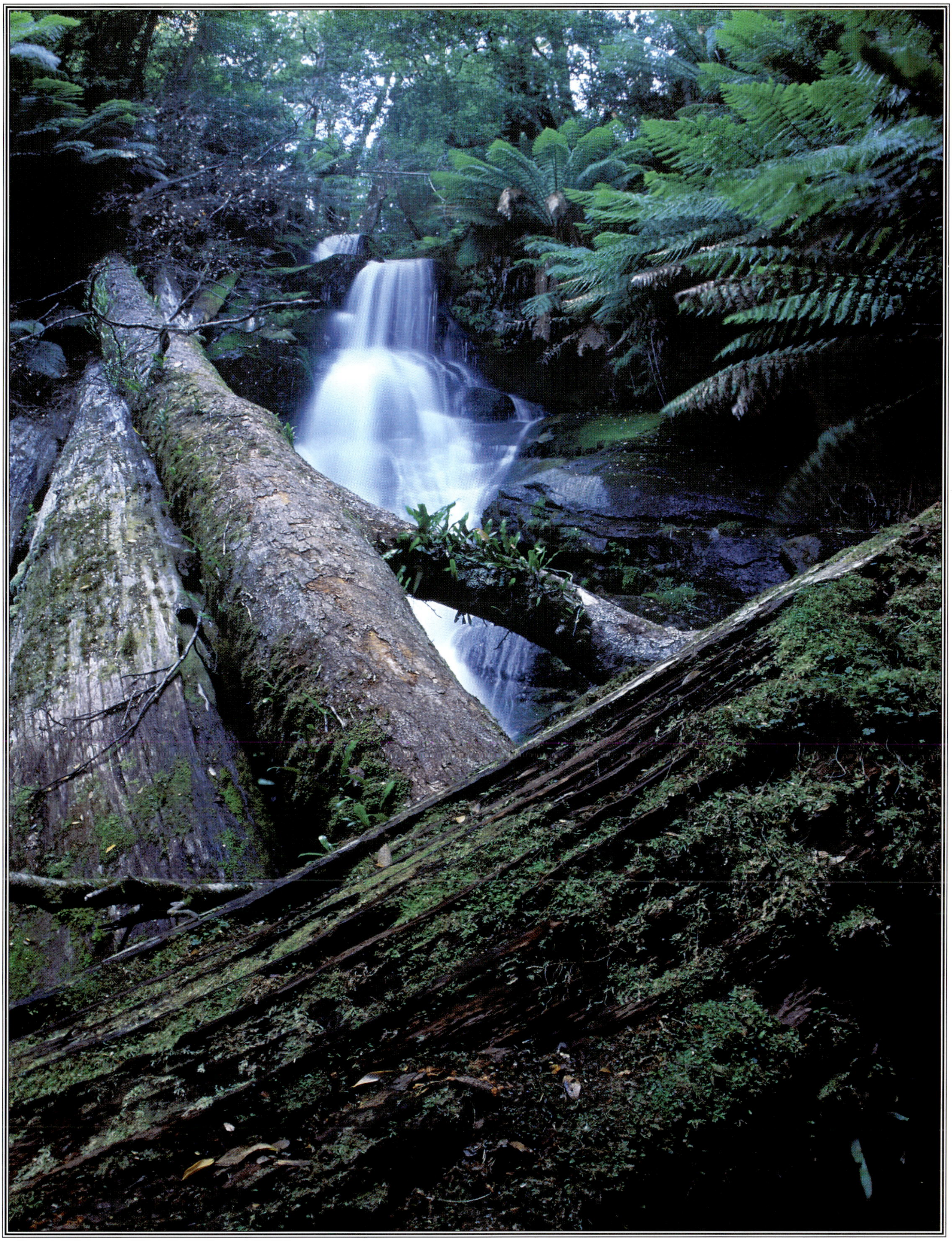

Fallen trees at Cuckoo Falls

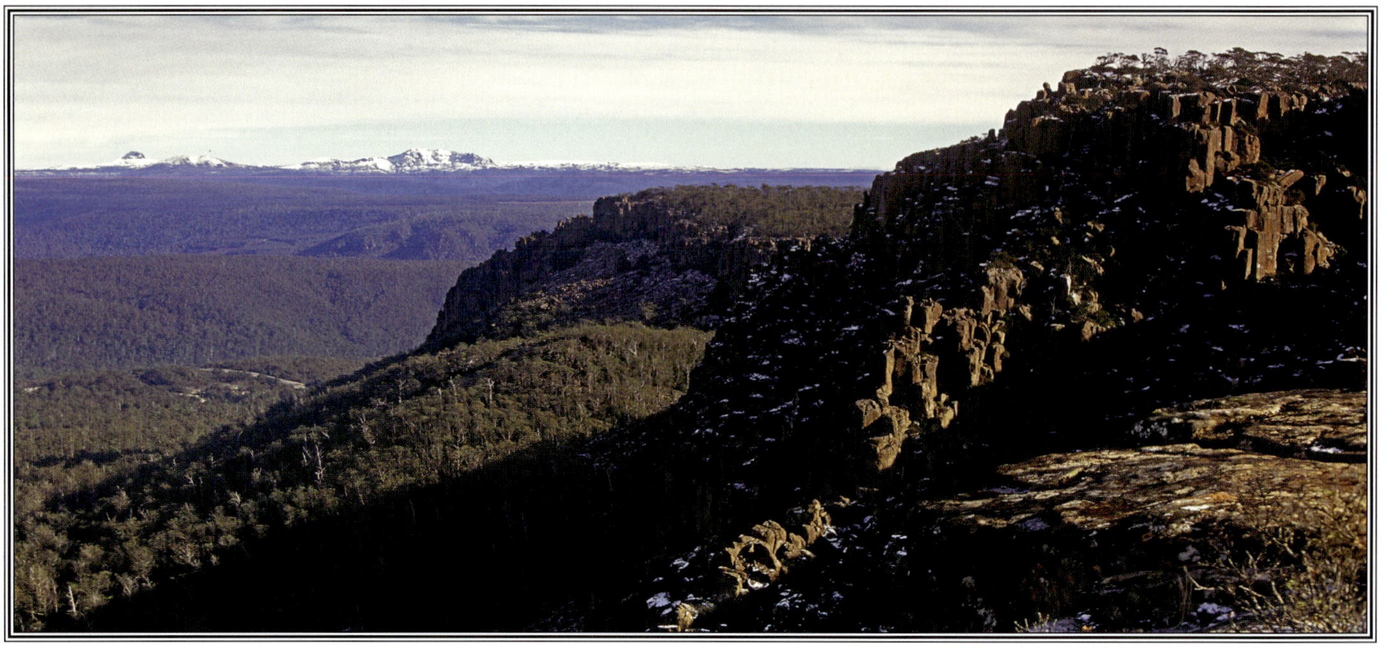

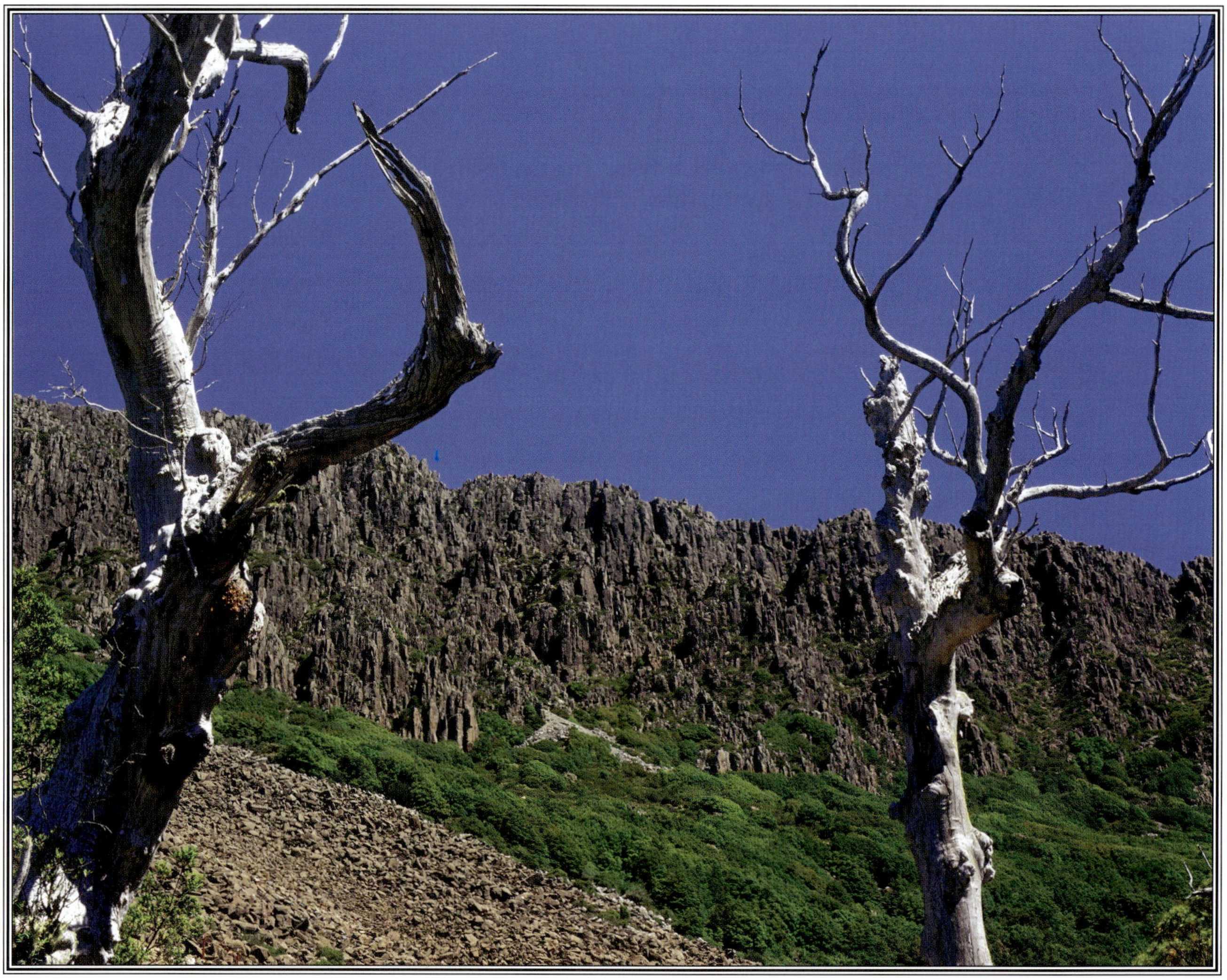

Top: *The Devils Gullet lookout - Great Western Tiers*
Bottom: *The dolerite cliffs of Mount Barrow*

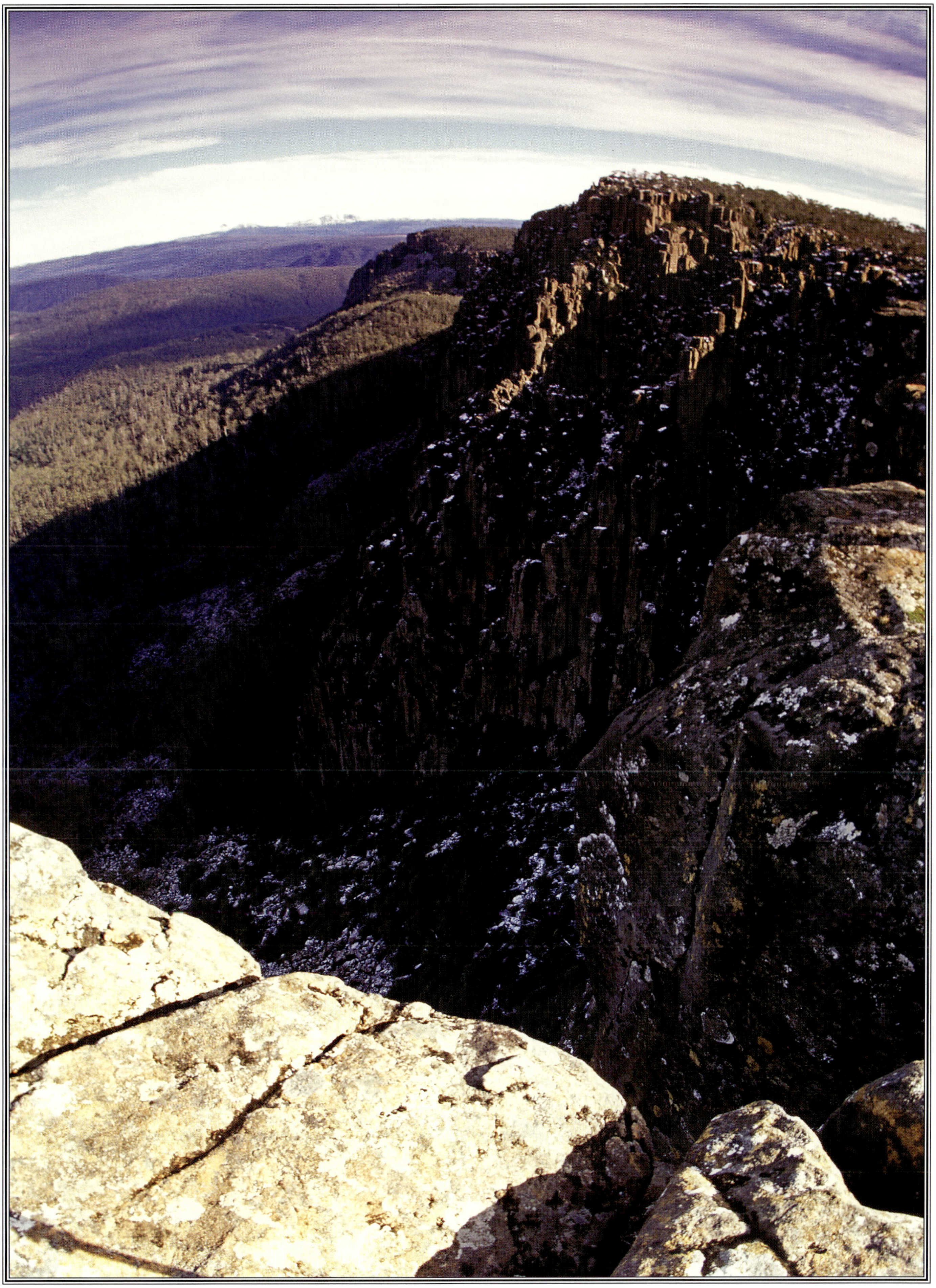

The Devils Gullet - Great Western Tiers

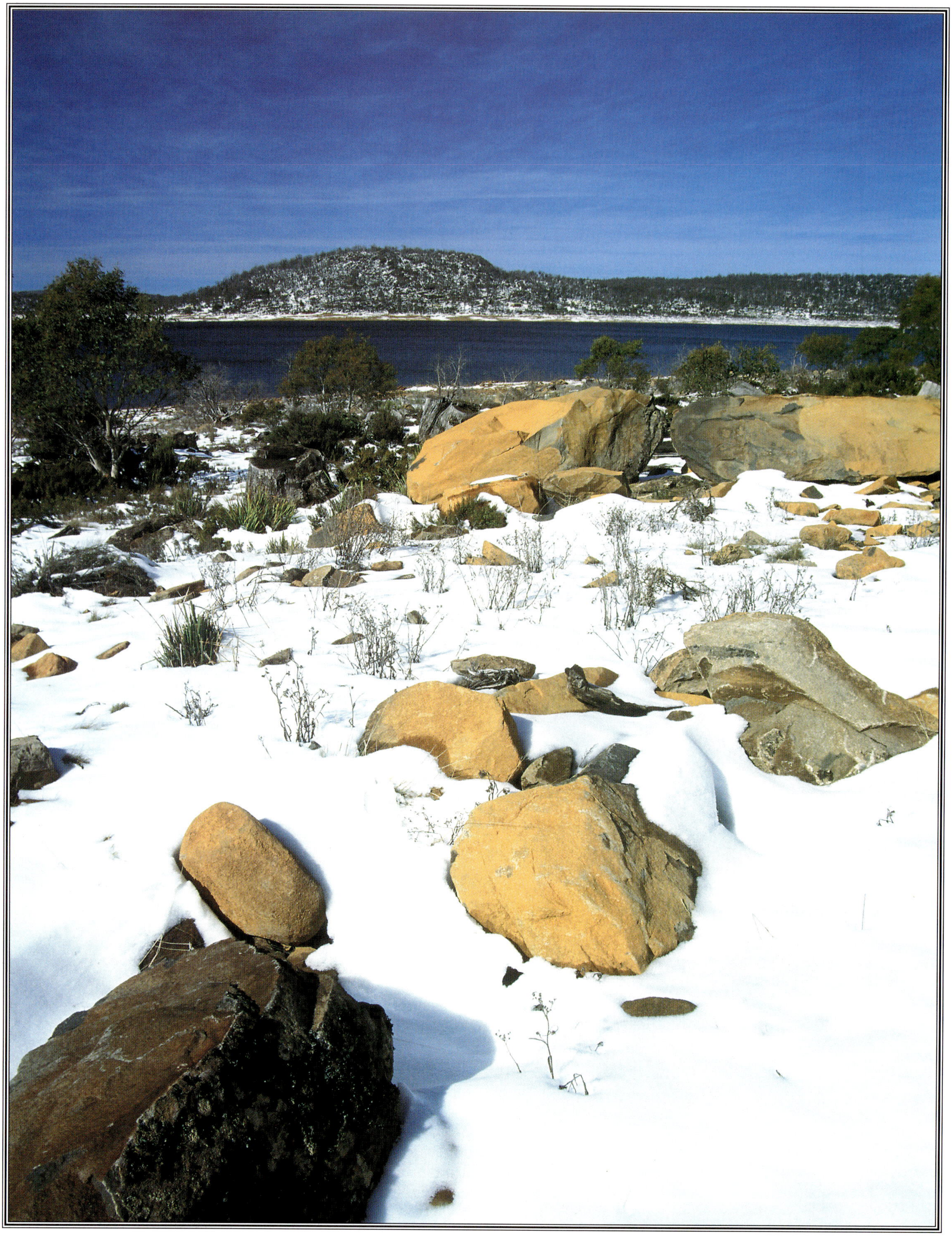

Fresh snow on the shore of The Great Lake

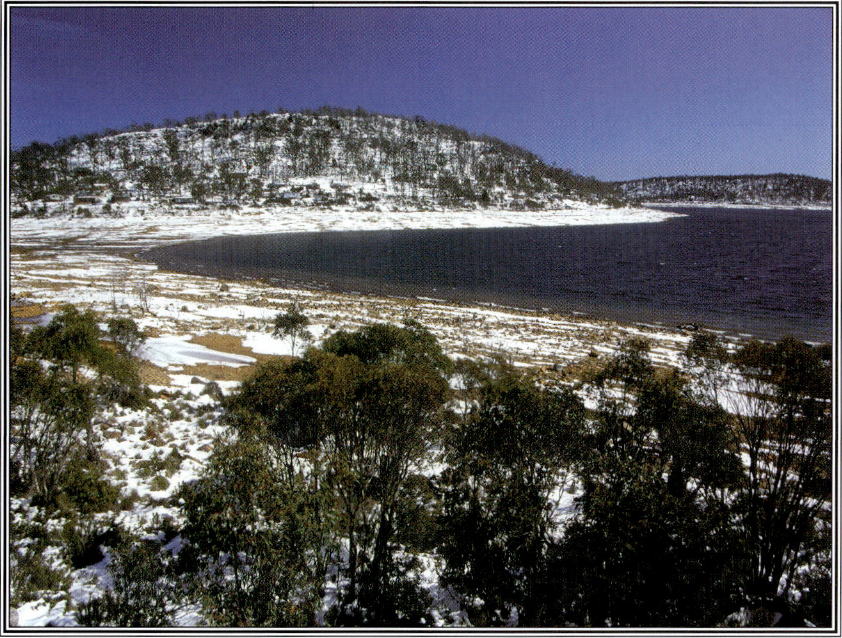

The Great Lake

South of the Great Western Tiers is Tasmania's lake region. The largest of these lakes is aptly named 'The Great Lake'.
During crisp winter days blankets of pure white snow contrast the dark waters of this magnificent expanse of fresh water.

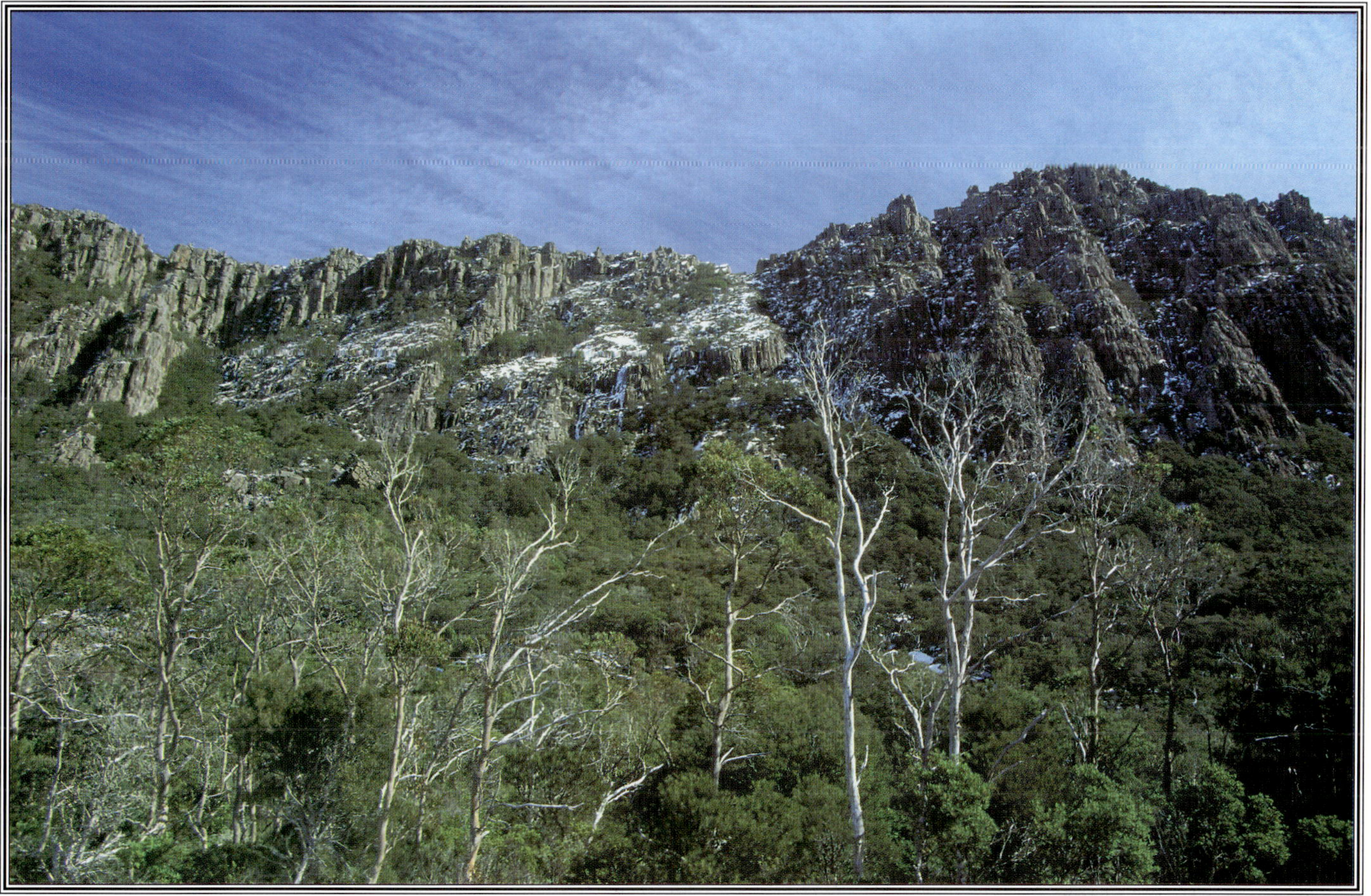

***Top**: A dusting of snow at The Great Lake*
***Bottom right**: The walls of the Great Western Tiers*

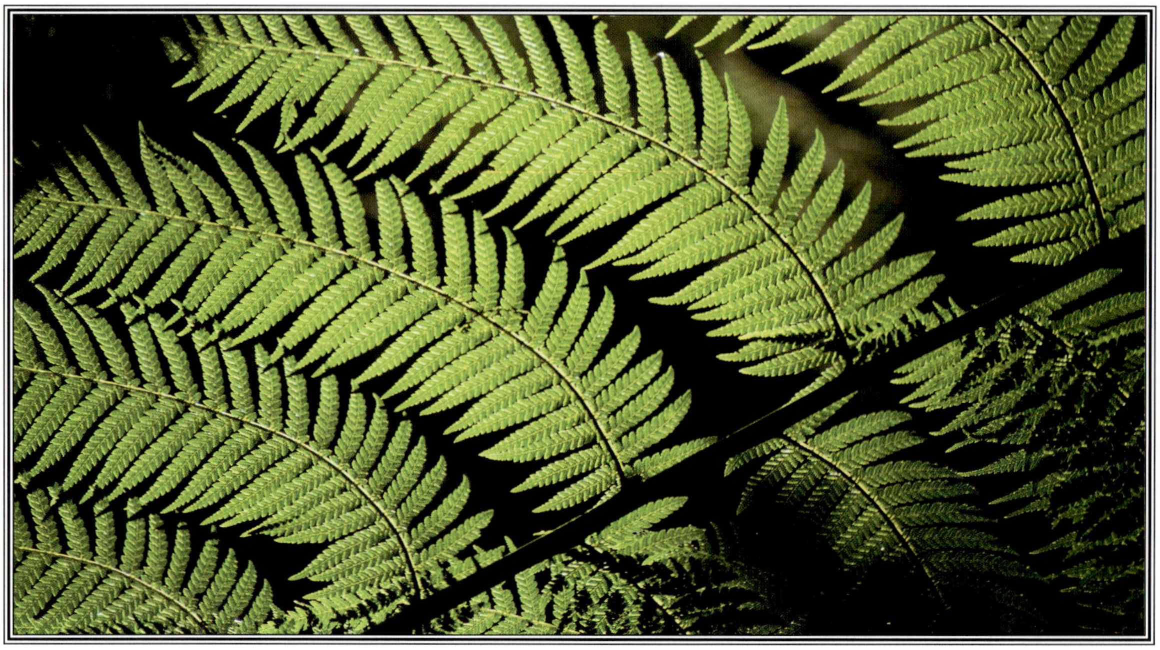

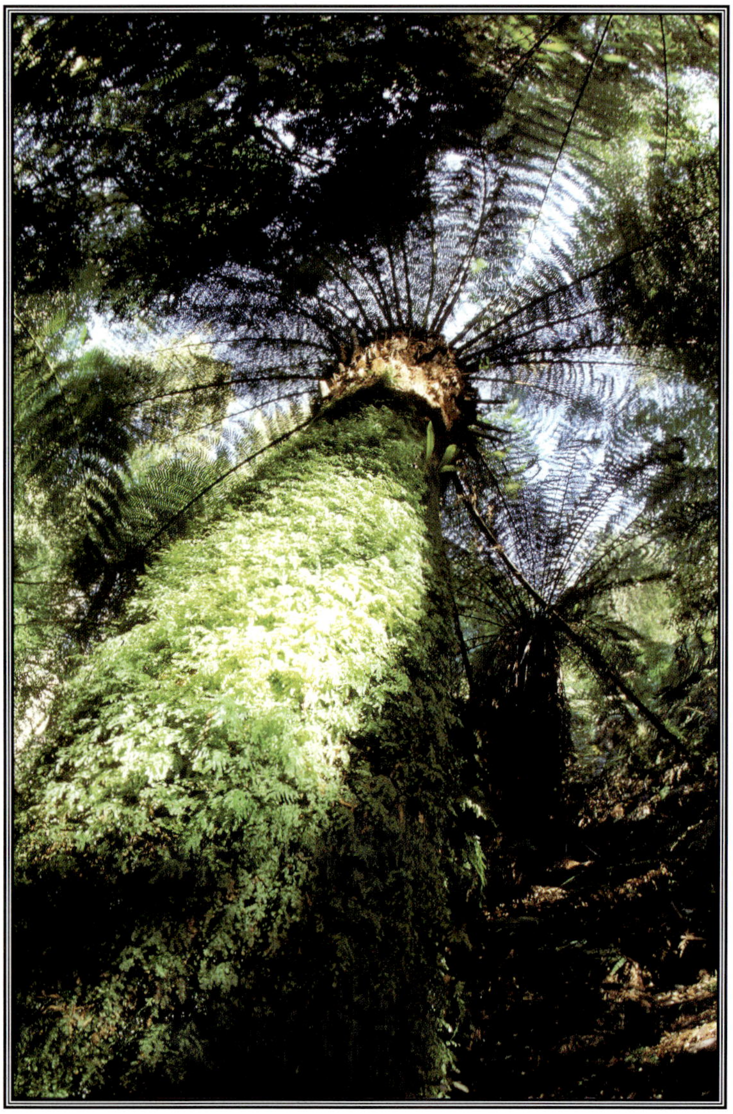

Liffey Falls

South East of Deloraine is a small forest called Liffey Forest Reserve. This reserve hosts one of the State's most beautiful bush walks, leading through lush forest on a track lined with giant tree ferns. The path follows a twisting river as it flows over three cascading waterfalls.

Shafts of dappled light are filtered through a dense canopy swaying gently in the breeze and dance on the forest floor.

***Top**: Abstract textures of a fern leaf*
***Bottom left**: Giant tree ferns line the track to Liffey Falls*

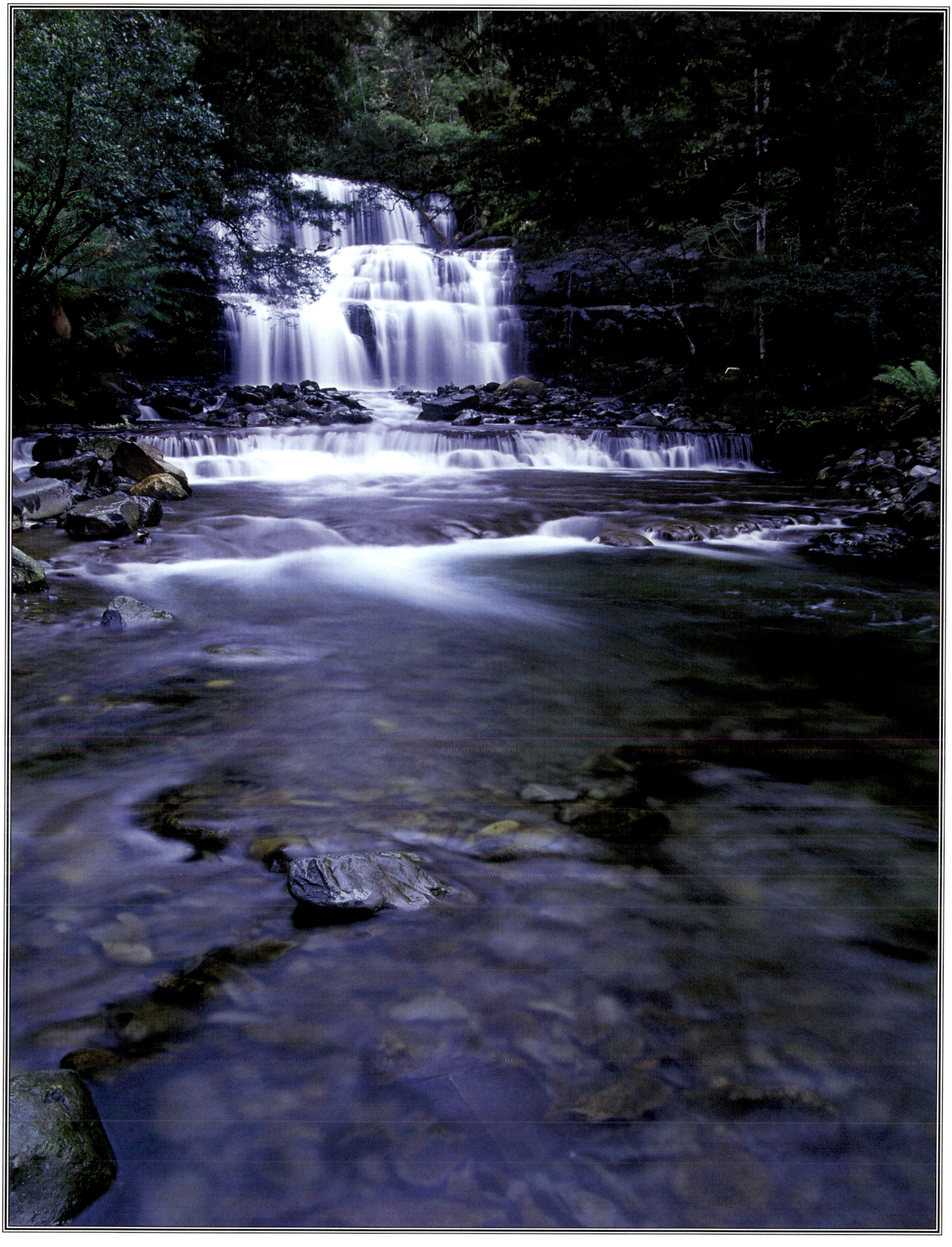

Clear icy waters falling over the lower cascade of Liffey Falls

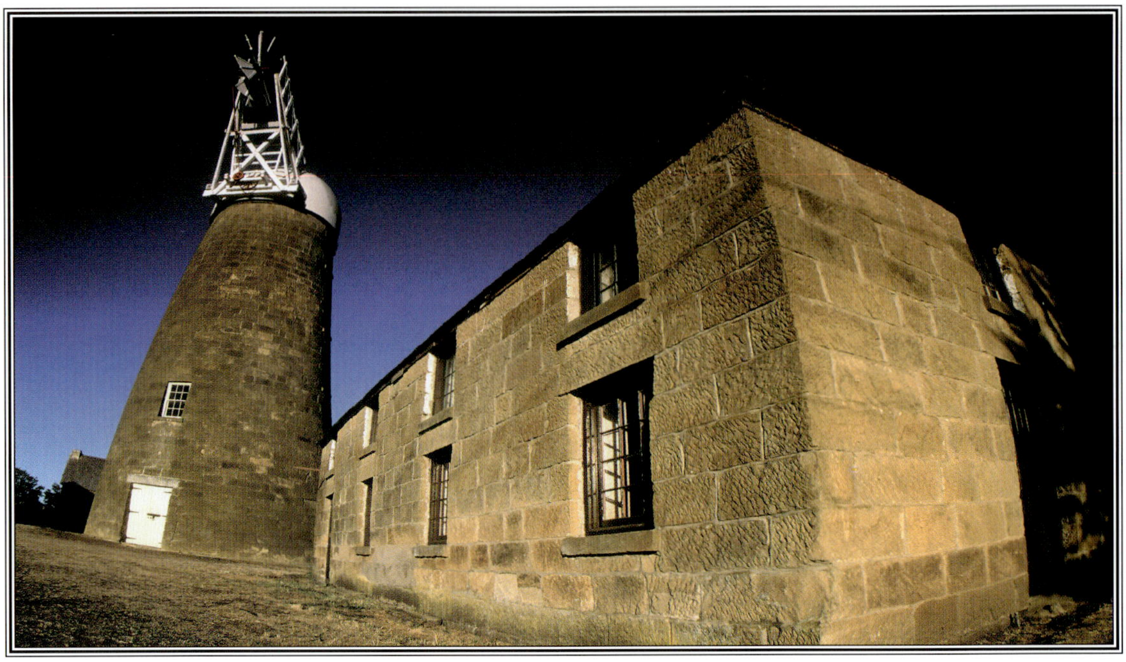

The Midlands

The Heritage Highway runs north / south and in Tasmania's centre plays host to a region named The Midlands. The historic townships of Tasmania's Midlands allow you to step back in time as you wander down their delightful streetscapes, enjoying the beauty of the Georgian era buildings and absorbing the ambiance of times gone by.

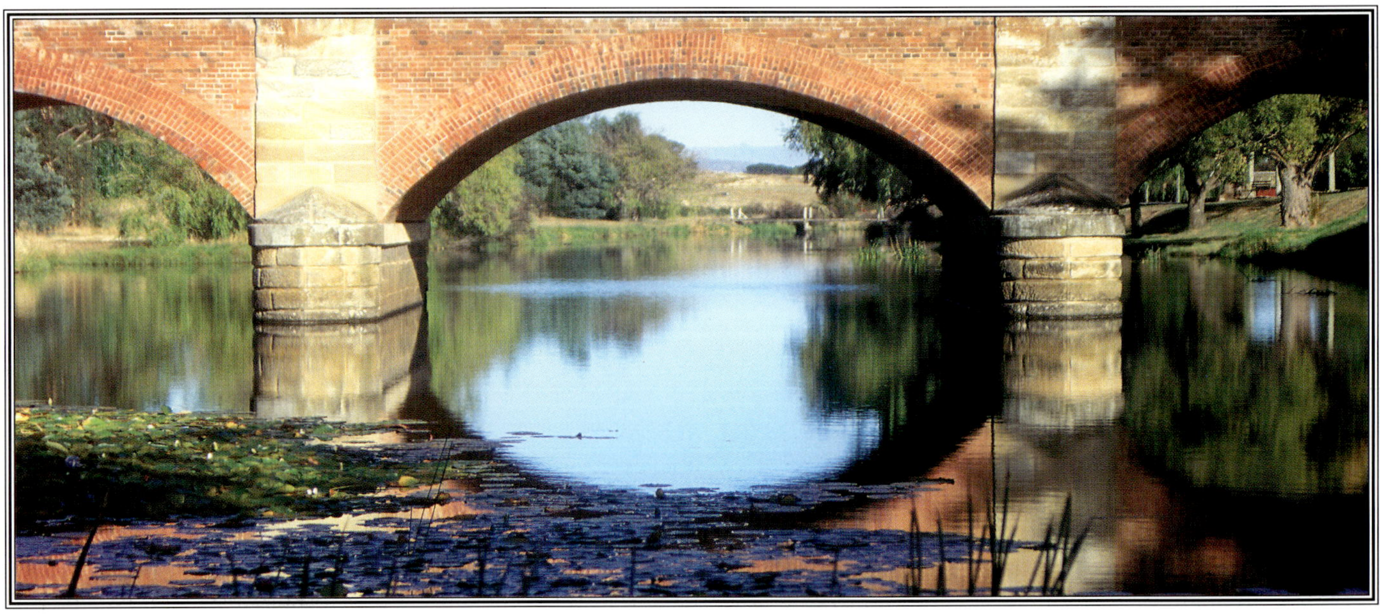

***Top**: The Callington Mill in Oatlands*
***Bottom**: Reflections of the Campbell Town Bridge*

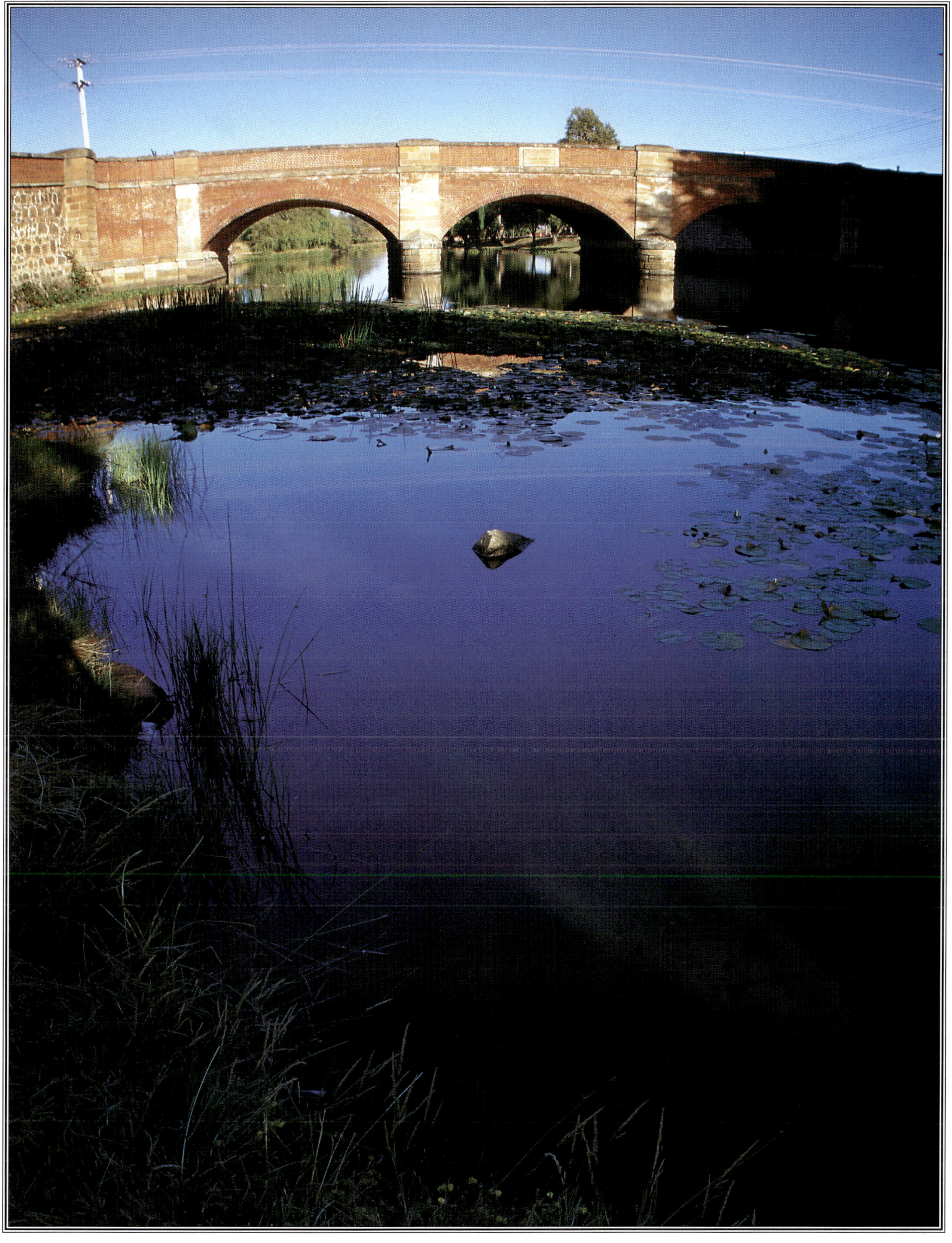

The Campbell Town bridge and river

Tasmania's South

From the bustling, cosmopolitan city of Hobart shadowed by the iconic majesty of Mt. Wellington, to the rugged coastal seascapes of Tasmania's southern tip and stretching across the 'Convict Trail', through Richmond and on to Port Arthur, Tasmania's south is a diverse combination of fascinating history, unique landscape and fine produce.

On a clear morning, make some time to venture to the top of Mt. Wellington and gaze in wonder at one of Australia's most inspiring panoramic views - Tasmania's south.

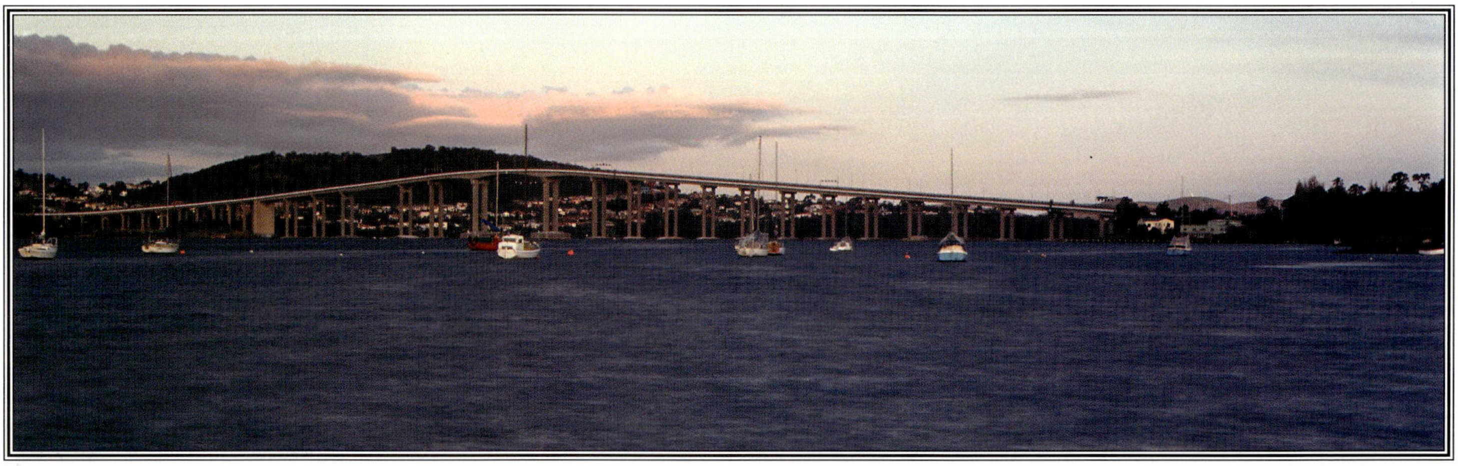

The Tasman Bridge spanning the River Derwent

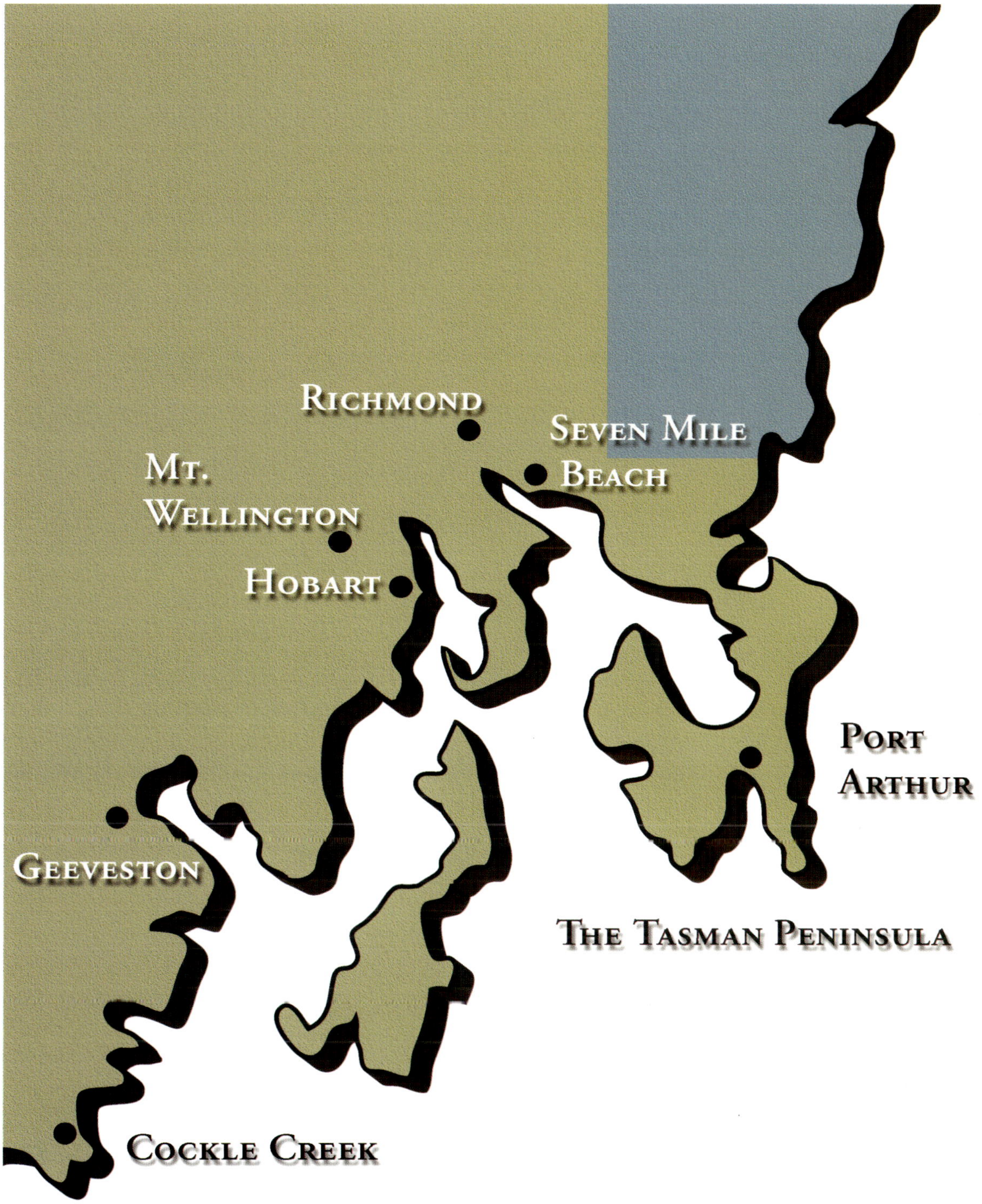
Richmond
Seven Mile
Beach
Mt.
Wellington
Hobart
Geeveston
Port
Arthur
The Tasman Peninsula
Cockle Creek

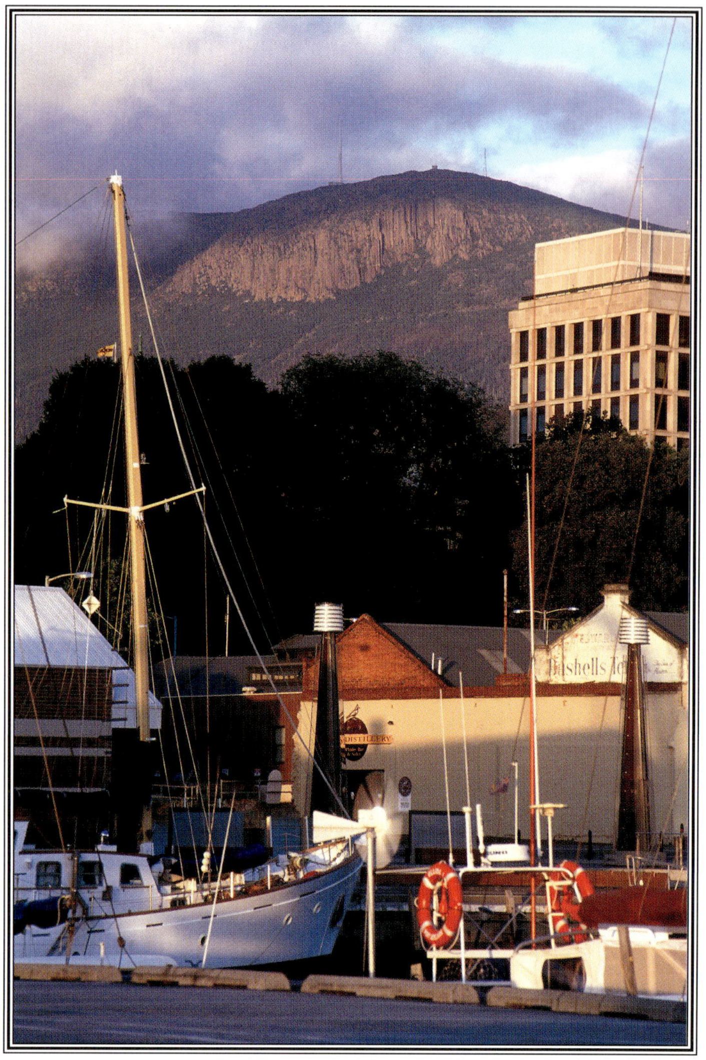

Hobart

Tasmania's capital city Hobart is a culmination of maritime history, picturesque sandstone buildings, colourful gardens and some of the finest seafood restaurants you could wish to find.

Discover the talents of local Tasmanian artisans by wandering through the bustling Salamanca Market. Admire the beautifully preserved historic buildings of Battery Point, or simply relax with a fine Tasmanian wine and watch the boats, gently rocking in the moonlight, from one of Hobart's waterfront restaurants.

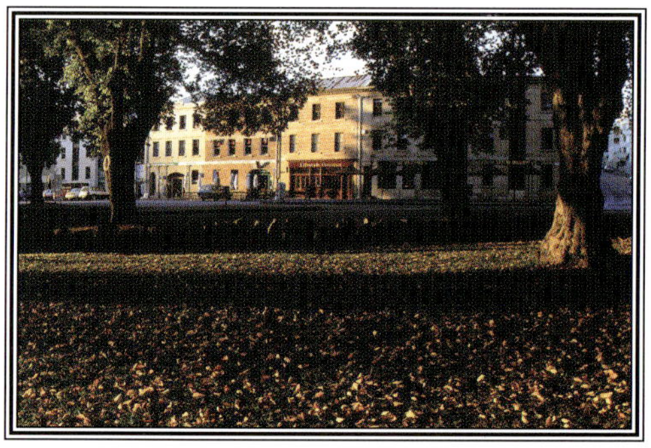

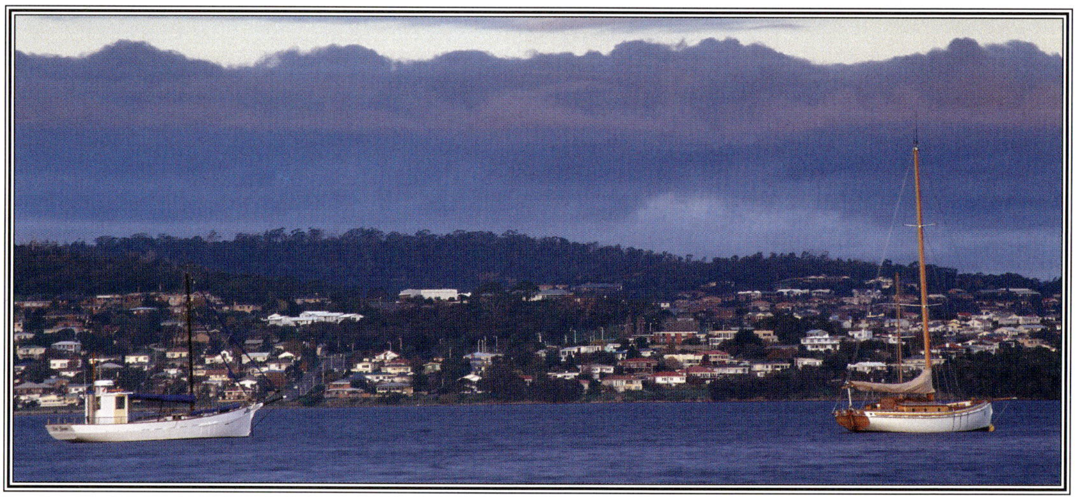

***Top:** Mt. Wellington towering over Hobart City*
***Centre:** Morning light at Salamanca Place*
***Bottom:** Boats on the River Derwent*

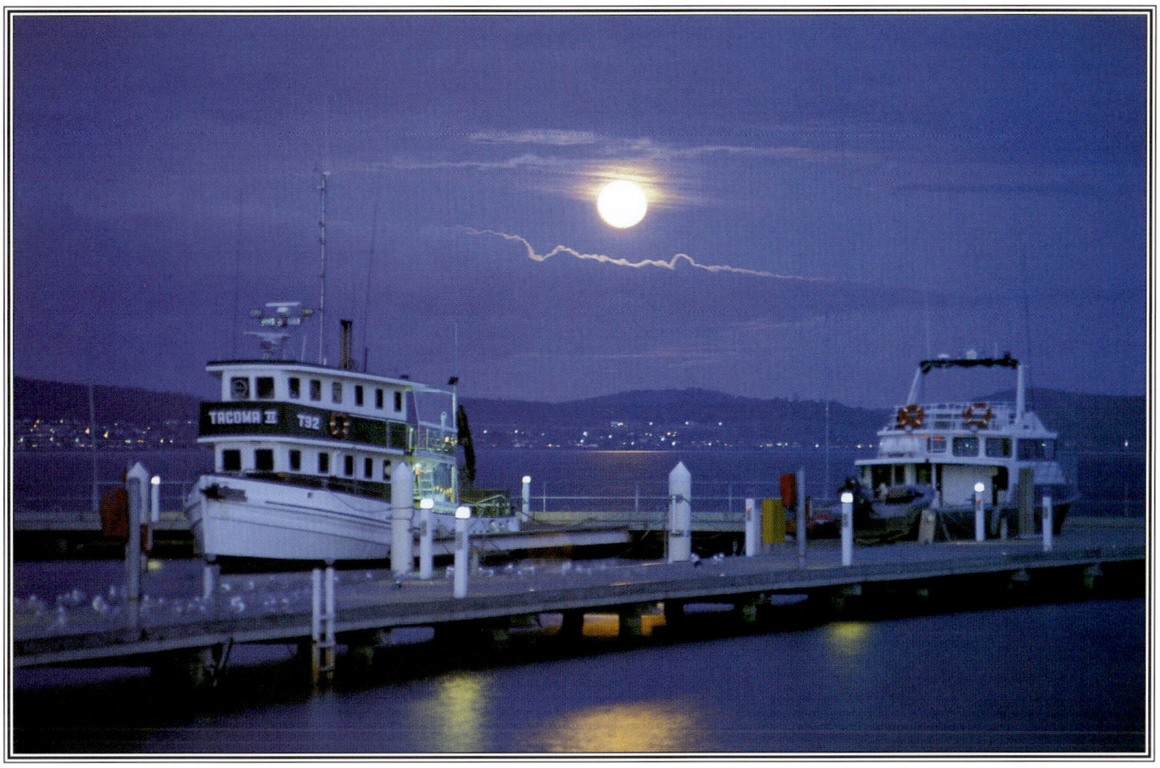

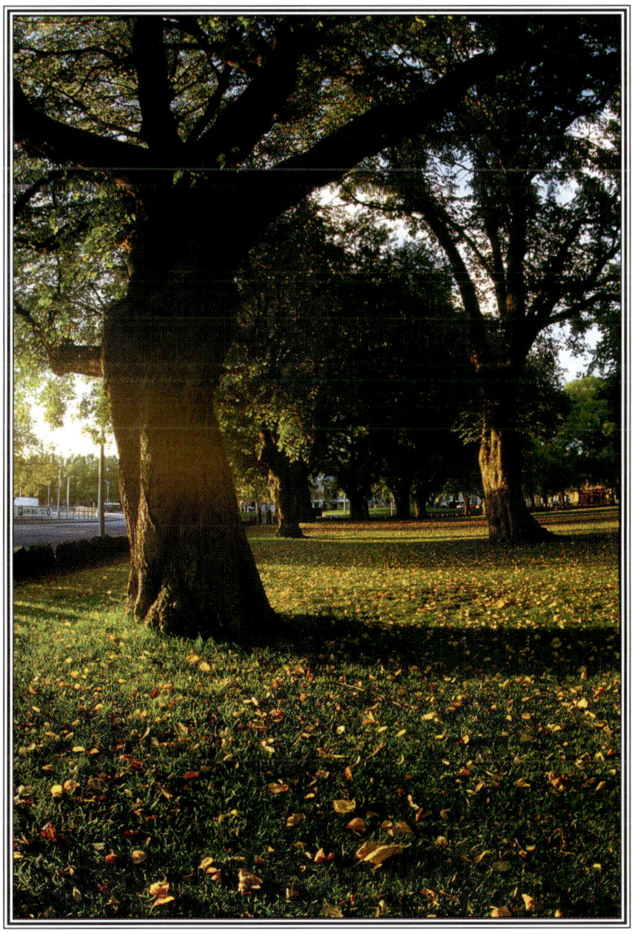

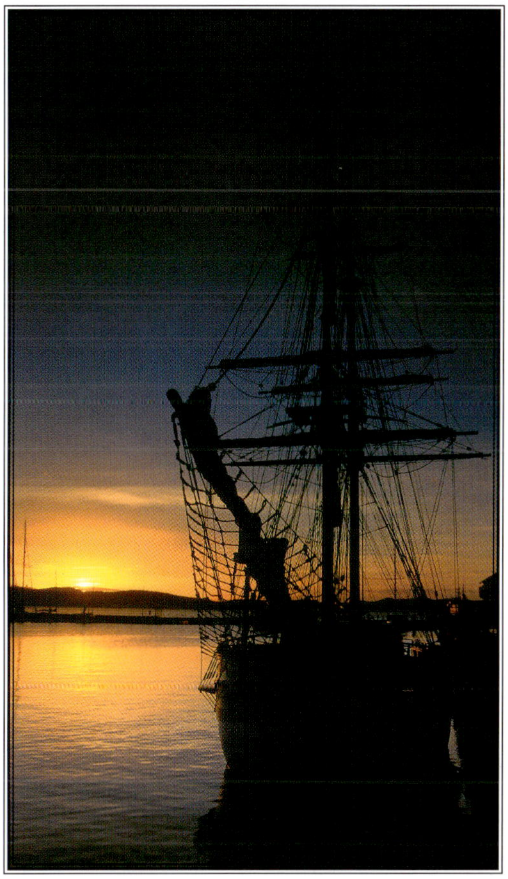

Top: *Moonrise over the river Derwent*
Bottom left: *Autumn at Salamanca*
Bottom right: *Silhouettes at dawn*

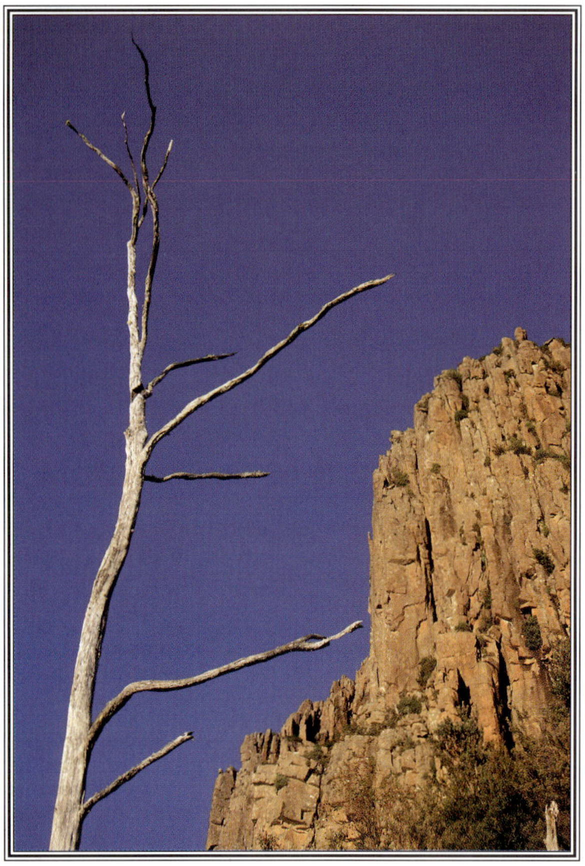

Mt. Wellington

Dominating the skyline, Mt. Wellington stands proudly behind the city of Hobart.

The forests of the mountain protect all manner of wildlife and provide a perfect backdrop for picnic areas and walking tracks.

The summit of the mountain boasts a huge, glass-lined lookout and boardwalks meander across its peak.

The awesome beauty of the jagged, orange dolerite columns and the breathtaking panoramic views from the summit are testimony to the majesty of the mountain.

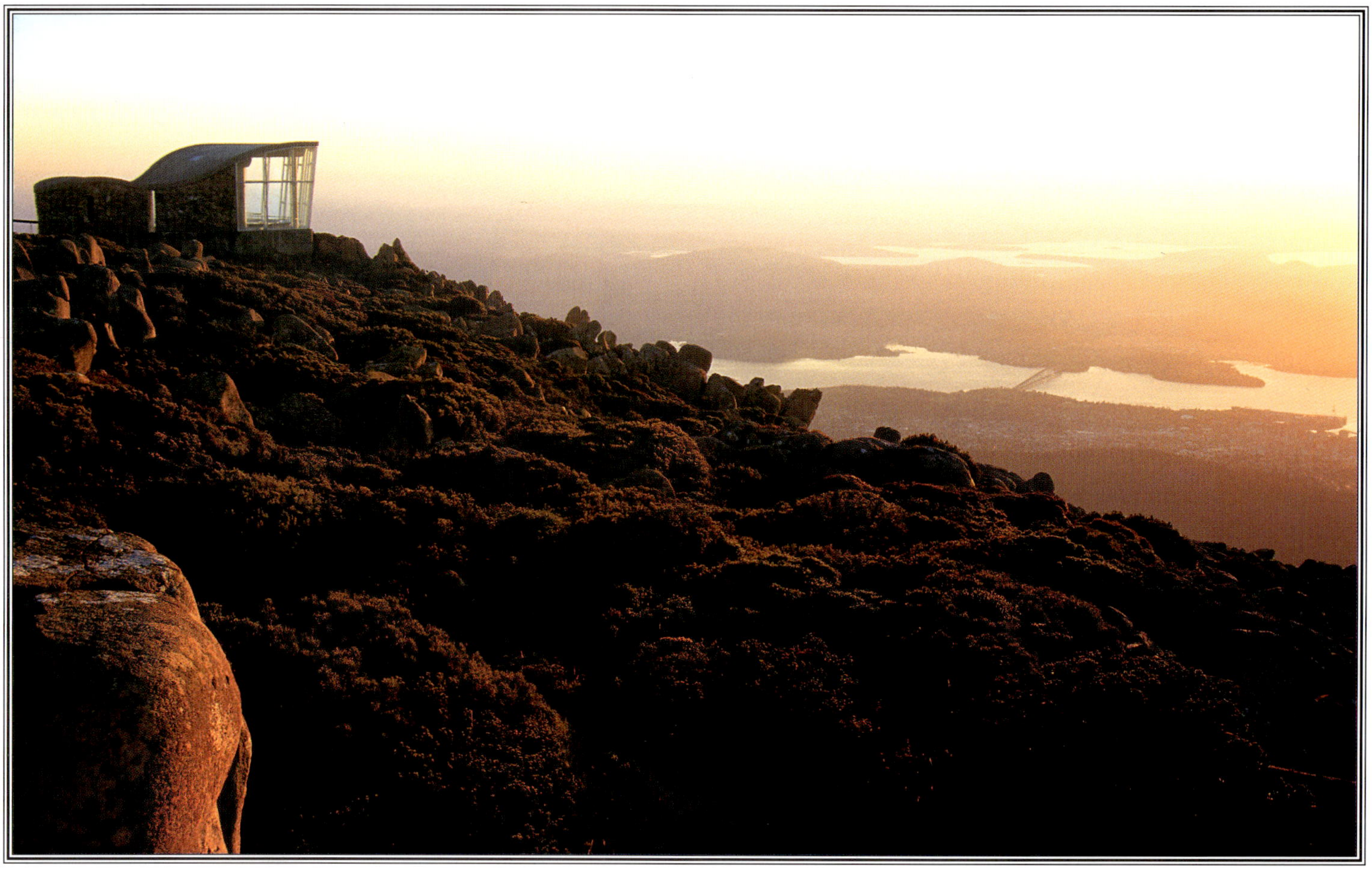

Top: *Mt. Wellington's Organ Pipes*
Bottom: *First light at the lookout*

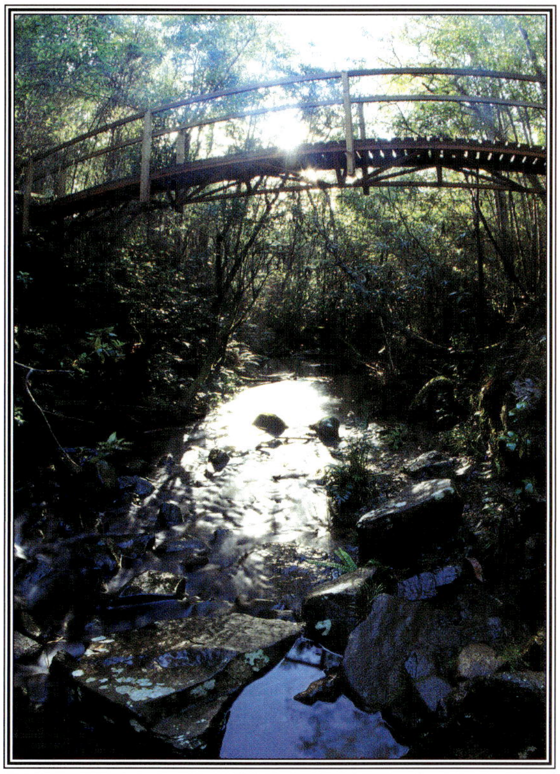

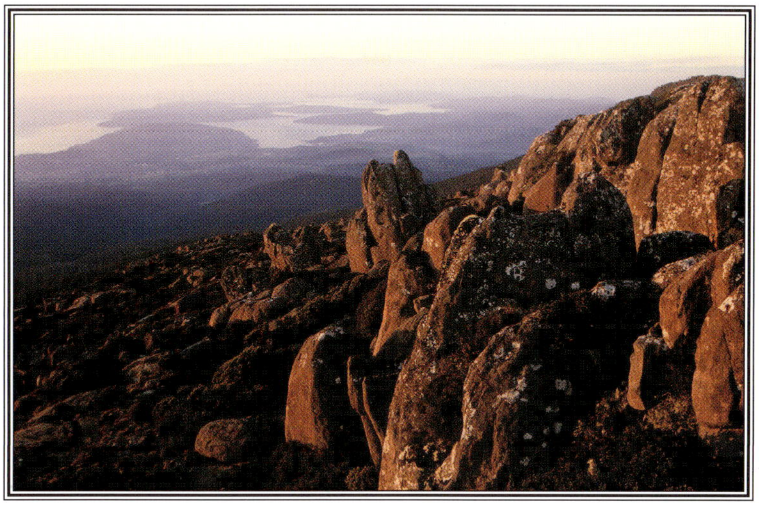

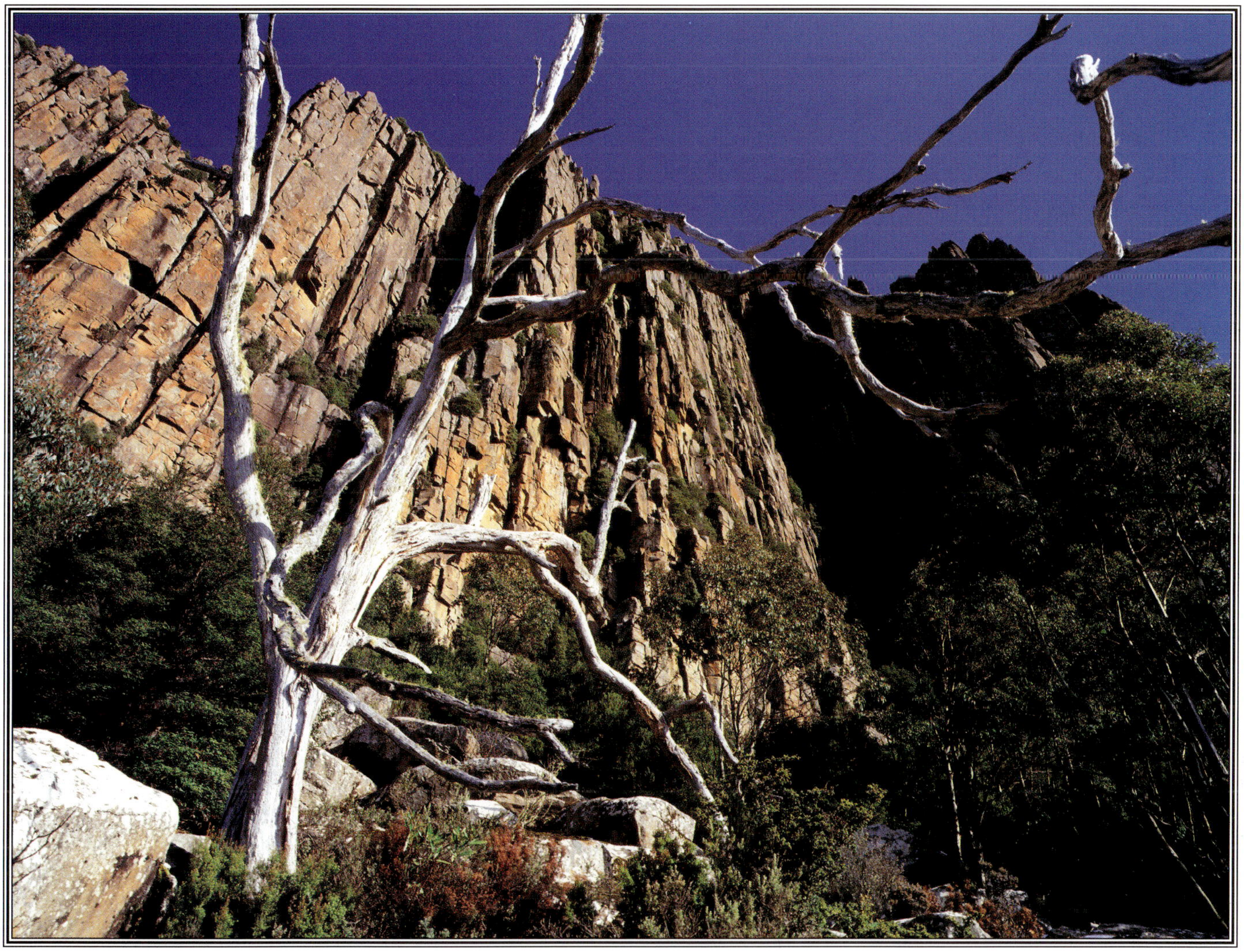

Top left: *Under the bridge at O'Grady's Falls*
Top right: *The view south from Mt. Wellington*
Bottom: *The Organ Pipes*

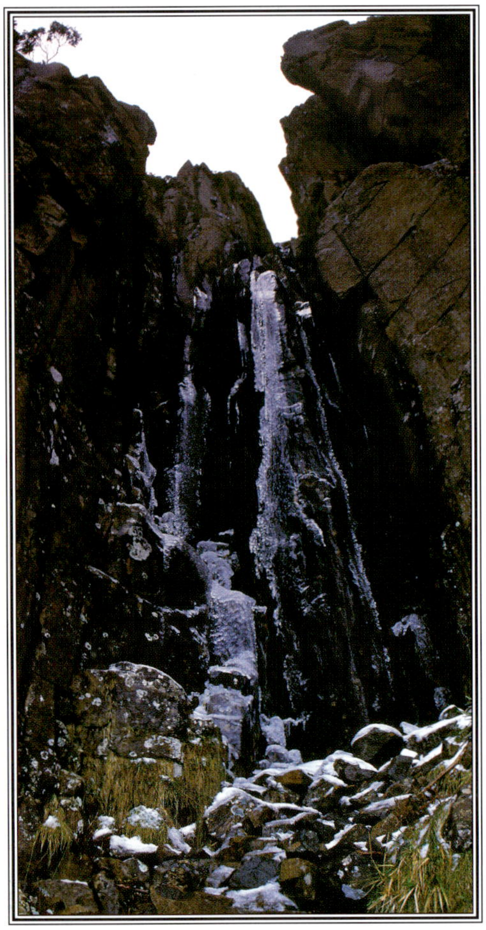

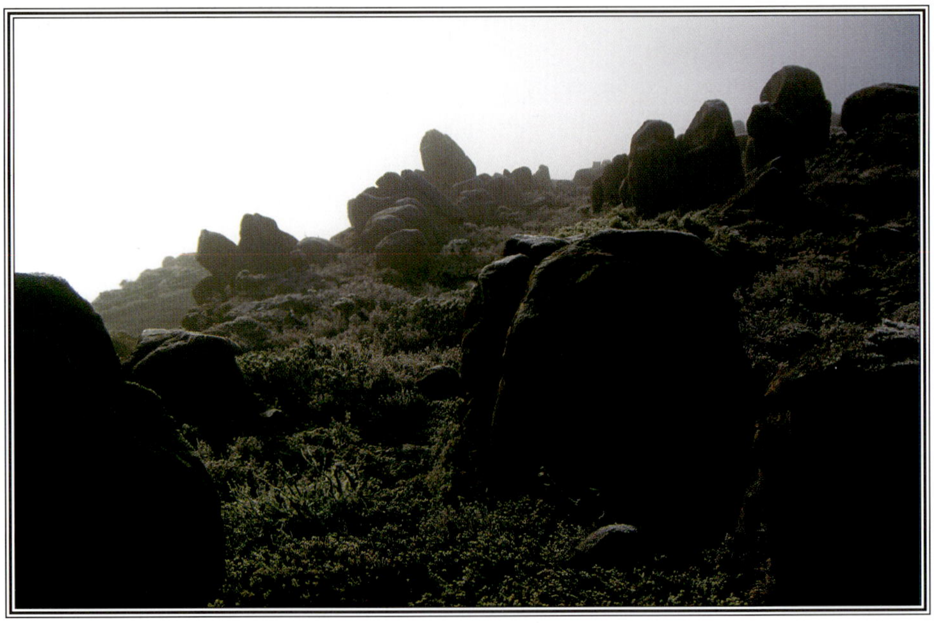

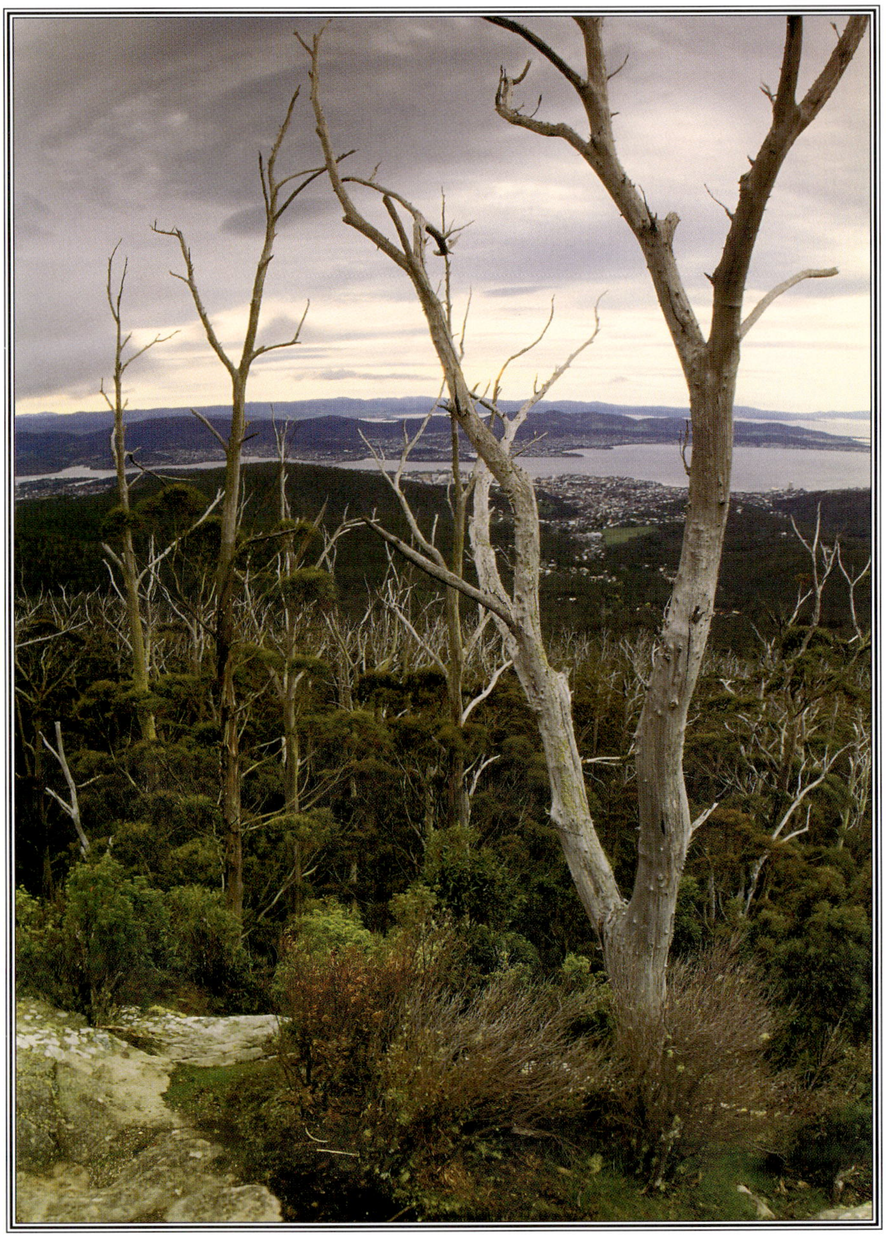

Top left: *Ice Falls at The Organ Pipes*
Top right: *Misty morning on Mt. Wellington's summit*
Bottom: *View to Hobart from Sphinx Rock lookout*

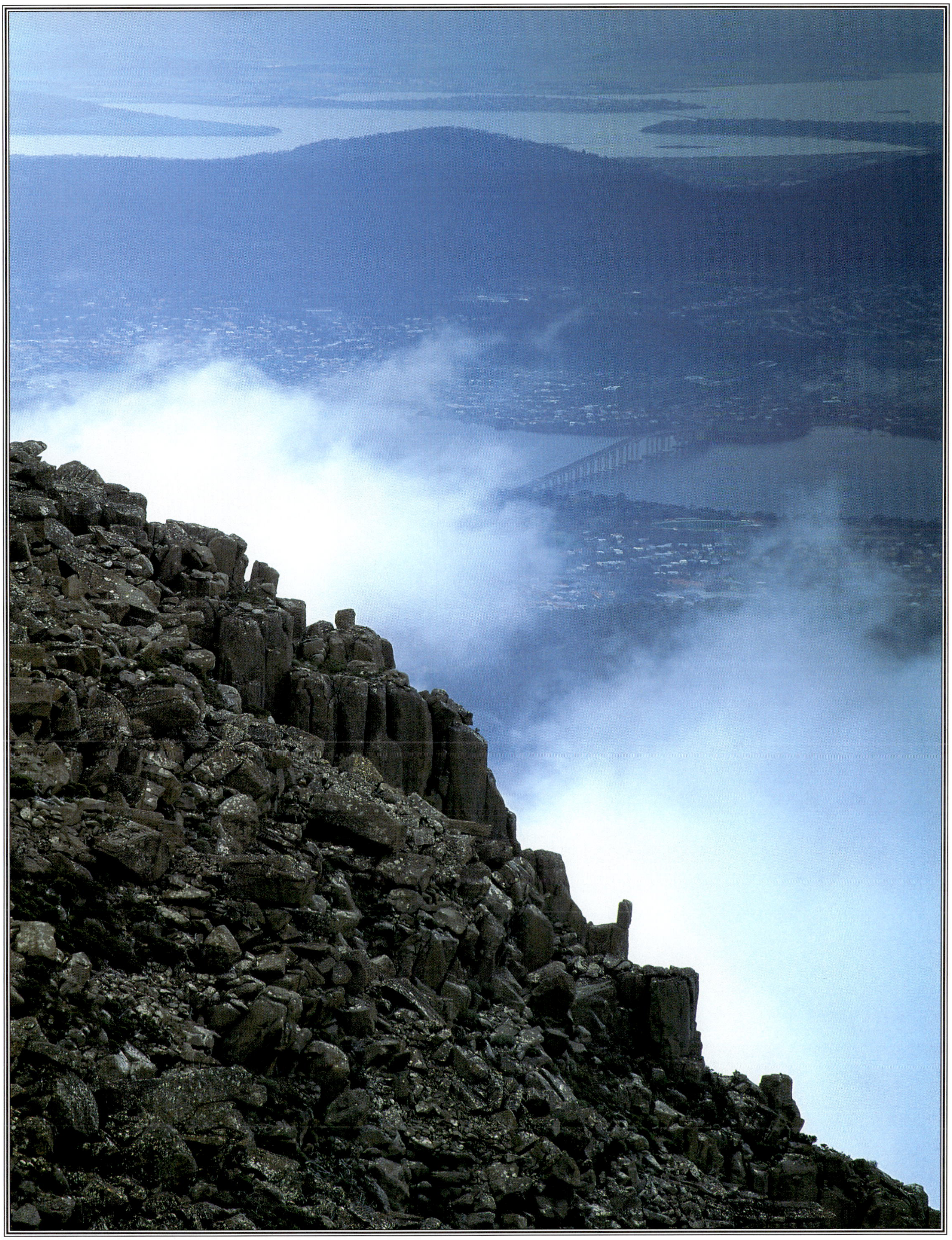

The Tasman Bridge from above the clouds

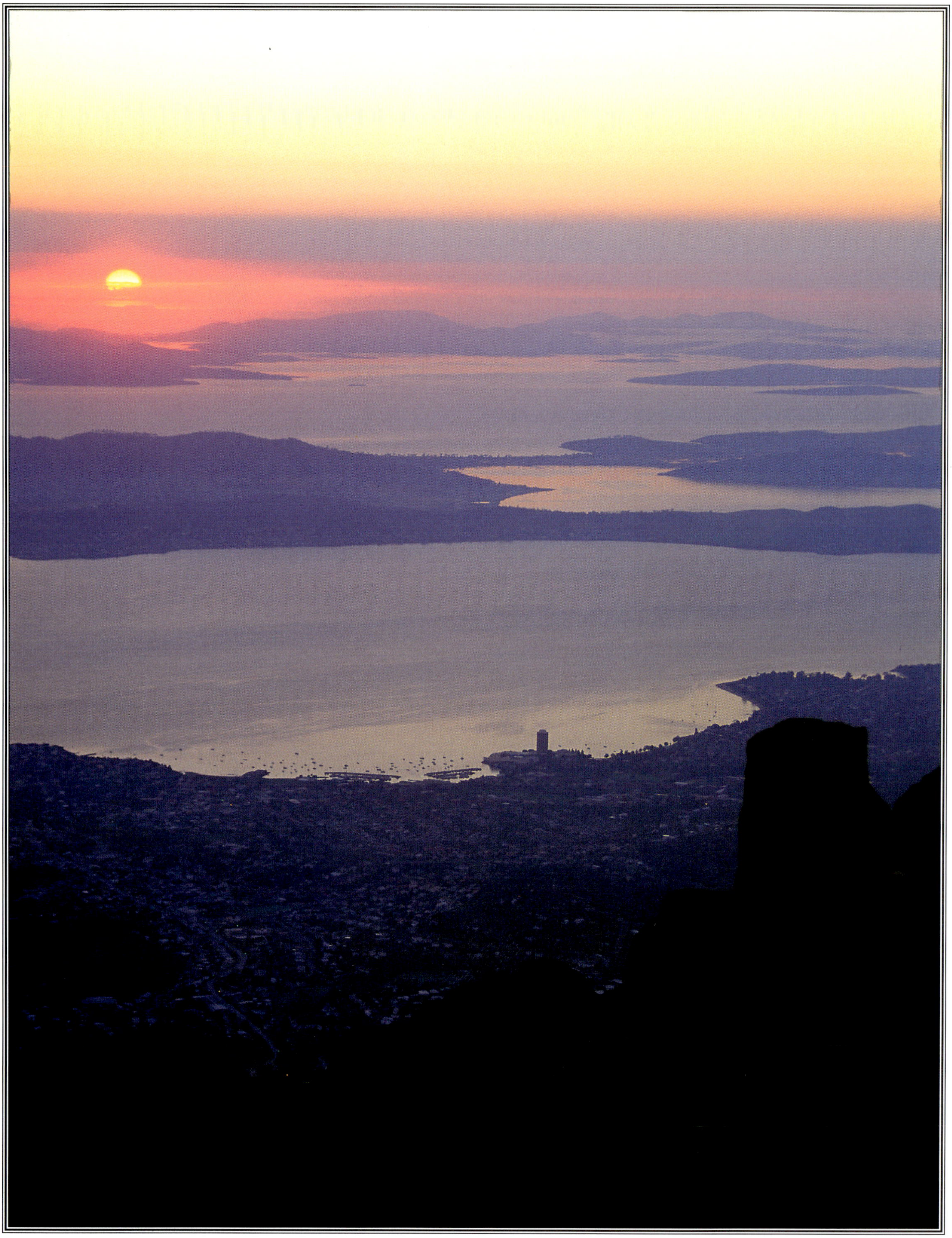

From Hobart to the Tasman Peninsula - sunrise from Mt. Wellington

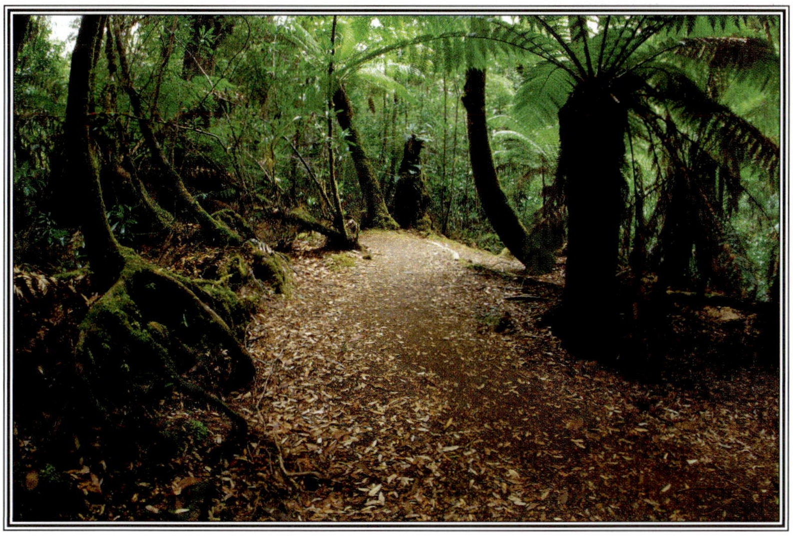

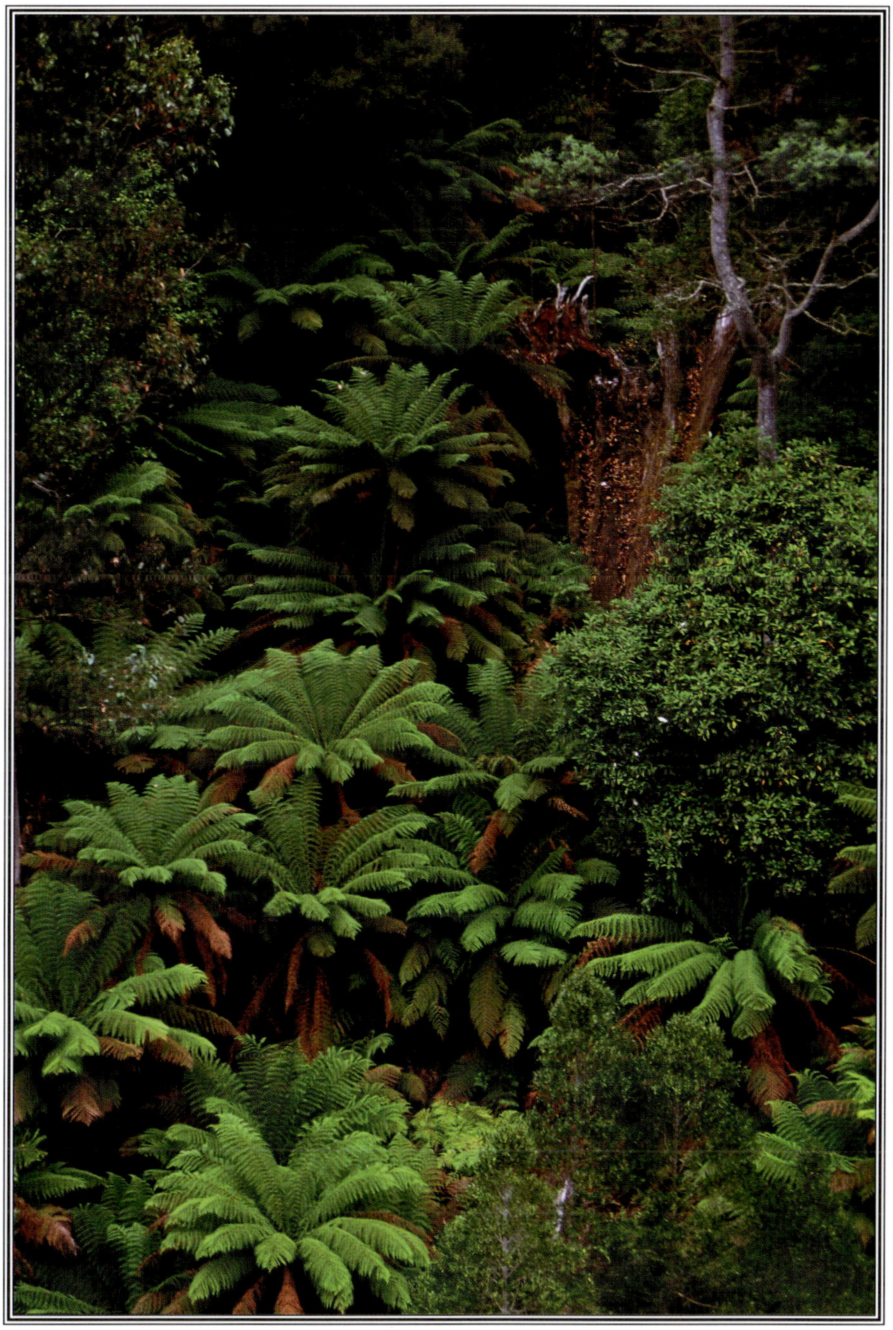

***Top:** A forest landscape in Tasmania's south*
***Bottom:** Tree ferns at Geeveston*

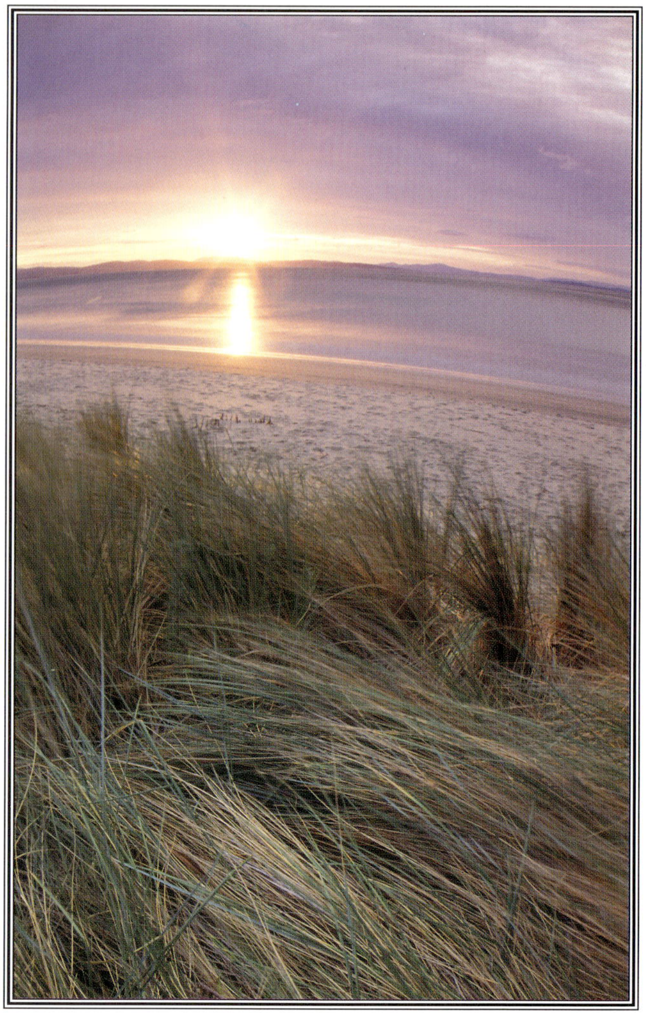

Seven Mile Beach,

Just fifteen minutes drive east of Hobart, past Mt. Rumney and bordering Frederick Henry Bay, Seven Mile Beach awaits exploration.

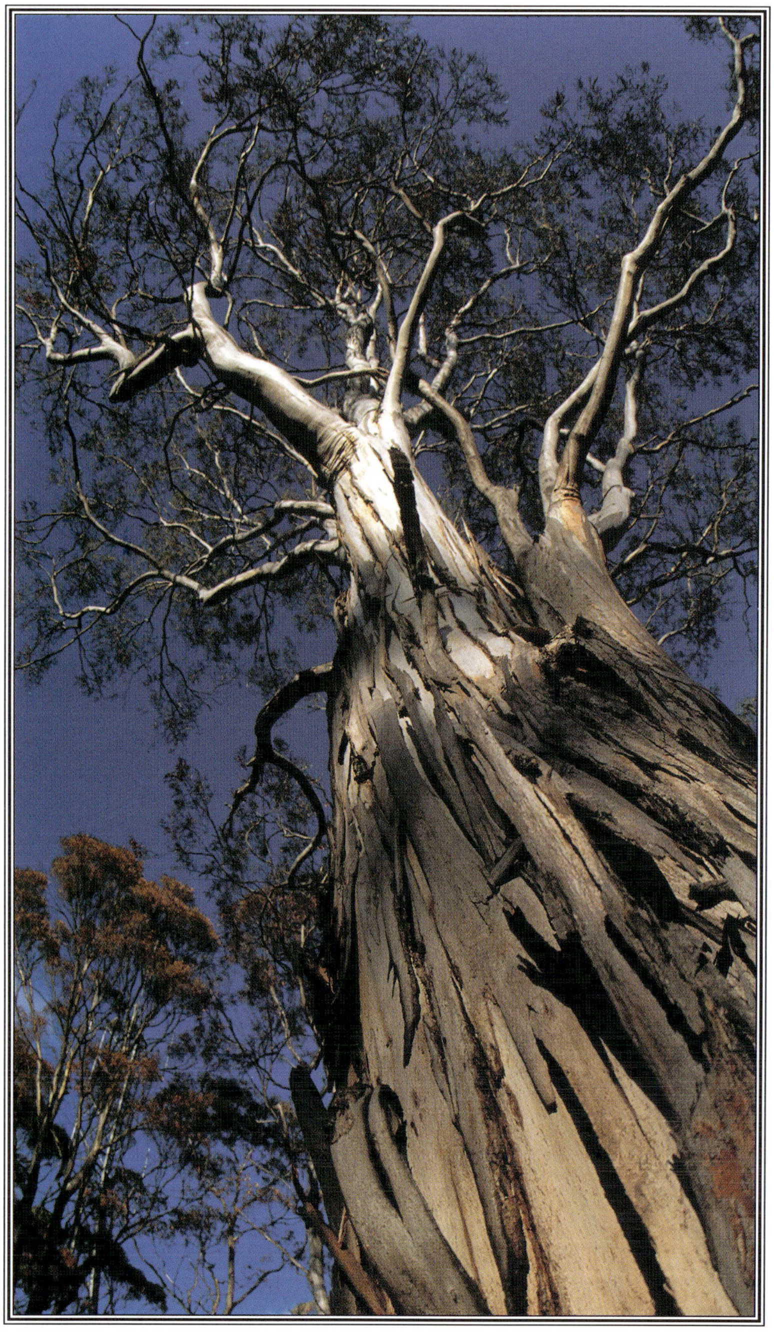

Although a popular recreational destination for local residents, the beach is large enough to ensure peaceful walks for contemplation or collection of the literally millions of shells scattered on its sands.

The combination of green spear-grass covered sand dunes; soft sand and abundant seashells make it a memorable beach for watching a golden sunrise.

Top: *The sand dunes of Seven Mile Beach*
Bottom: *Towering gum trees at Mt. Rumney*

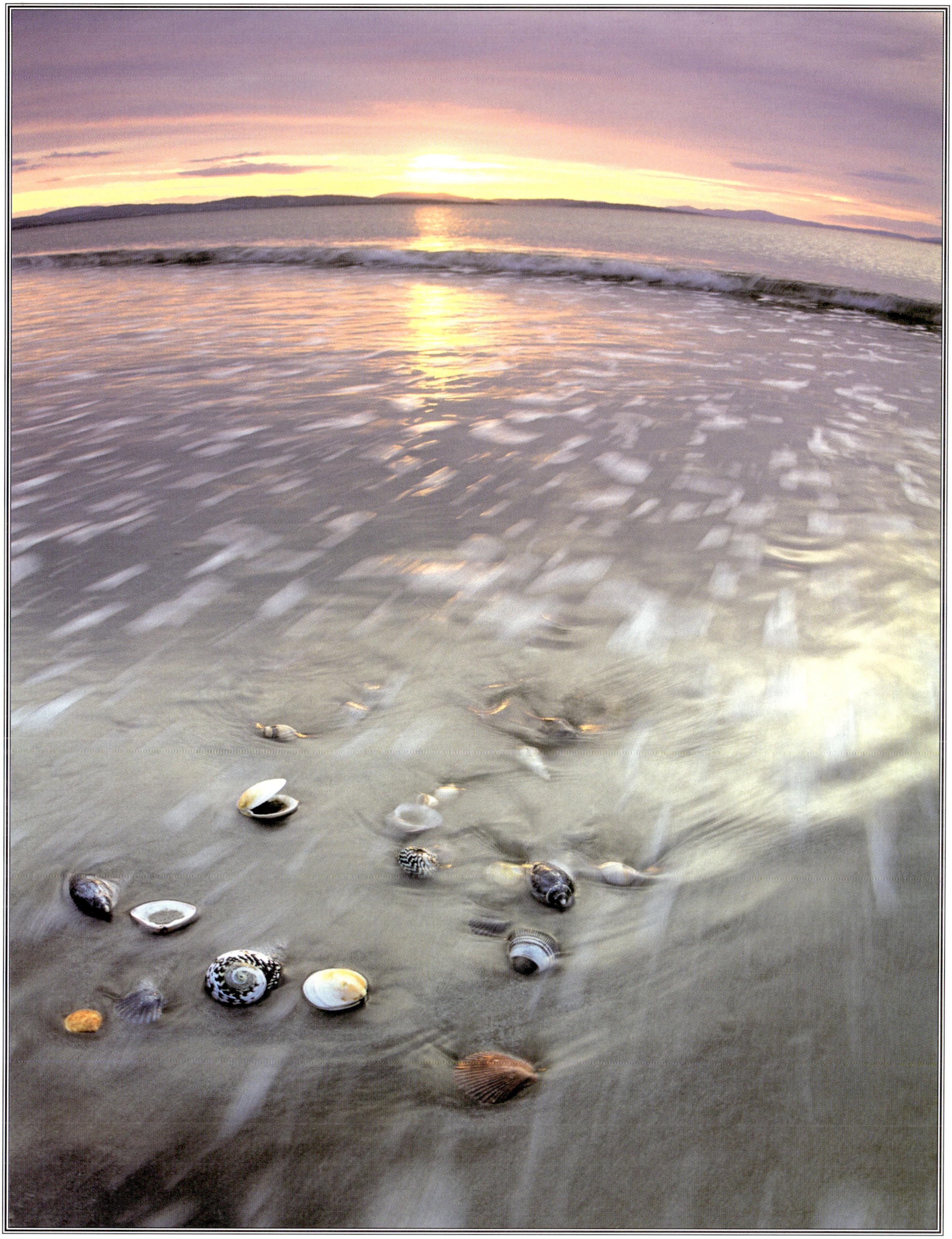

Colourful seashells in the waves of Seven Mile Beach at sunrise

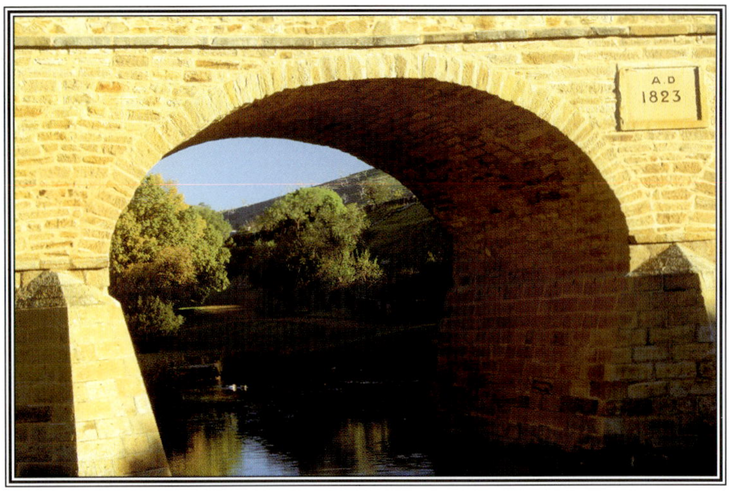

Richmond

Twenty five kilometers north east of Hobart, following the 'Convict Trail', is the historic township of Richmond, home to Australia's oldest stone bridge, built in 1823.

Browse through the galleries, craft and antique shops or simply unwind with a hot drink in the traditional ambiance of one of its many tearooms.

Marvel as the sandstone bridge takes on the golden hues of sunlight during an autumn afternoon, whilst flocks of ducks parade on the riverbanks, demanding the attention of visitors.

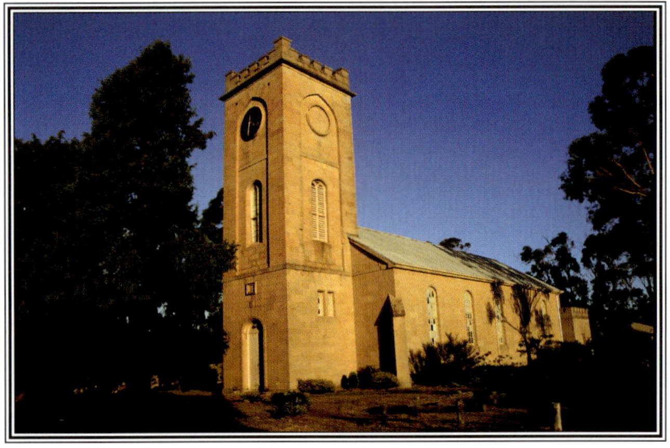

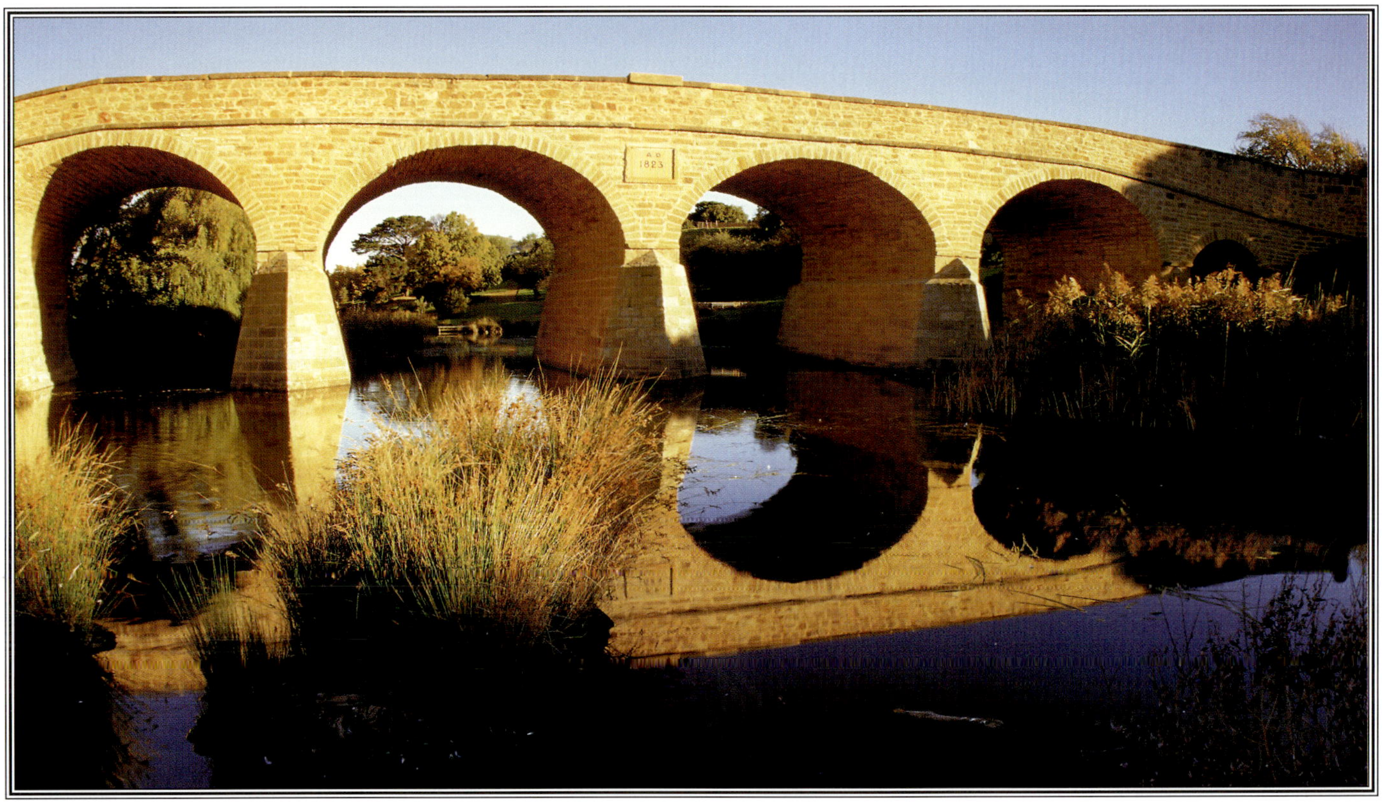

Top: *The sandstone arches of Richmond Bridge*
Centre: *The Anglican Church in Richmond*
Bottom: *Australia's oldest bridge in afternoon sun*

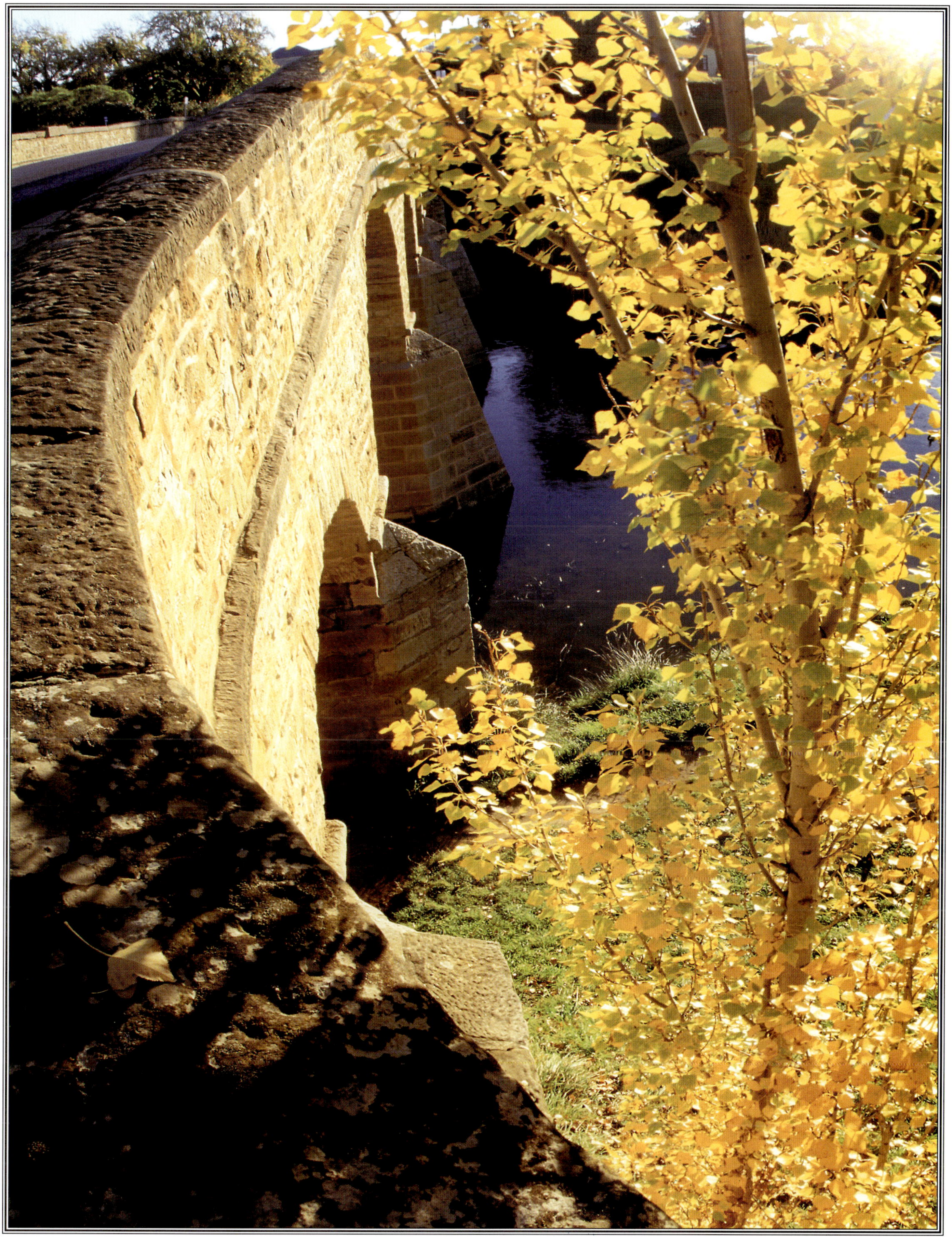

Richmond Bridge in autumn colours

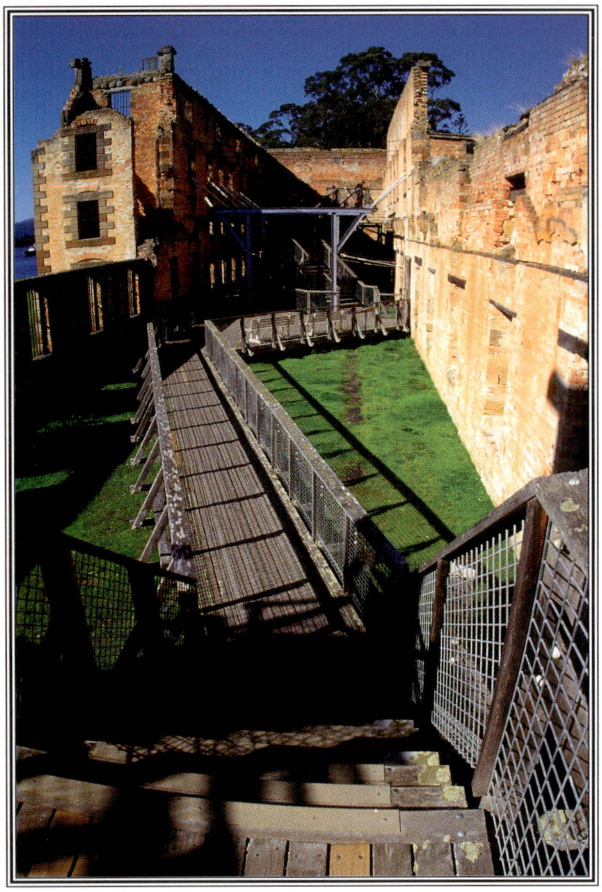

Port Arthur

Following the 'Convict Trail' south east from Hobart will eventually lead to Port Arthur, the site of a former convict penitentiary. Wander the ruins, whilst learning of their history, or catch a ferry and explore the 'Isle of the Dead'.

The tranquillity and peaceful beauty of Port Arthur is polarised by its sad and often tragic past.

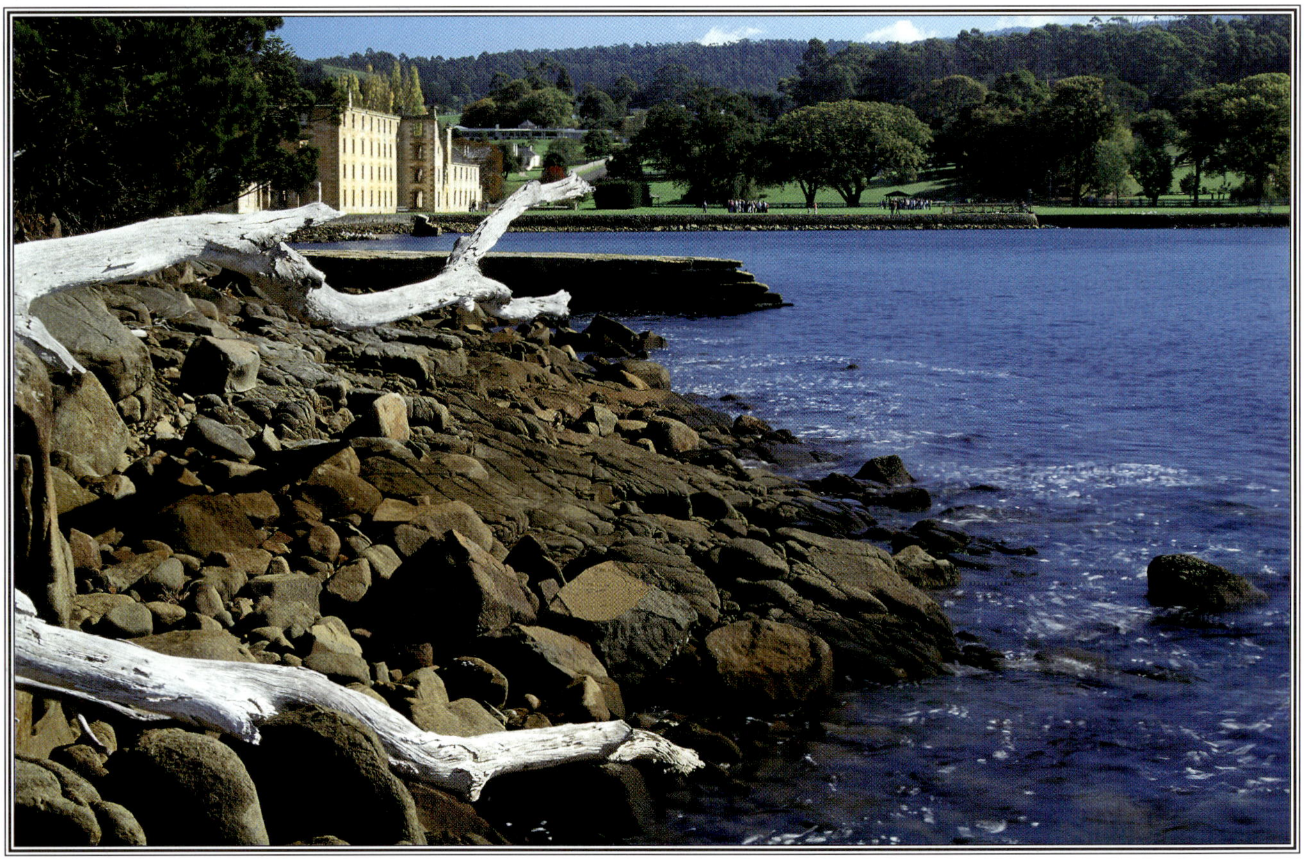

Top: *Explore the penitentiary*
Bottom: *The peaceful tranquillity of Port Arthur*

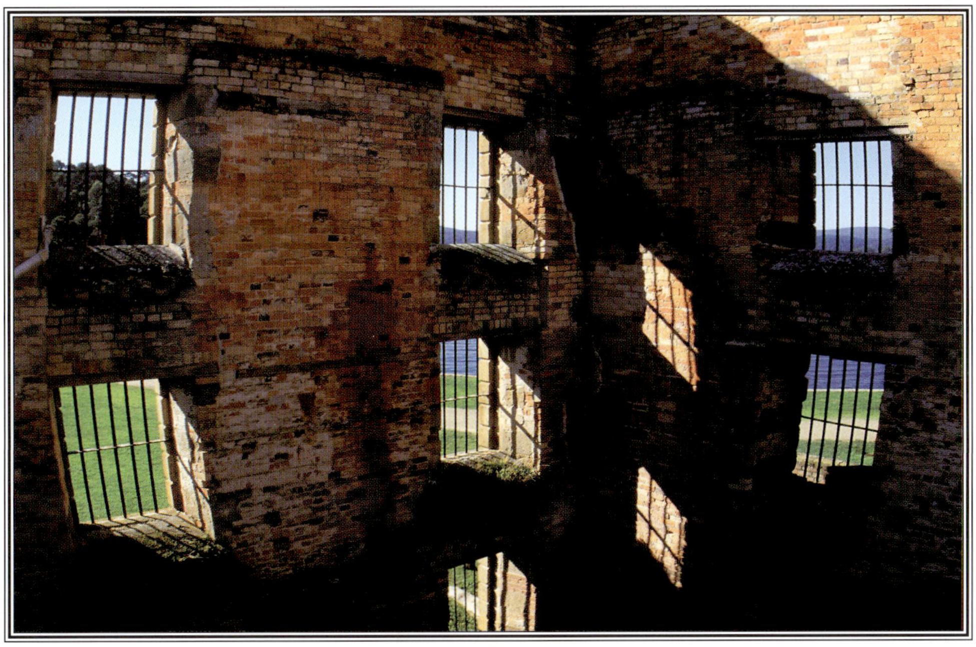

Top: *A convict's view of Port Arthur*
Bottom: *The penitentiary building at Port Arthur*

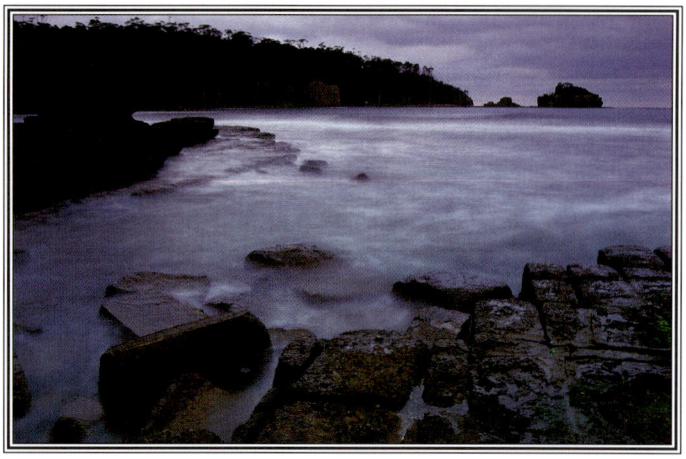

The Tasman Peninsula

The rugged, sheer cliffs, exposed to rough seas and strong winds define the dramatic coastal landscape of the Tasman Peninsula.
This bushwalker's paradise offers everything, from dramatic cliff top treks, to gentle strolls along remote and pristine sandy beaches.

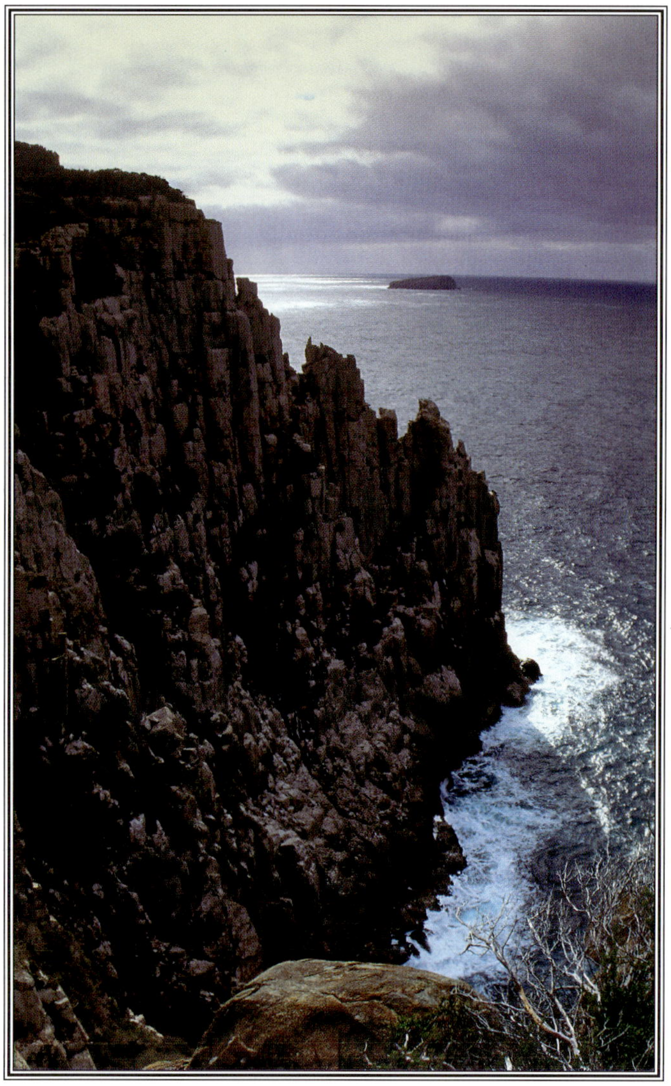

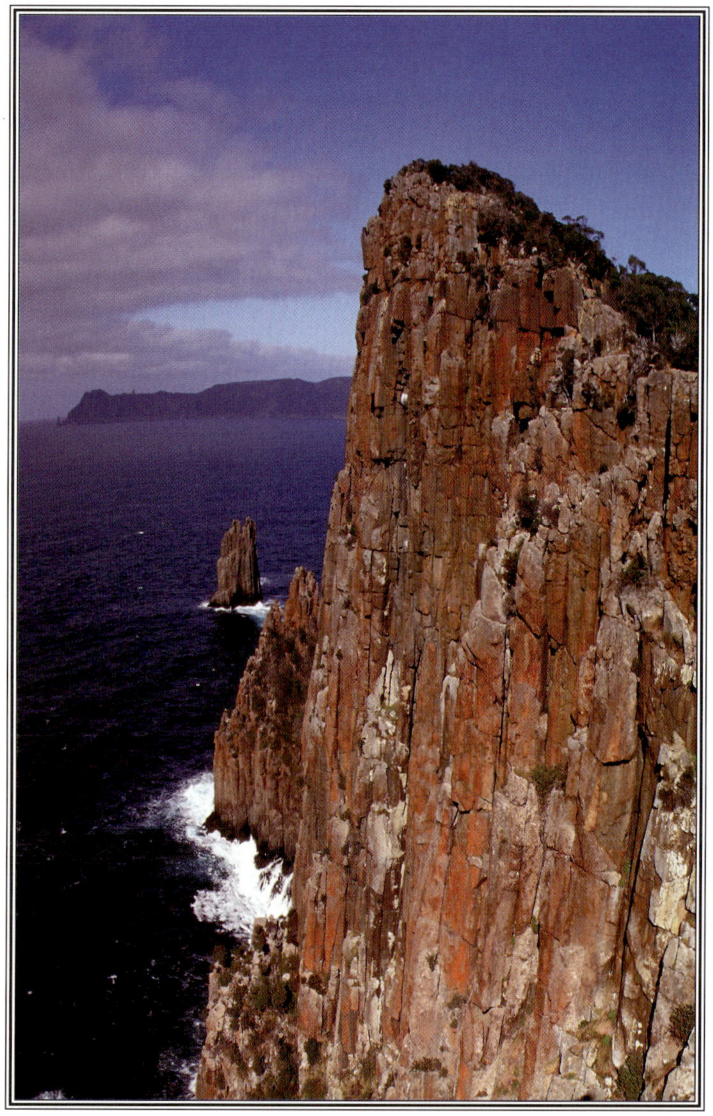

Top left: *The Tessellated Pavement*
Bottom left and right: *The dramatic cliffs of Cape Hauy*

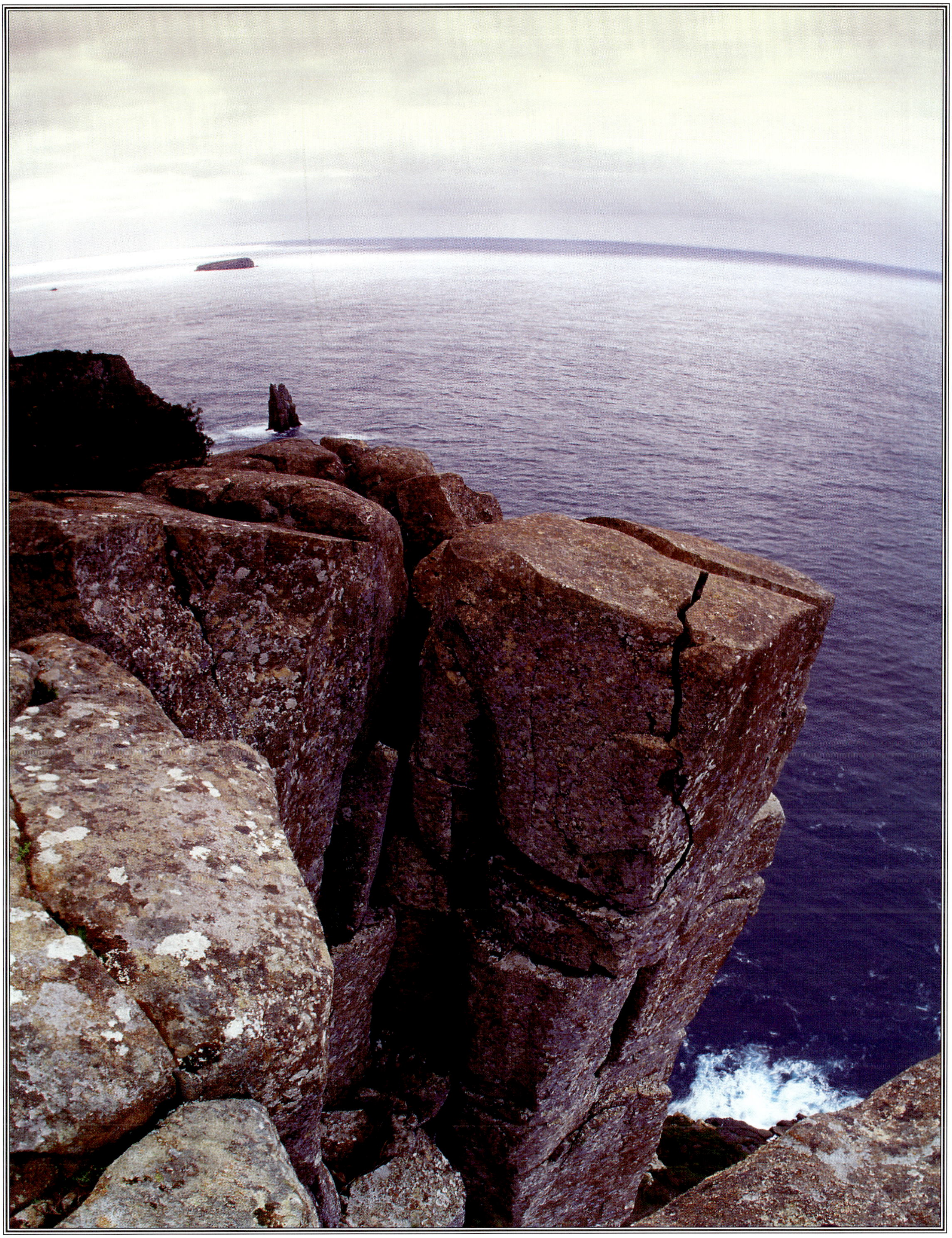

Sheer cliffs towering over the sea on the Cape Hauy walk

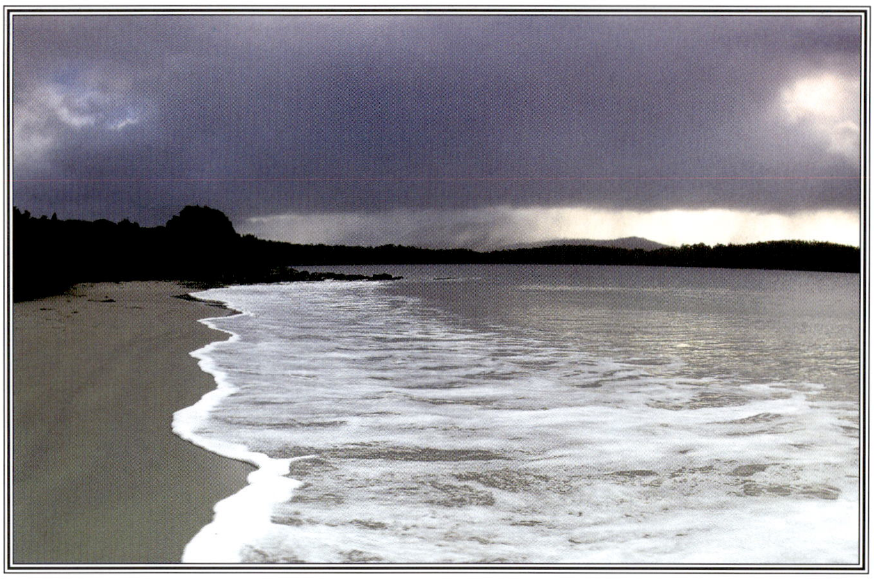

Cockle Creek

The southern tip of Tasmania is home to Cockle Creek, a unique landscape of tree-lined beaches and kelp filled waters. Amble along four beaches to 'Fishers Point' and discover the ruins of the house, used by the Harbour Pilot, during early settlement. The gentle rhythm of waves lapping on the beaches is punctuated only by the sound of cockleshells being crushed underfoot.

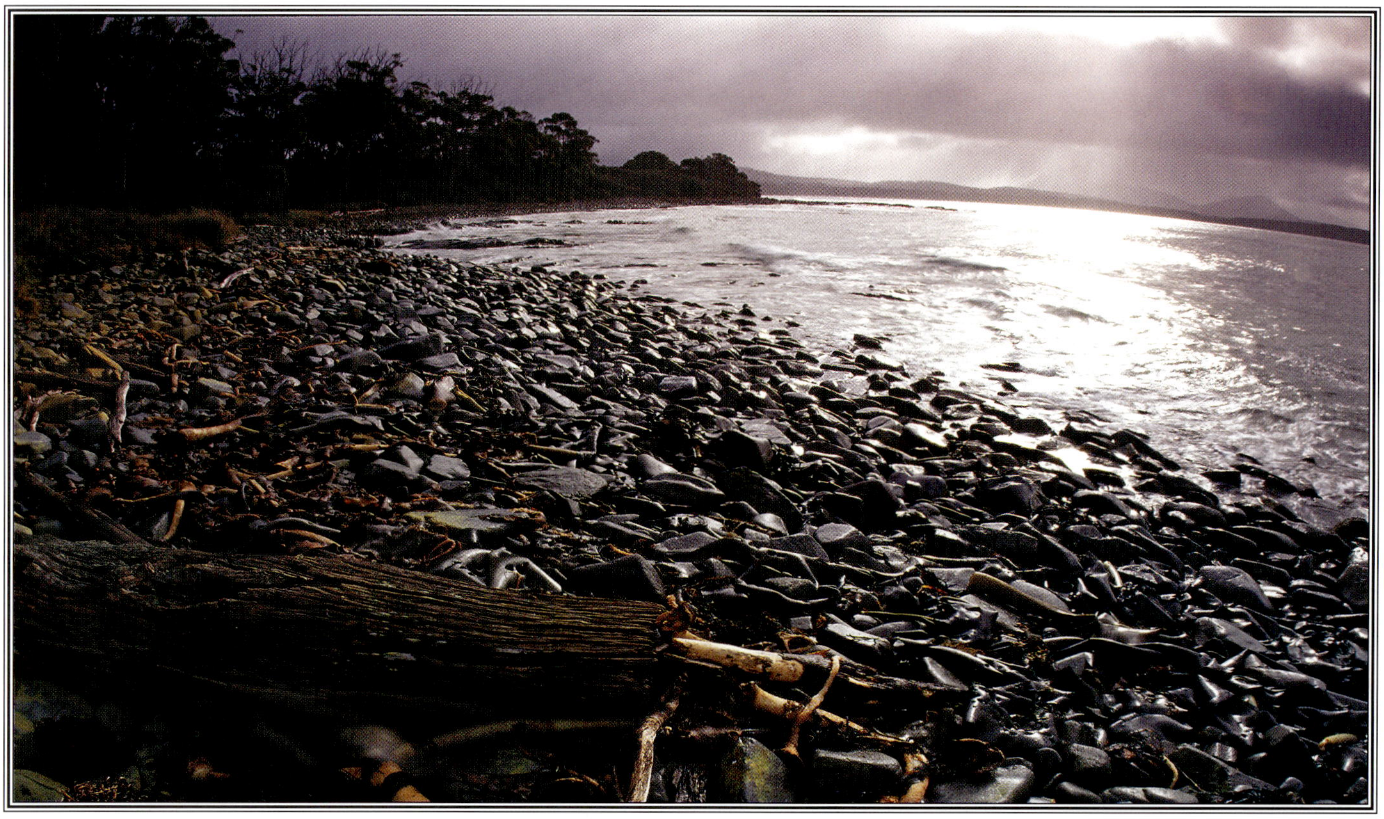

Top: *Storms brewing at Cockle Creek*
Bottom: *Tree lined beaches at Fishers Point*

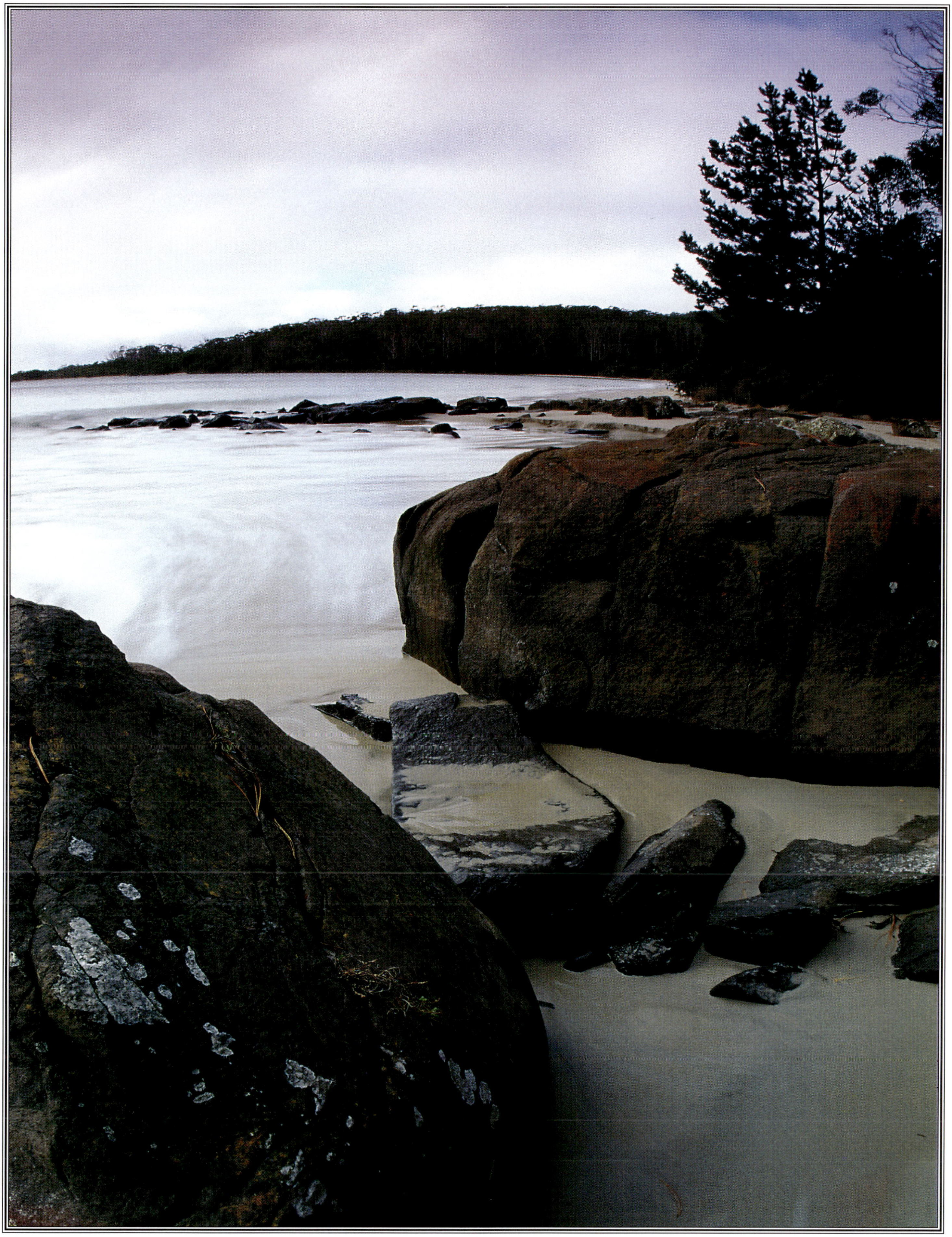

Beach walking at Cockle Creek

Tasmania's East

Tasmania's east coast beaches are amongst the most beautiful in Australia. Powder-white sand, so fine that it gently squeaks underfoot, interspersed with colourful boulders, diverse in both shape and texture, all reflect in the clear azure waters of the Tasman Sea.

Whether relaxing on unspoiled wild beaches in summer, or fossicking for shells on clear, blue-sky days in winter, visiting the east coast of Tasmania is an unforgettable experience.

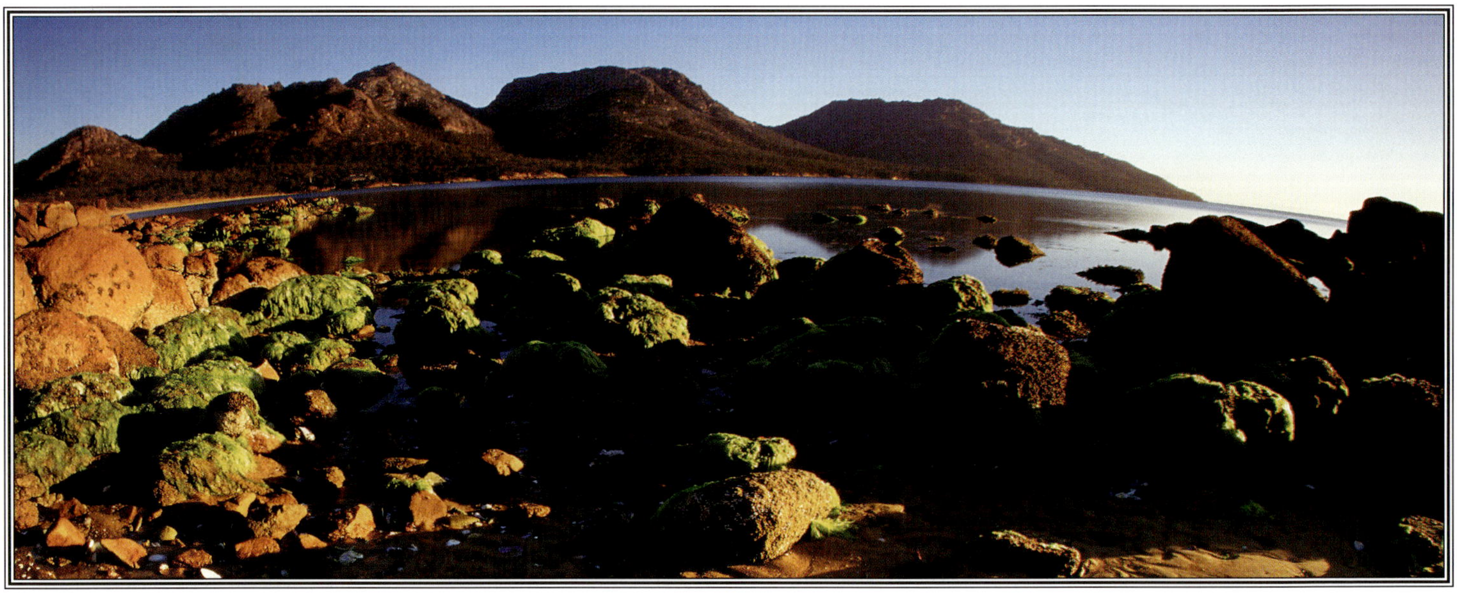

Evening light paints the Hazards at Coles Bay

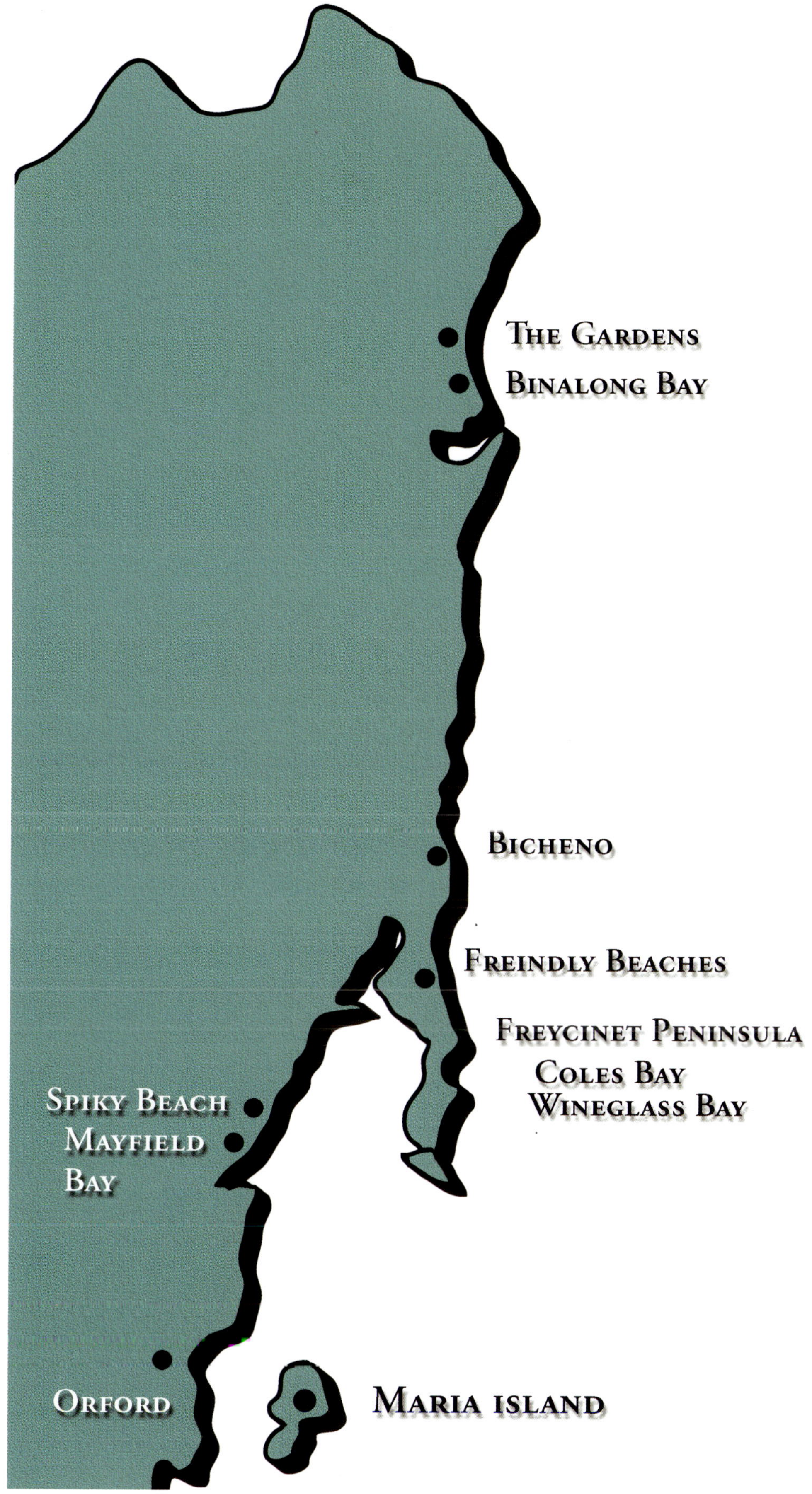
The Gardens
Binalong Bay
Bicheno
Freindly Beaches
Freycinet Peninsula
Coles Bay
Wineglass Bay
Spiky Beach
Mayfield
Bay
Orford
Maria island

Spiky Beach

South of Swansea lies an unassuming stretch of seascape called Spiky Beach, a soft stretch of sand bordered by rugged, dark rocks upon which grows a contrasting bright orange-coloured lichen.

Stand on the rocks and look out over Great Oyster Bay toward the Freycinet Peninsula or simply wonder at the shapes and textures of the bull kelp washed upon the sand.

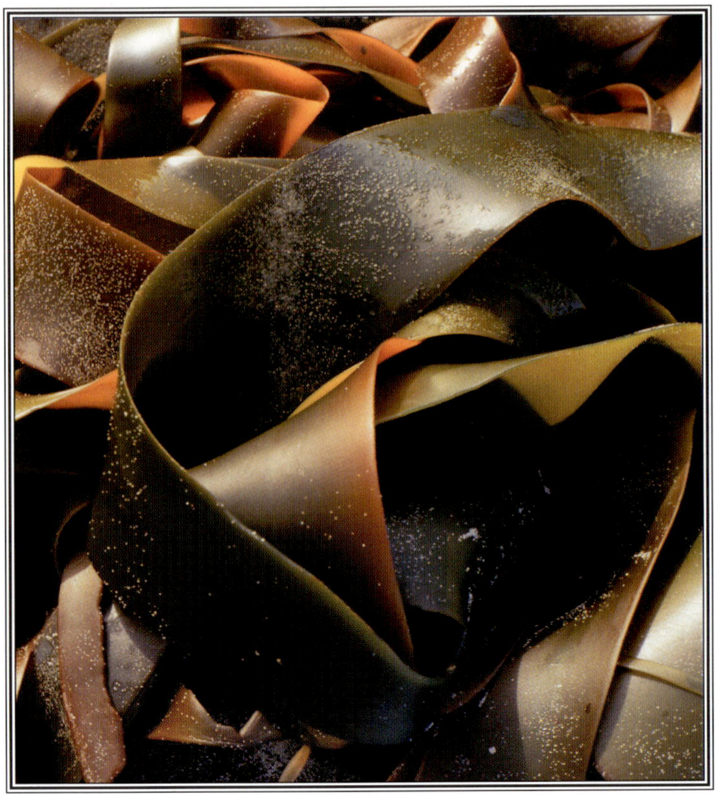

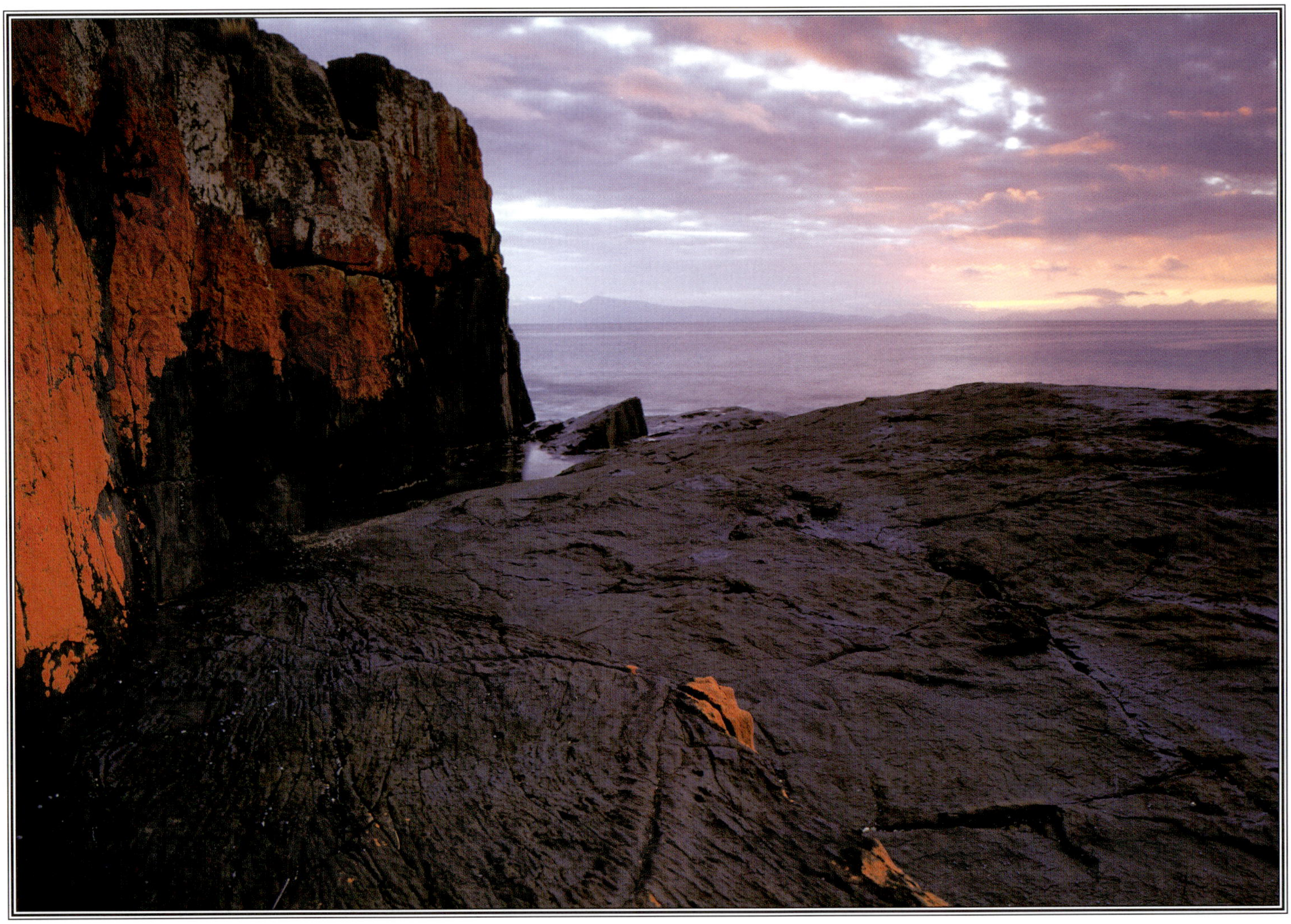

Top: *Giant kelp leaves deposited on the beaches*
Bottom: *Orange lichen covered rocks intensify the sunrise*

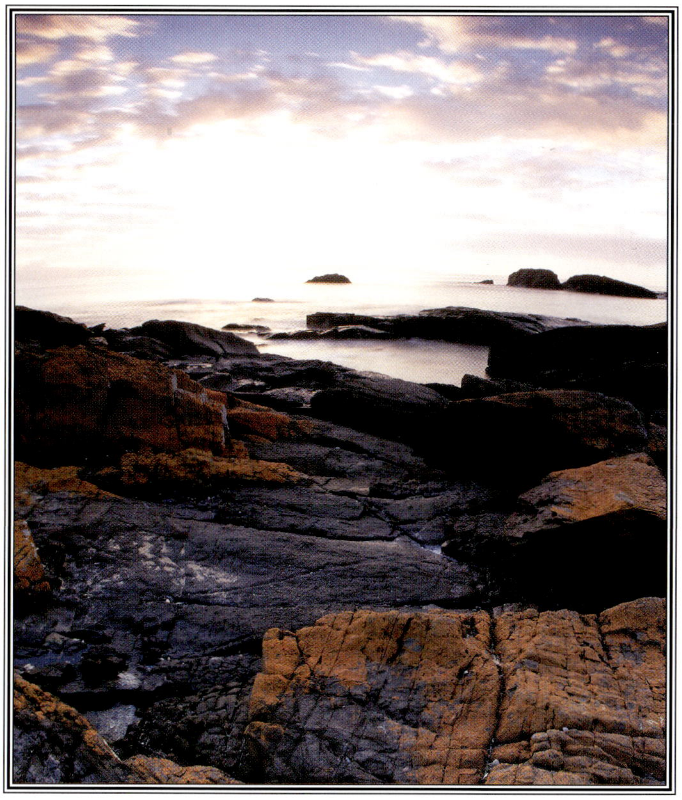

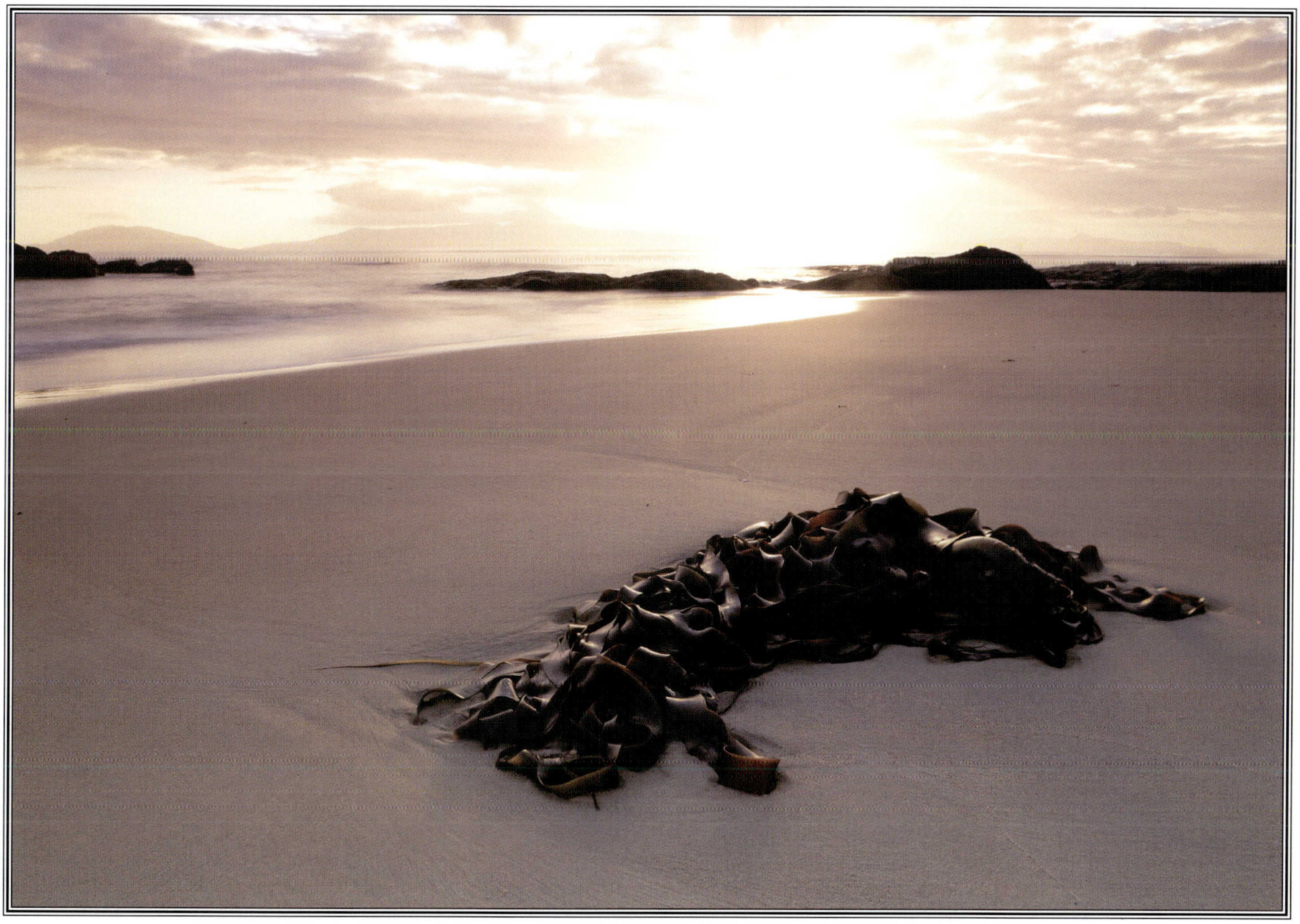

Top and bottom: *Sunrise over Great Oyster Bay from Spiky Beach*

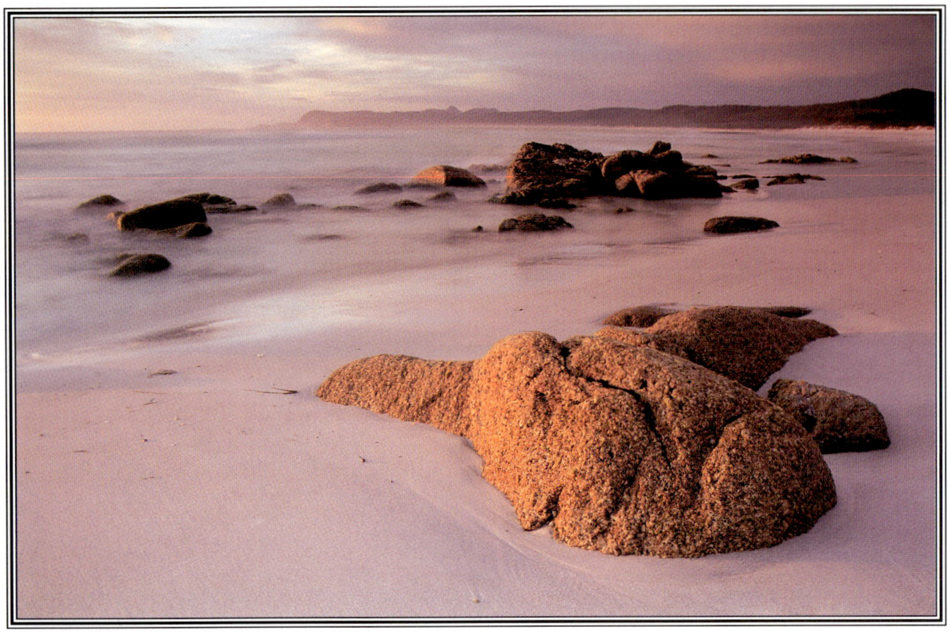

Friendly Beaches

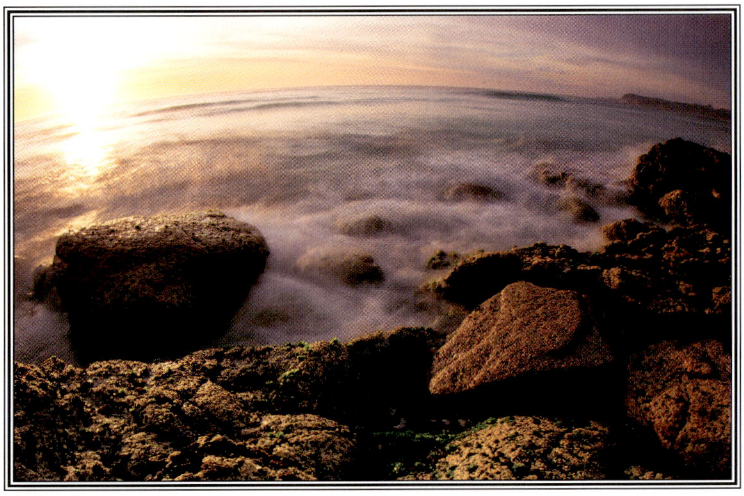

Friendly Beaches is a picturesque expanse of beach wilderness found whilst travelling to Coles Bay and the Freycinet Peninsula.

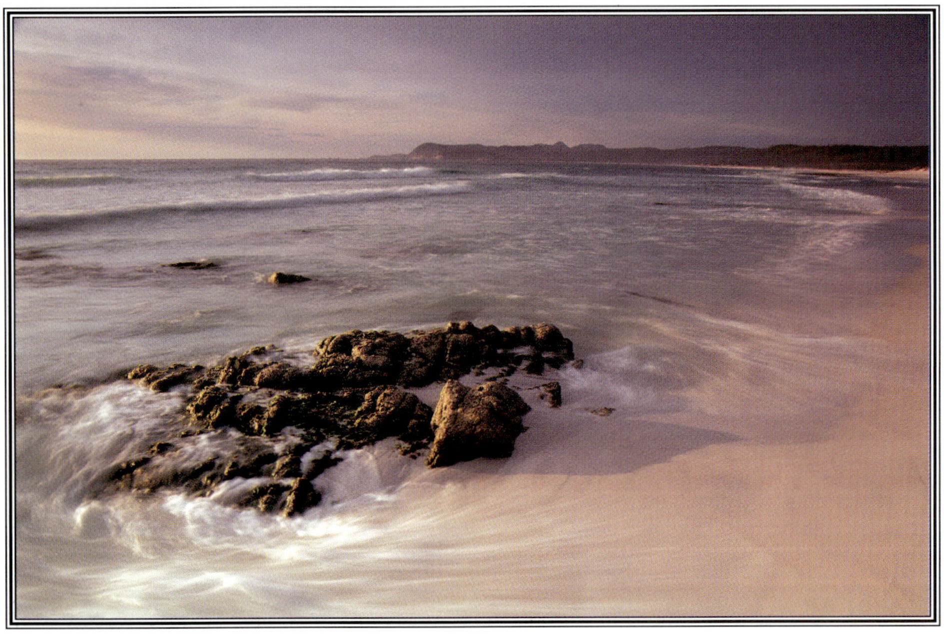

Generally deserted, long expanses of squeaky fine sand offer an opportunity for reflection whilst beachcombing one of the most pristine beach areas Tasmania has to offer.

The gentle colours of morning on Friendly Beaches

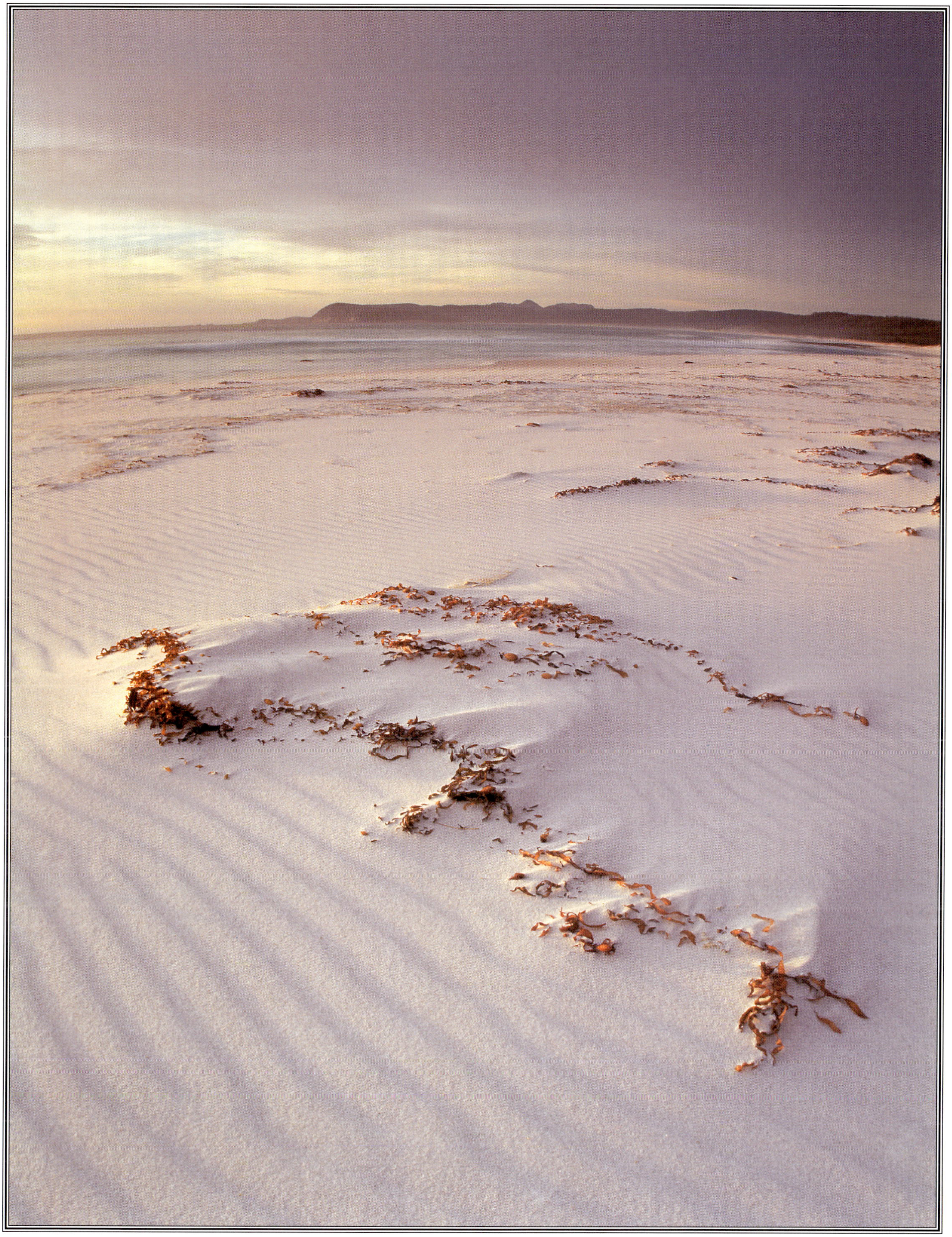

The windblown corrugations in the sand of Friendly Beaches

Freycinet Peninsula

Coles Bay is the gateway to the Freycinet Peninsula National Park. Protecting that gateway are 'The Hazards', three mountains that divide the land from the peninsula.

Scramble between these mountains to the lookout and discover the beauty of Wineglass Bay and the Freycinet Peninsula, or simply marvel as the Hazards turn a fiery red in the last rays of a setting sun.

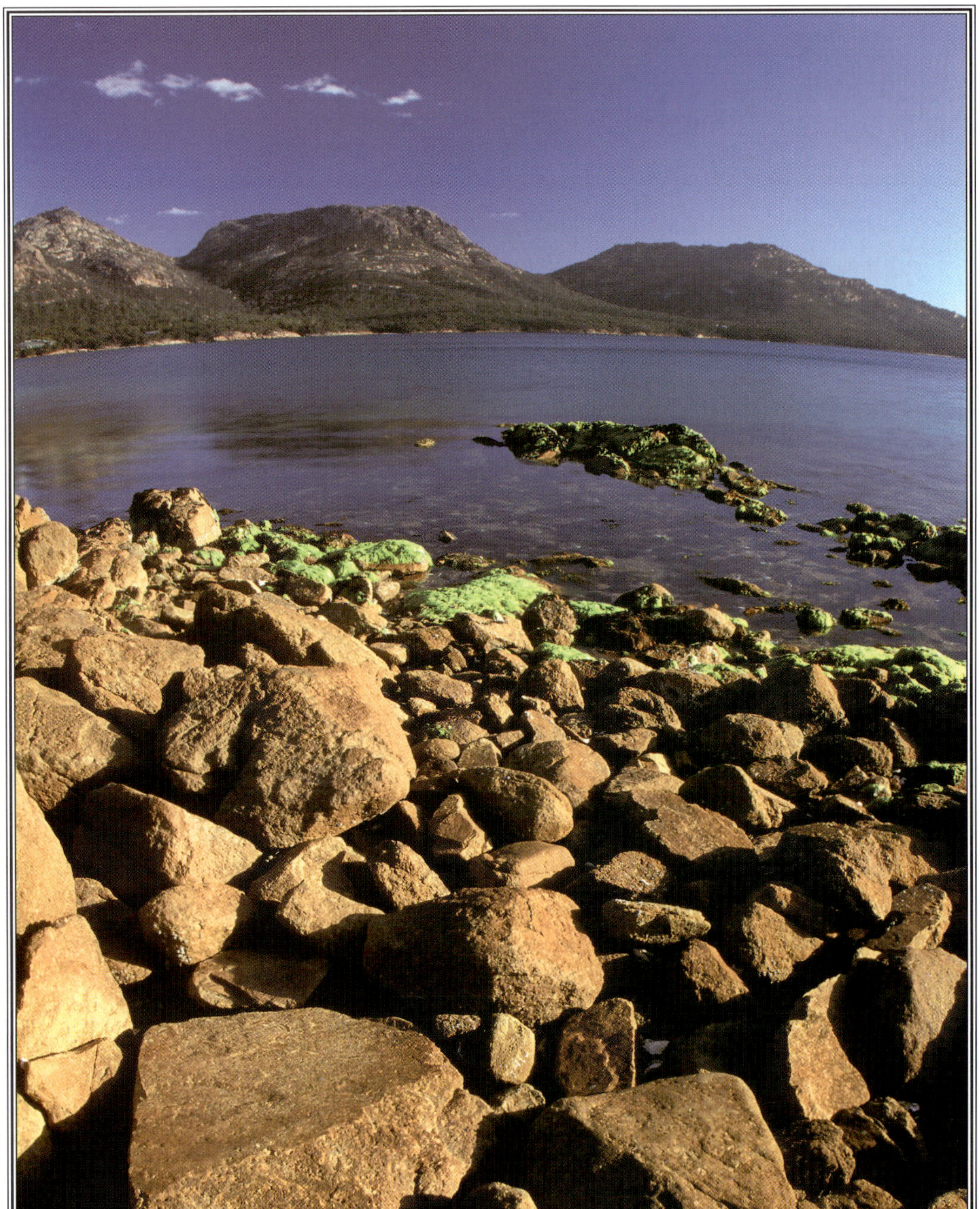

The Hazards from Richardson's Beach

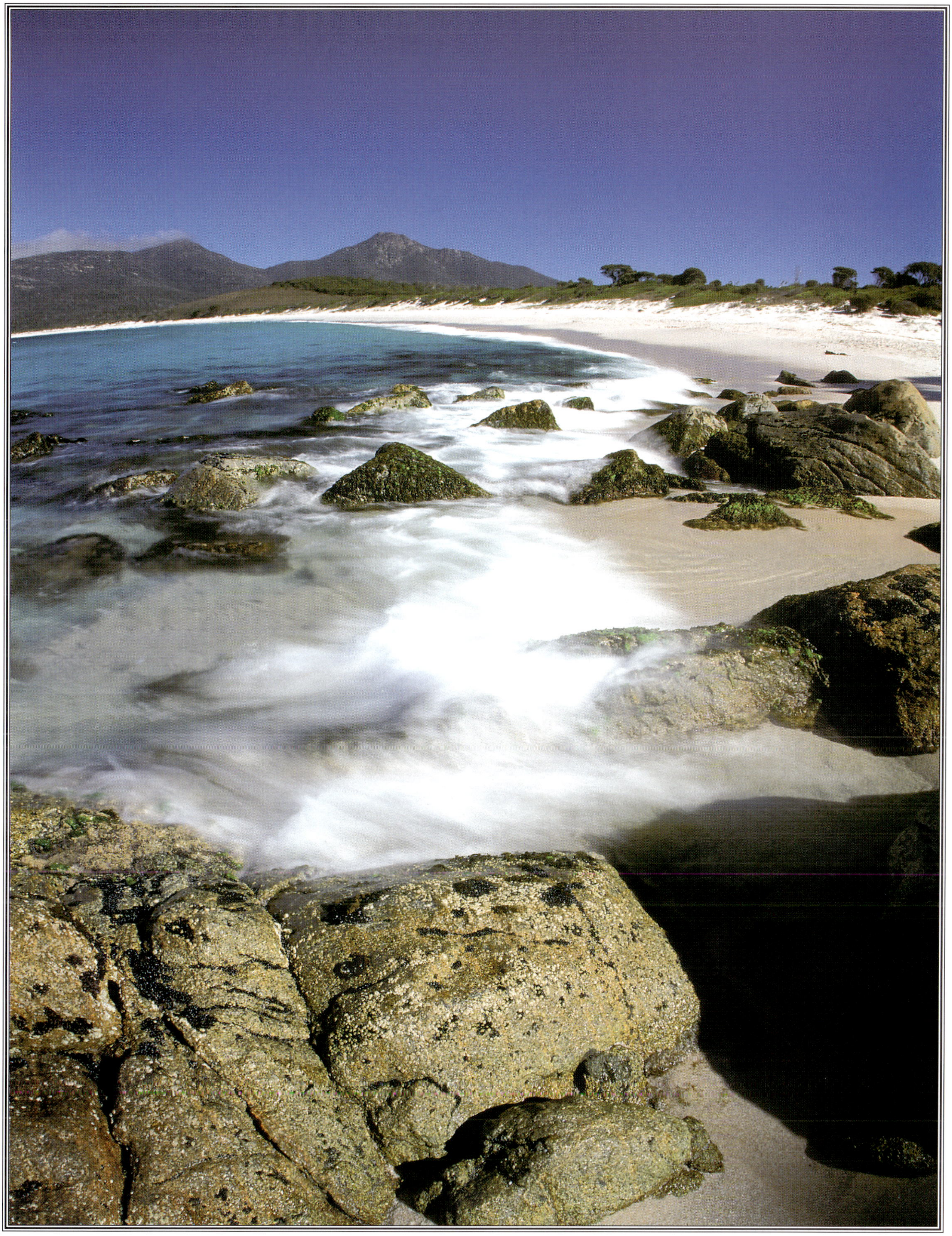

The pure white sands and deep blue water of Wineglass Bay

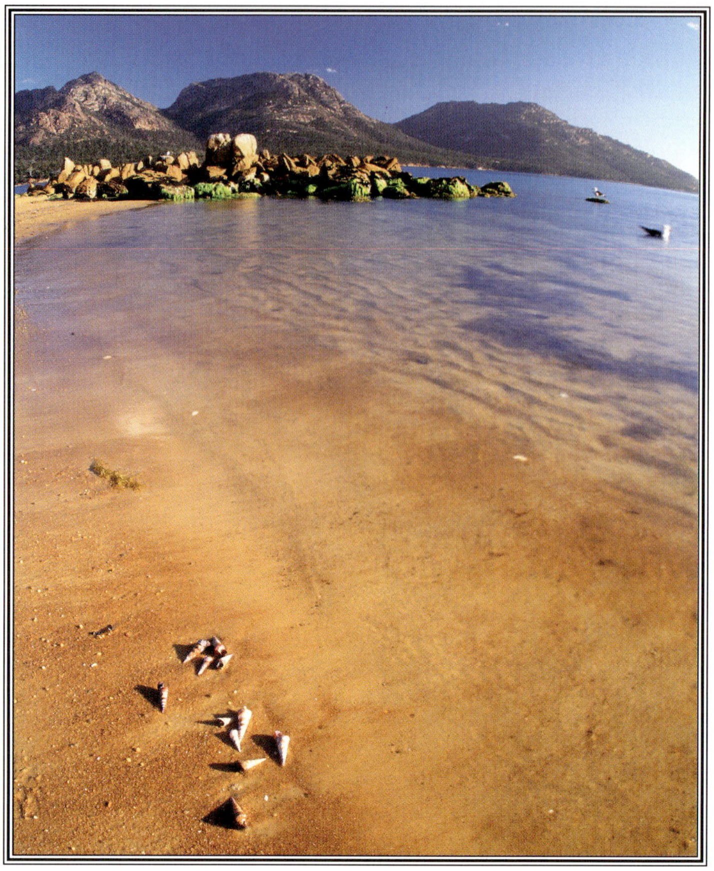

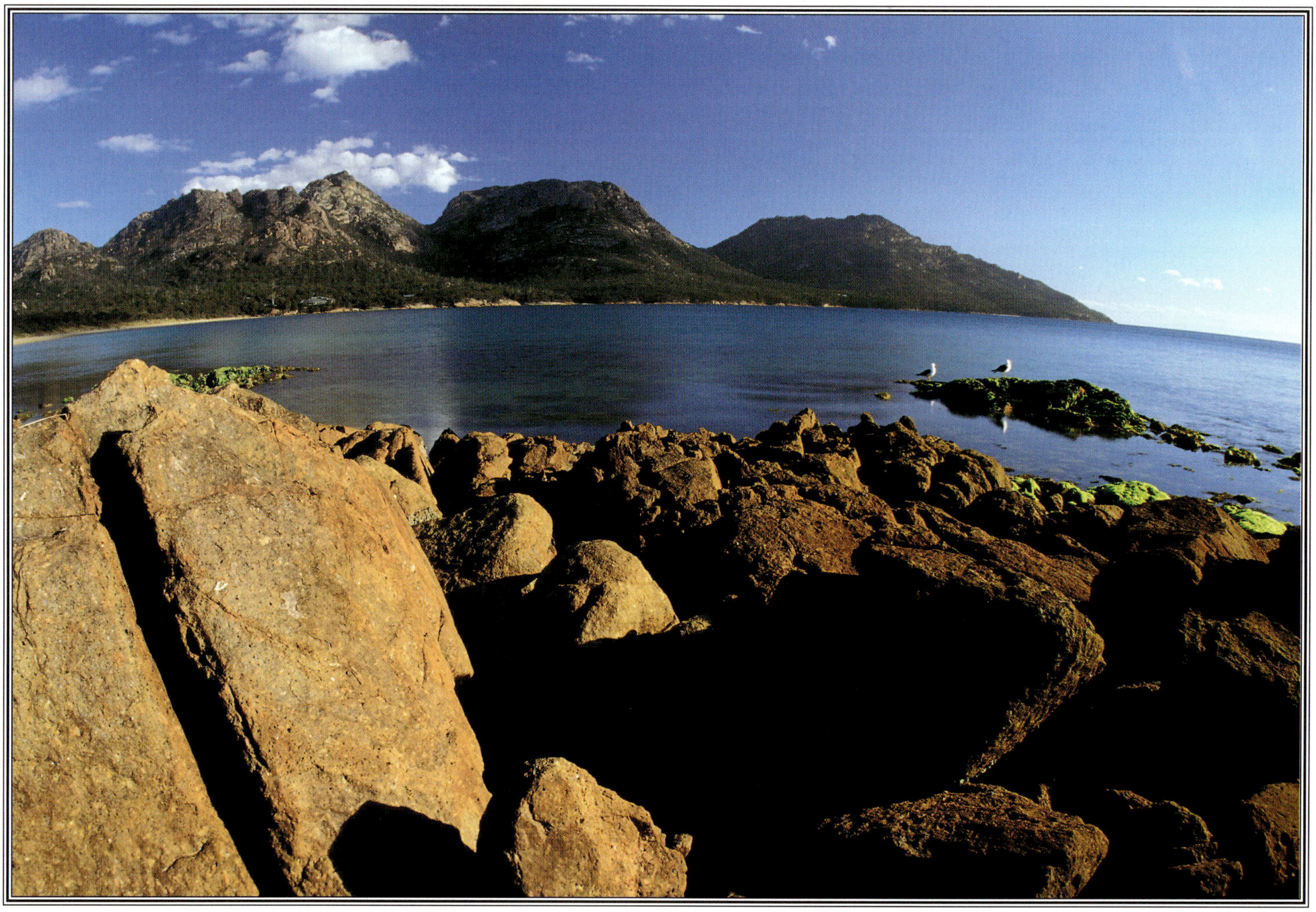

The Hazards from the beaches of Coles Bay

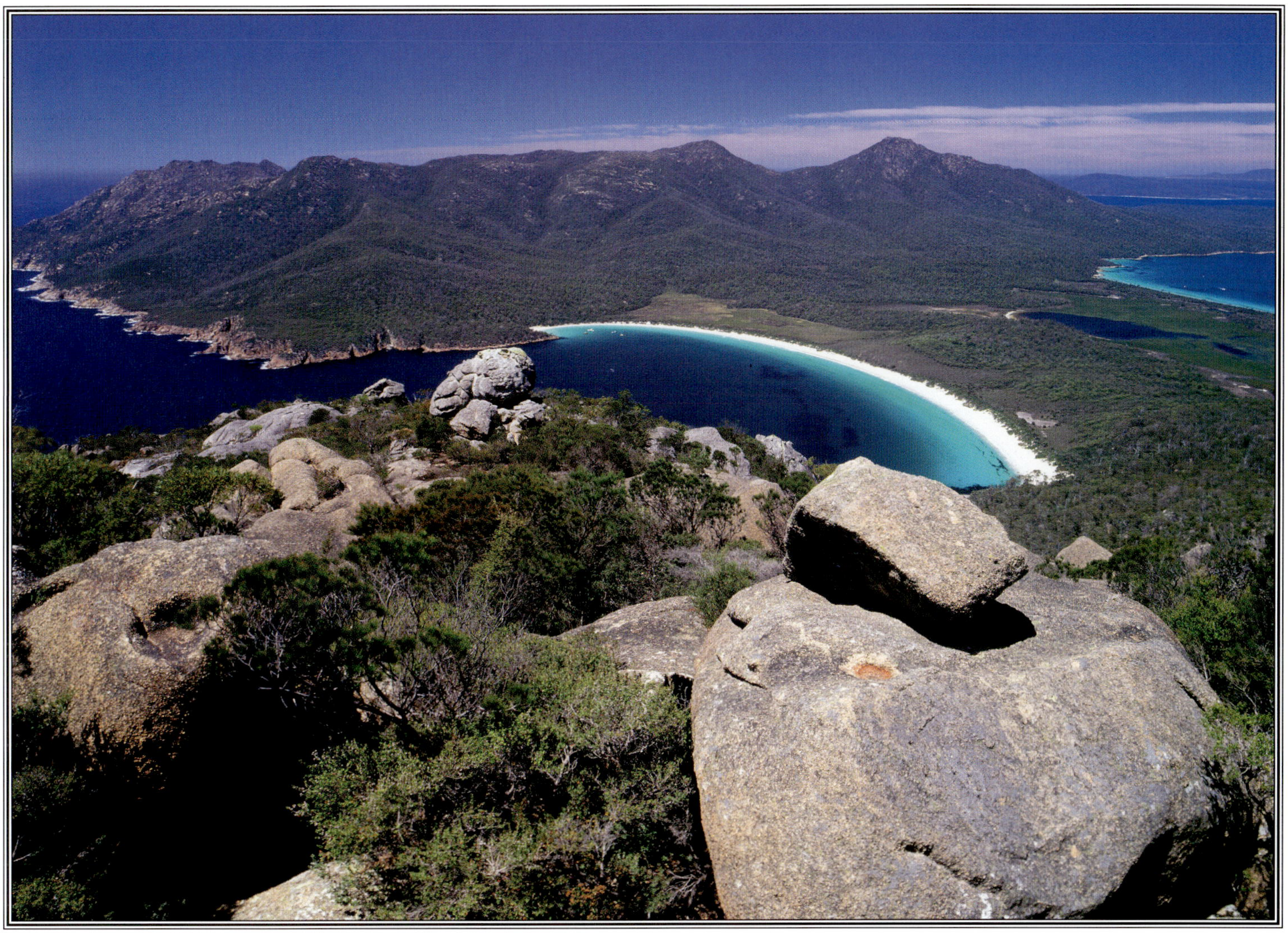

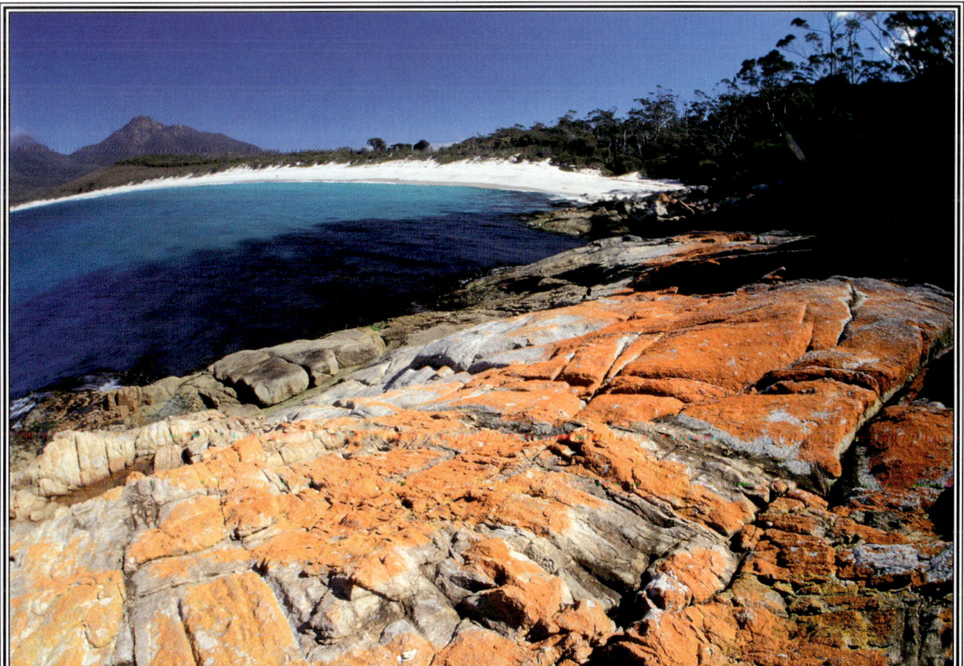

Top: *View of Wineglass Bay from Mt. Amos*
Bottom: *Orange lichen covered rocks at Wineglass Bay*

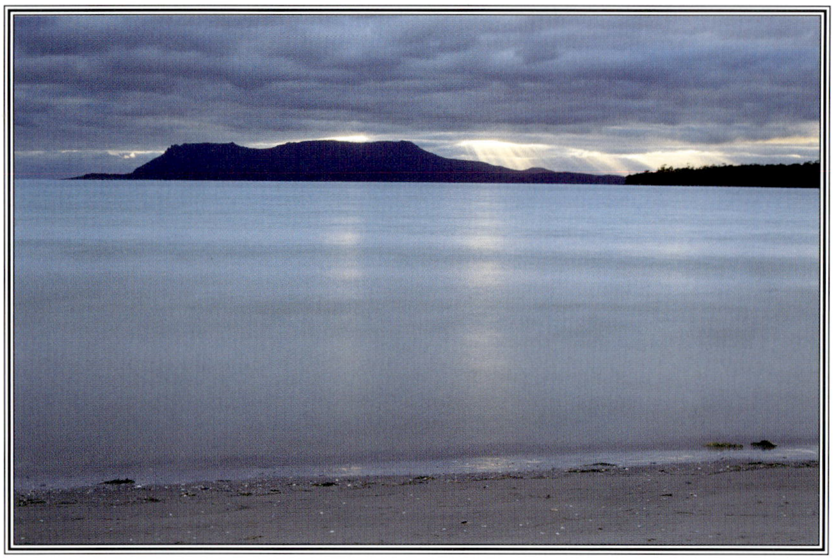

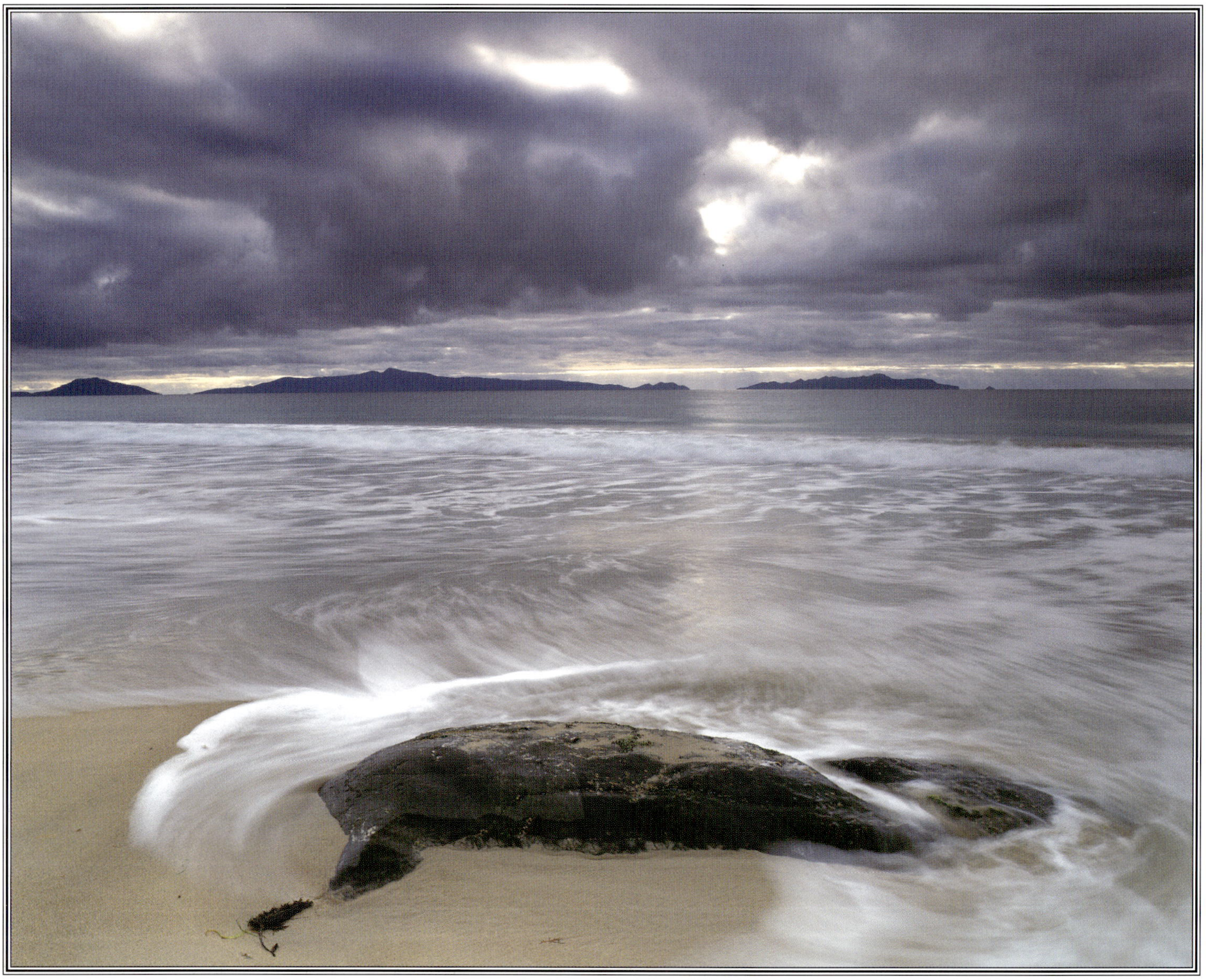

Top: *View to Maria Island, across Prosser Bay*
Bottom: *Mayfield Bay looks out to Freycinet National Park*

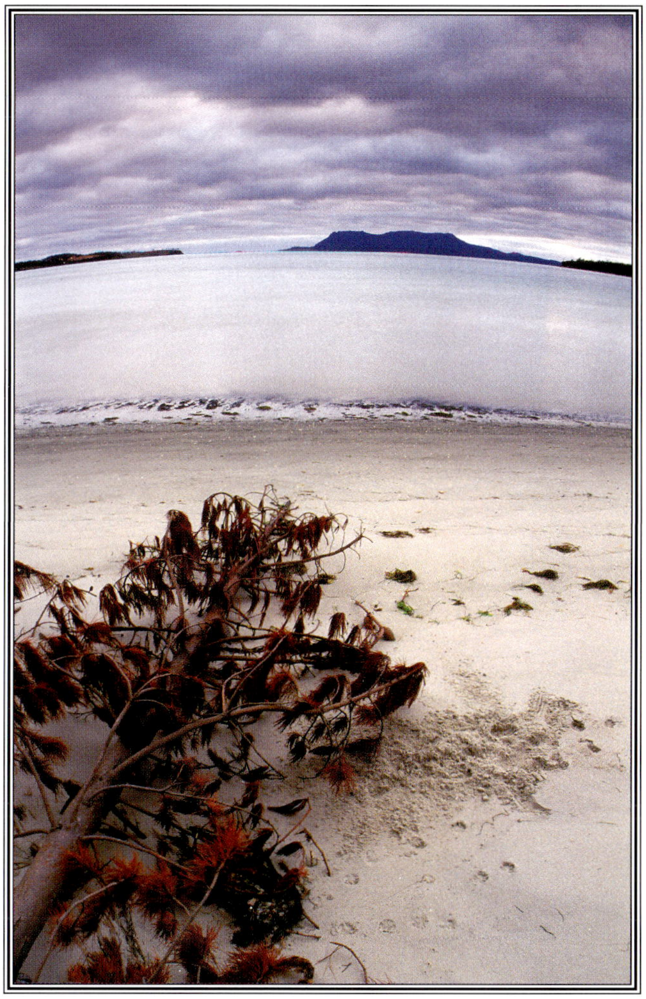

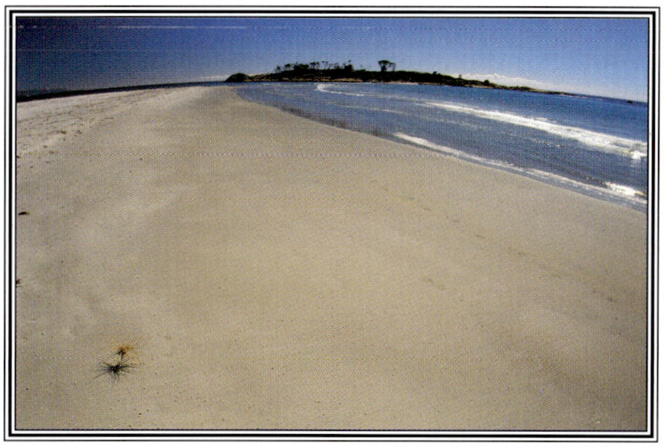

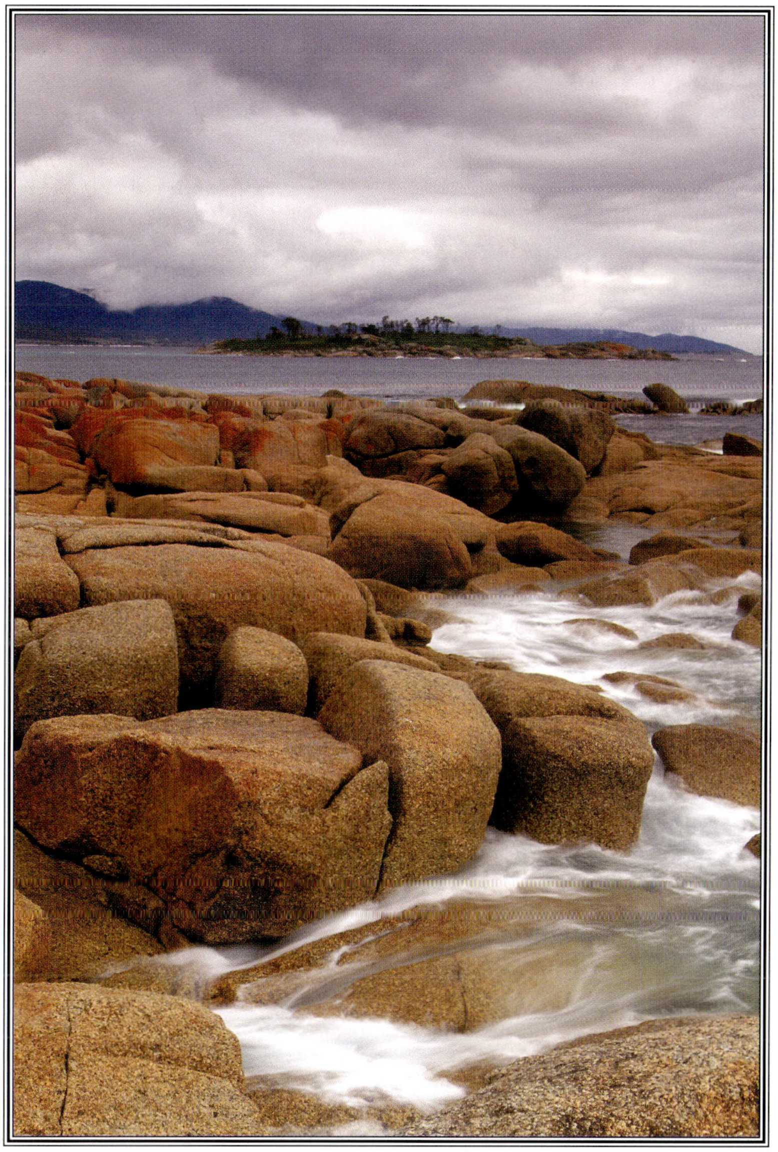

Top left: *Maria Island from Orford*
Top right: *Bicheno beaches*
Bottom right: *Diamond Island from the rocks of Bicheno*

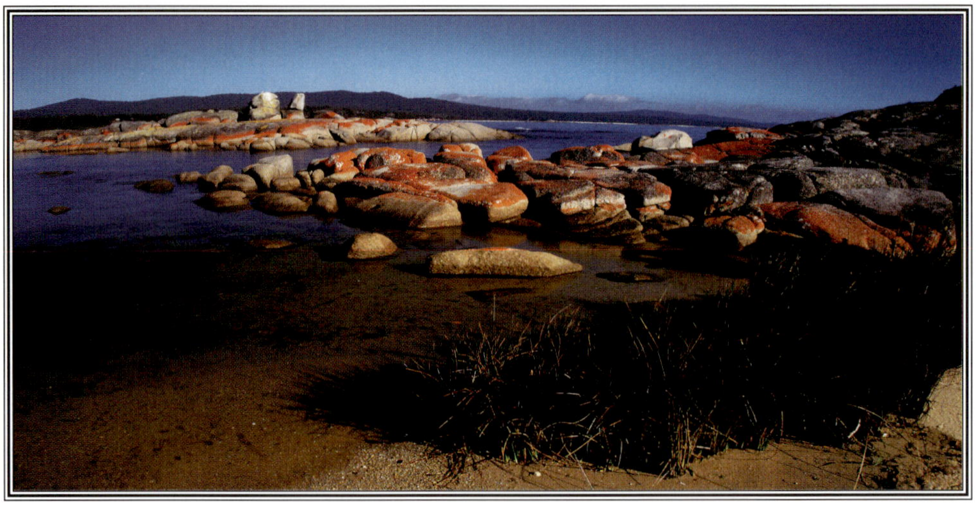

Binalong Bay

To the North East of St. Helens is the small coastal town of Binalong Bay. Popular for its combination of soft white sands and crystal clear, blue waters, Binalong Bay is a favourite with both visitors and locals alike. Huge boulders representing all the colours of the rainbow contour the inspiring landscape of this seaside paradise, guaranteeing an enduring memory for all those who witness its beauty.

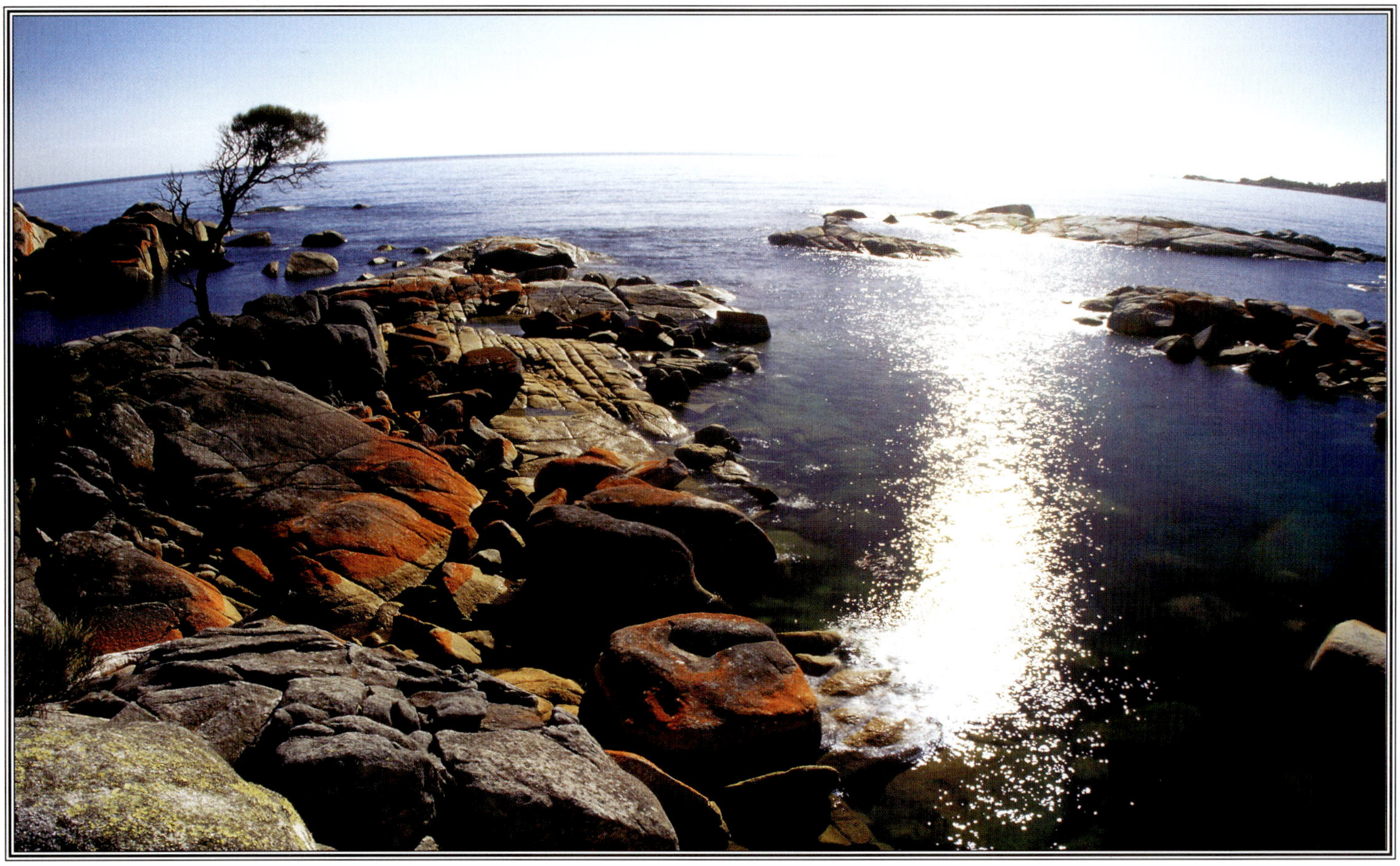

Top and Bottom: *The rock formations and colours of Binalong Bay*

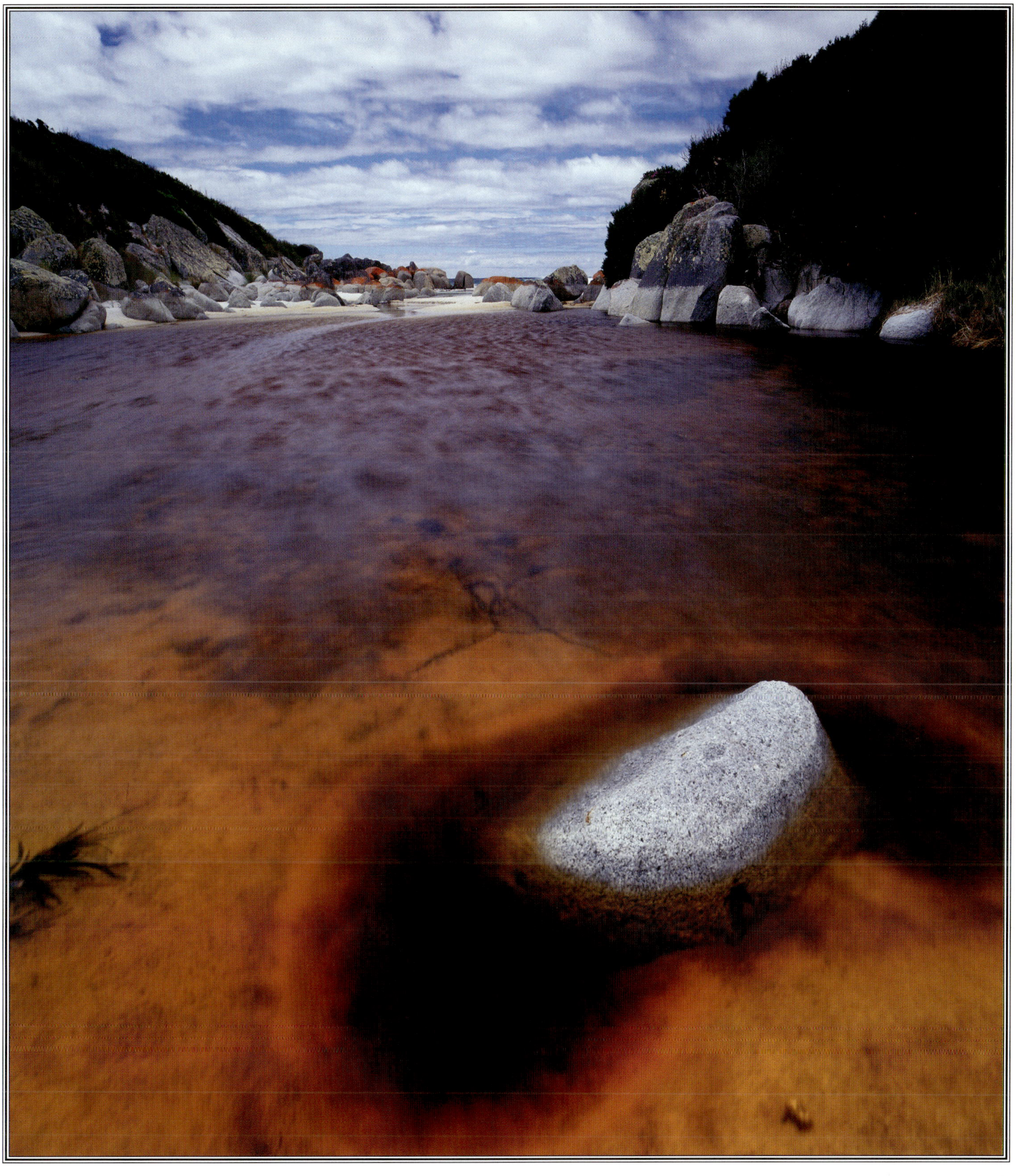

Tannin stained water flowing into the Bay of Fires - The Gardens

Binalong Bay beach

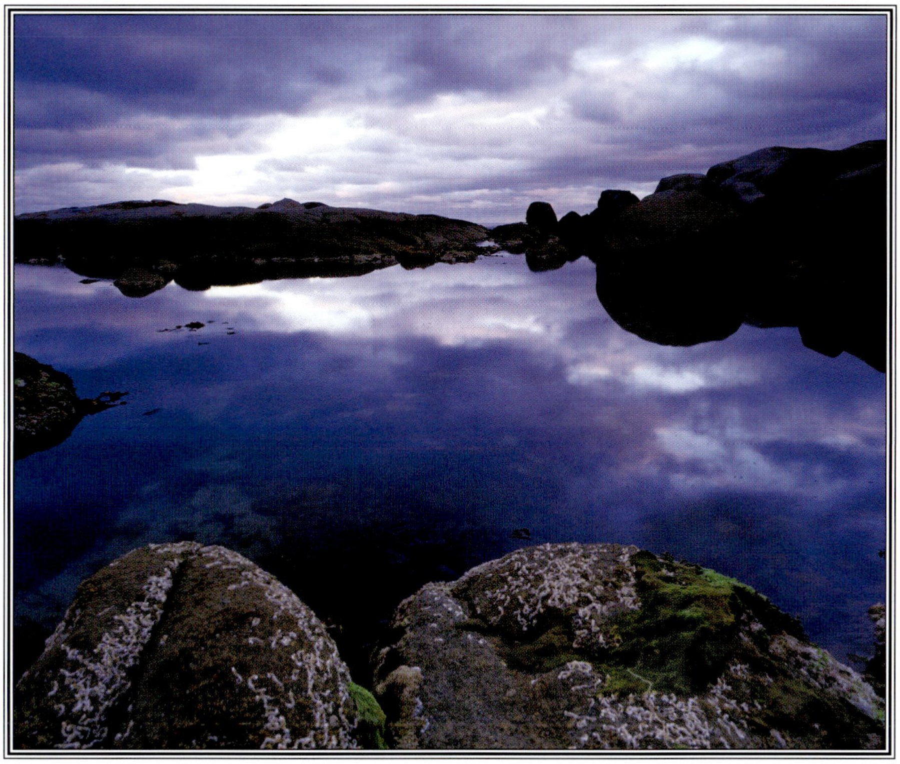

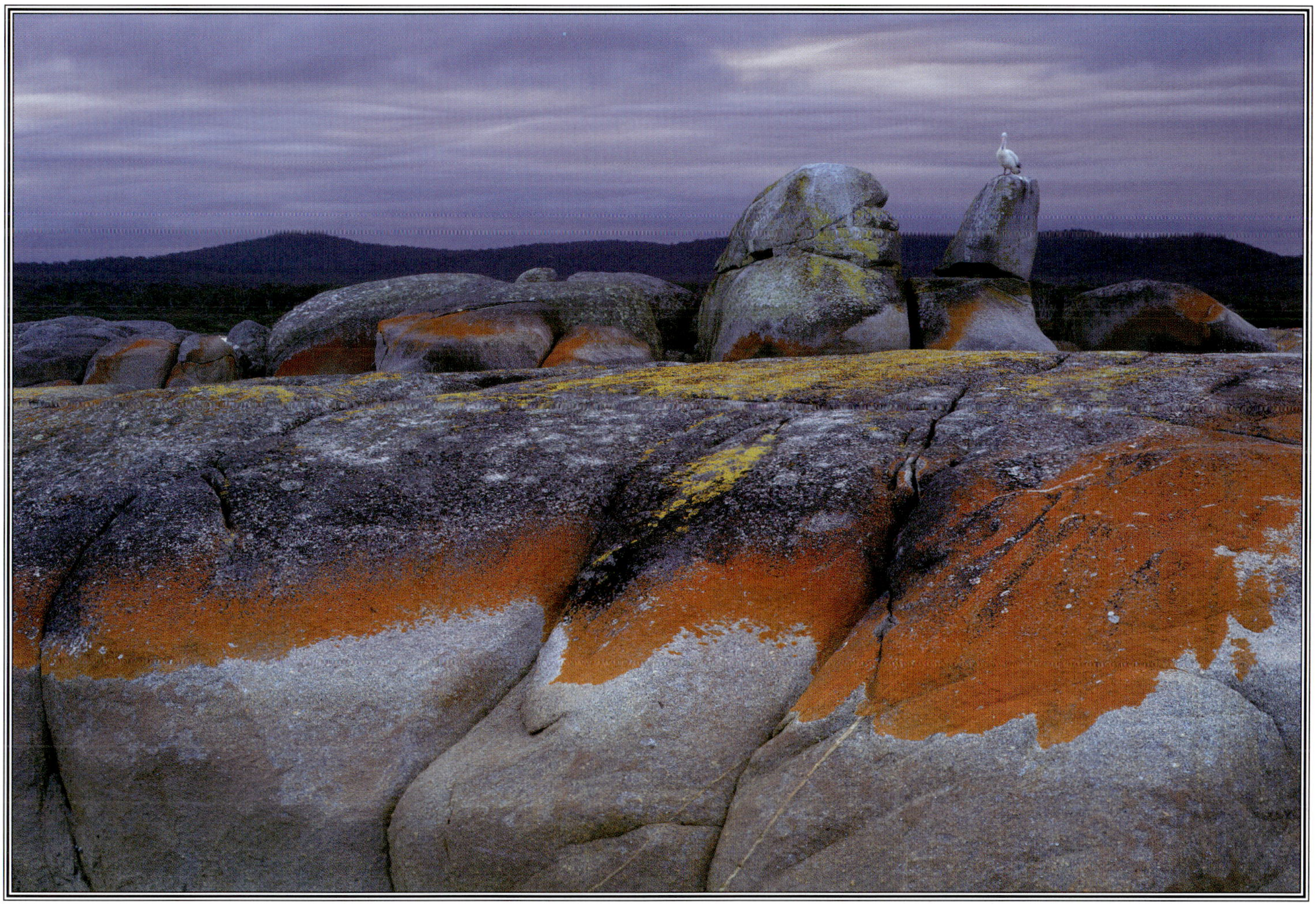

Top: *Pool reflections at nightfall*
Bottom: *Pelican resting on the rocks at Binalong Bay*

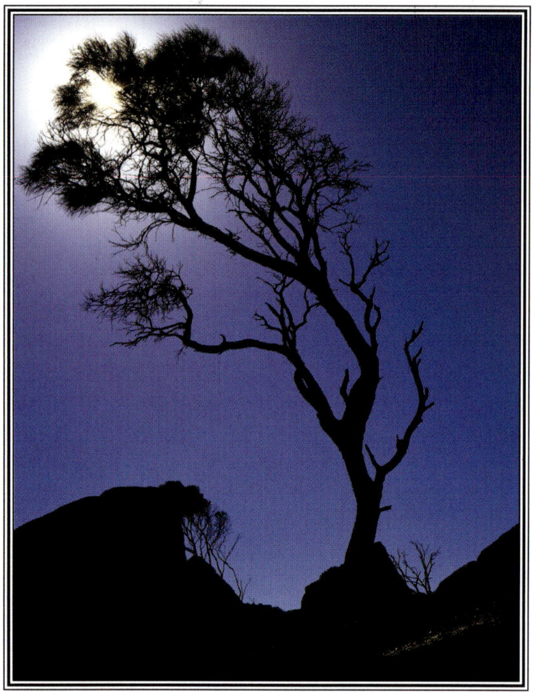

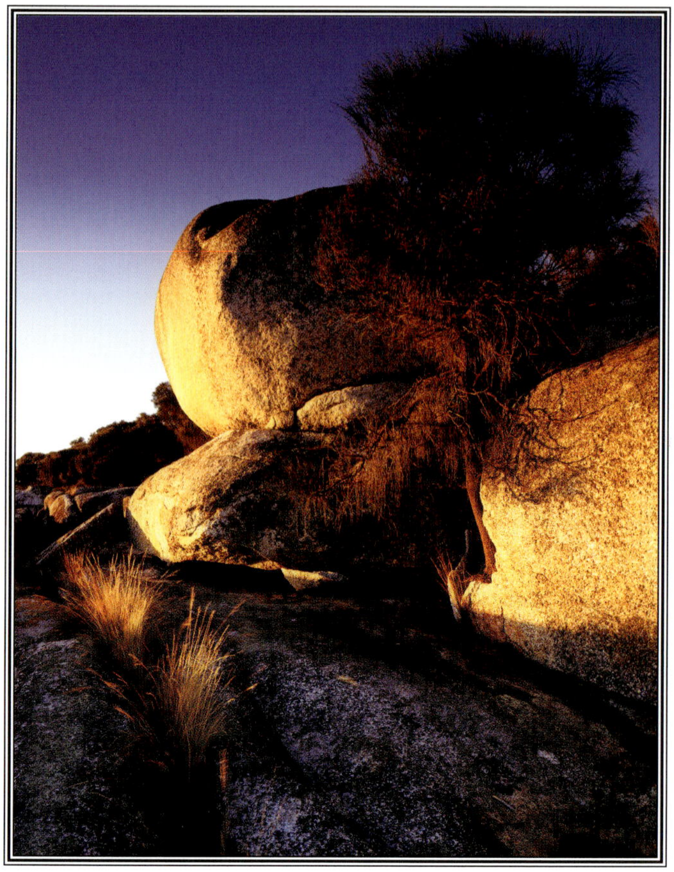

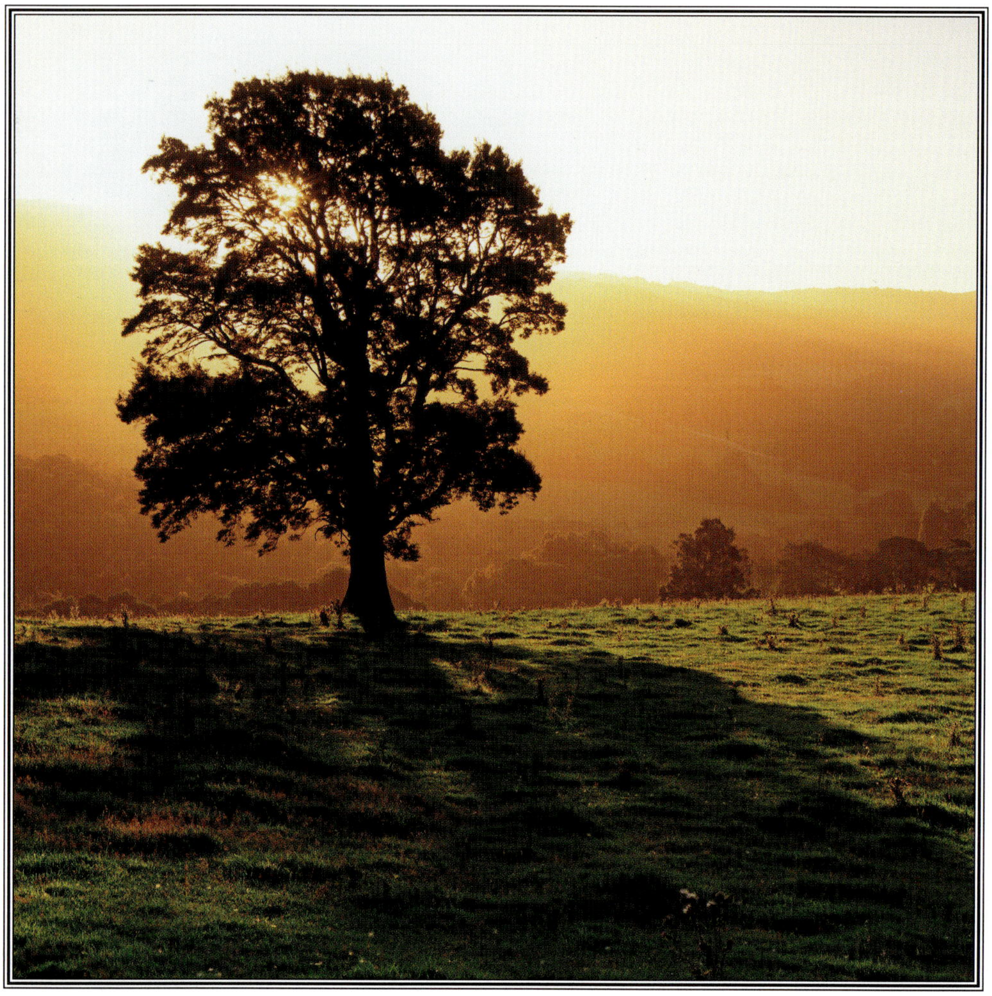

The beautiful landscape surrounding the east coast beaches of Tasmania

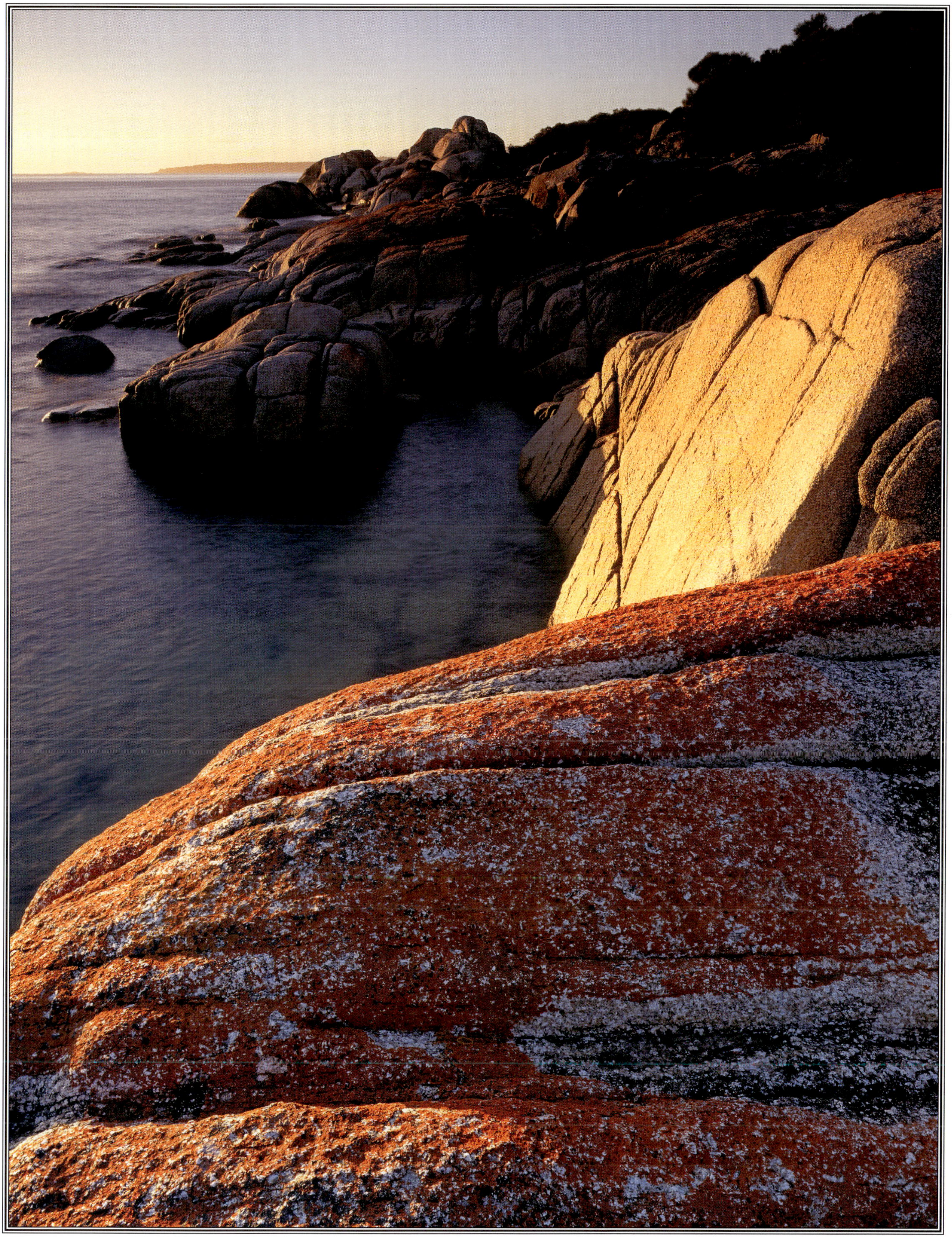

Morning light at Sloop Reef

Tasmania's West

One fifth of Tasmania is listed as a 'World Heritage' area and most of this protected landscape can be found in Tasmania's west.

Craggy mountain peaks and impenetrable forest surround sweeping button-grass plains, teeming with native wildlife. Meandering highland streams find their way to unspoiled beaches and release their tannin-stained waters to an often-treacherous ocean.

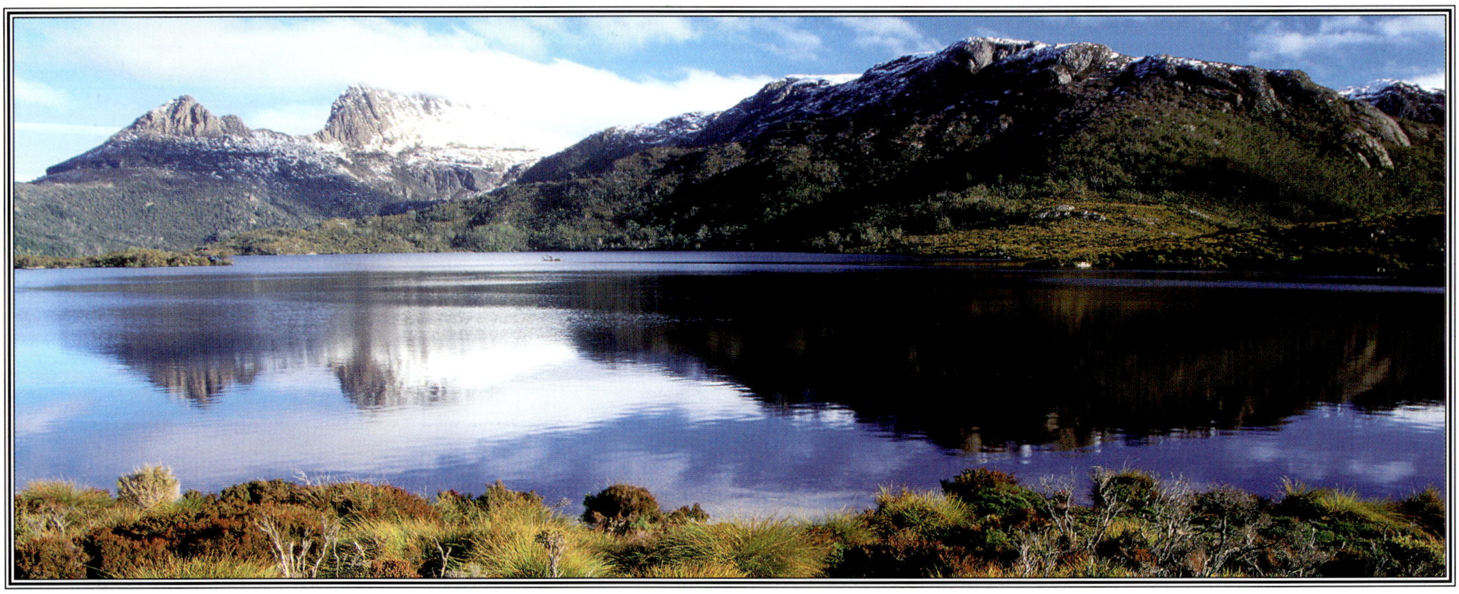

Cradle Mountain from the shore of Dove Lake

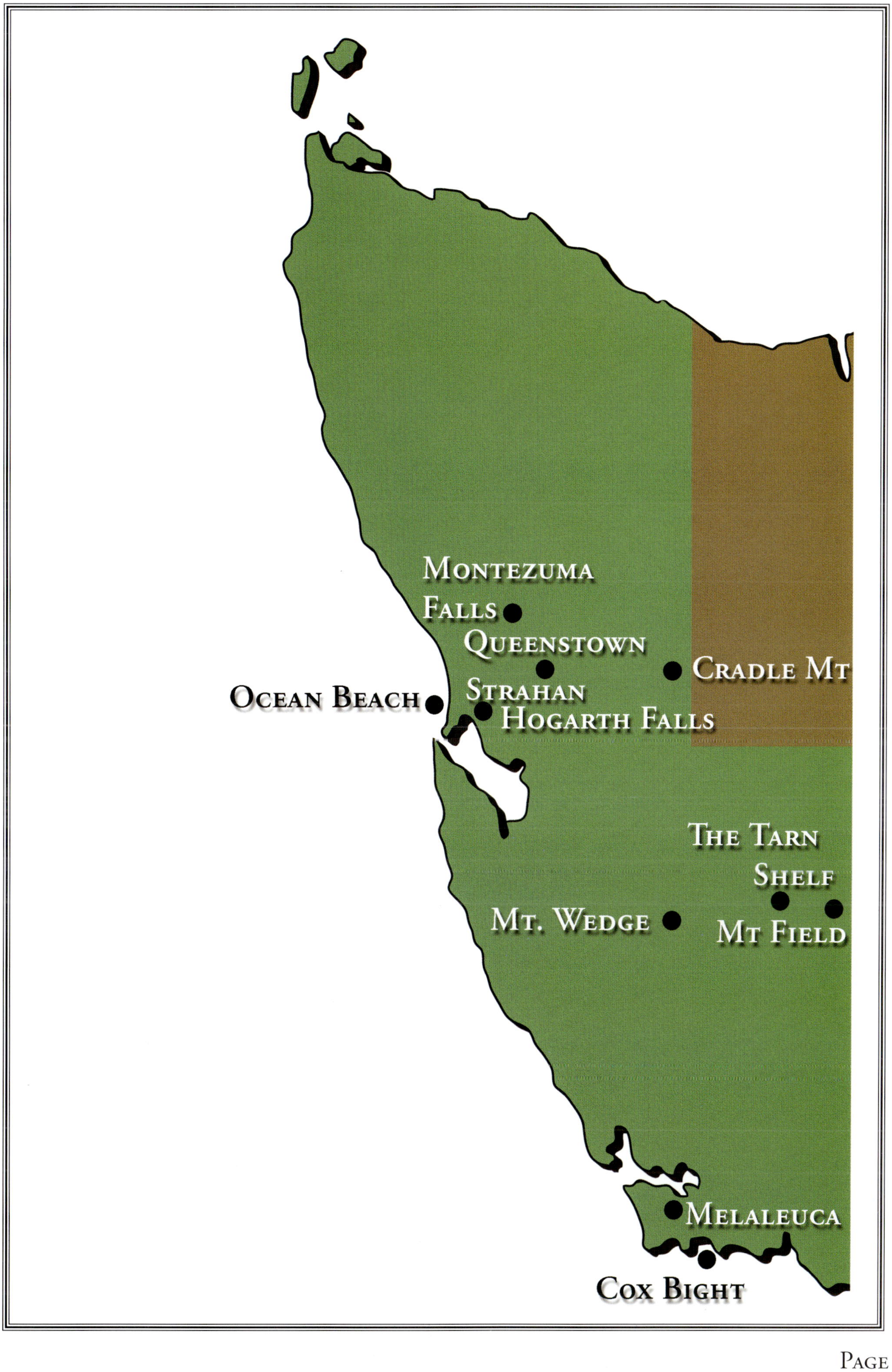
Montezuma Falls
Queenstown
Cradle Mt
Ocean Beach
Strahan
Hogarth Falls
The Tarn Shelf
Mt. Wedge
Mt Field
Melaleuca
Cox Bight

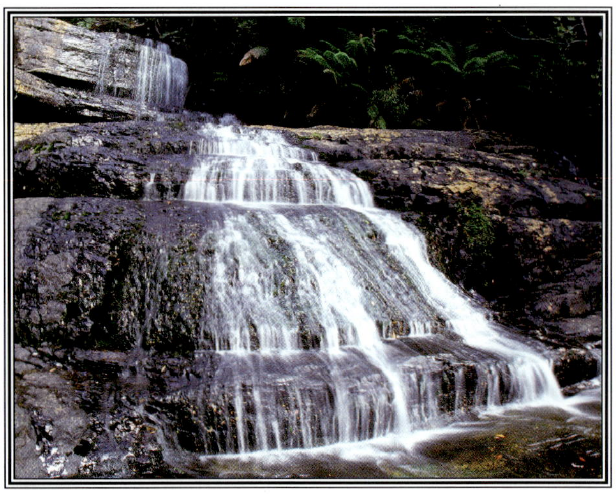

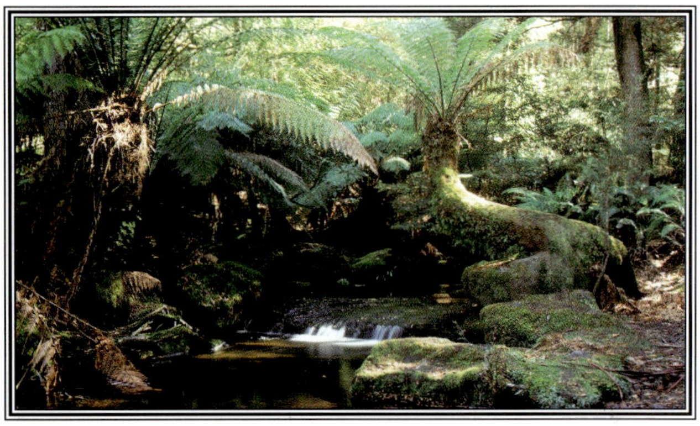

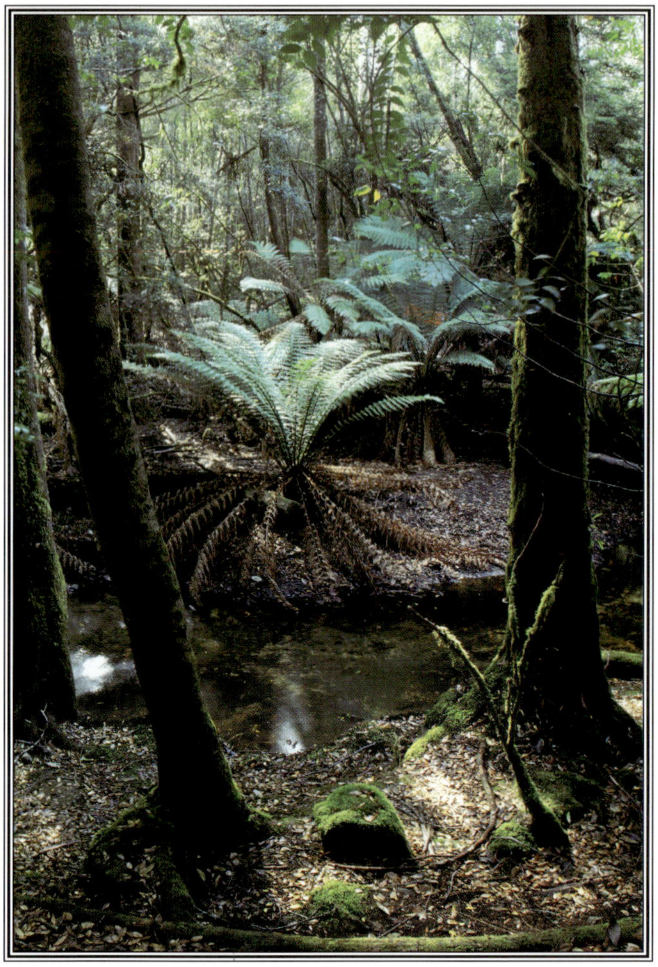

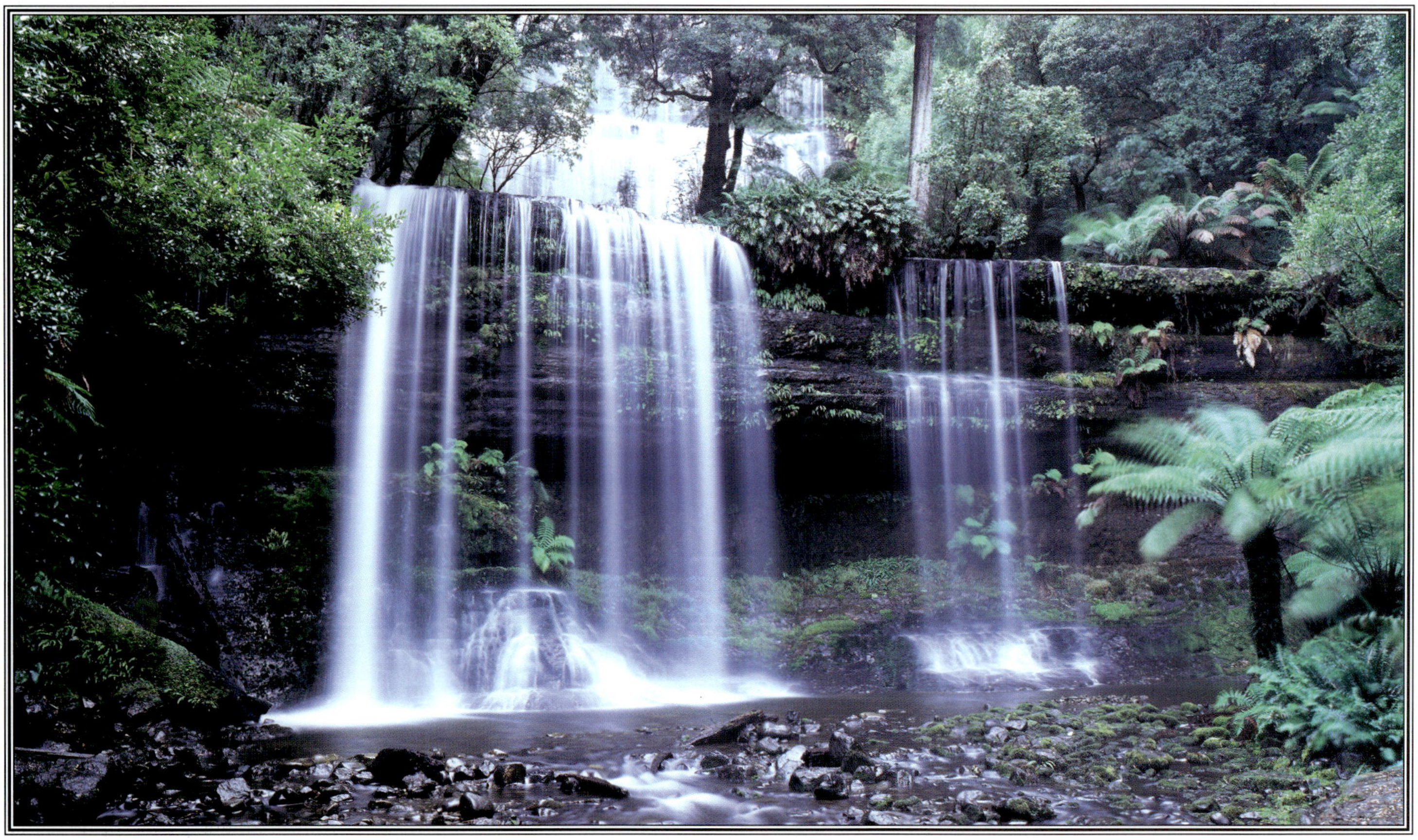

***Top left:** Lady Barron Falls **Top right:** The track to Russell Falls*
***Centre:** Meandering streams flow through Mt. Field National Park*
***Bottom:** Ancient rock layers behind Russell Falls*

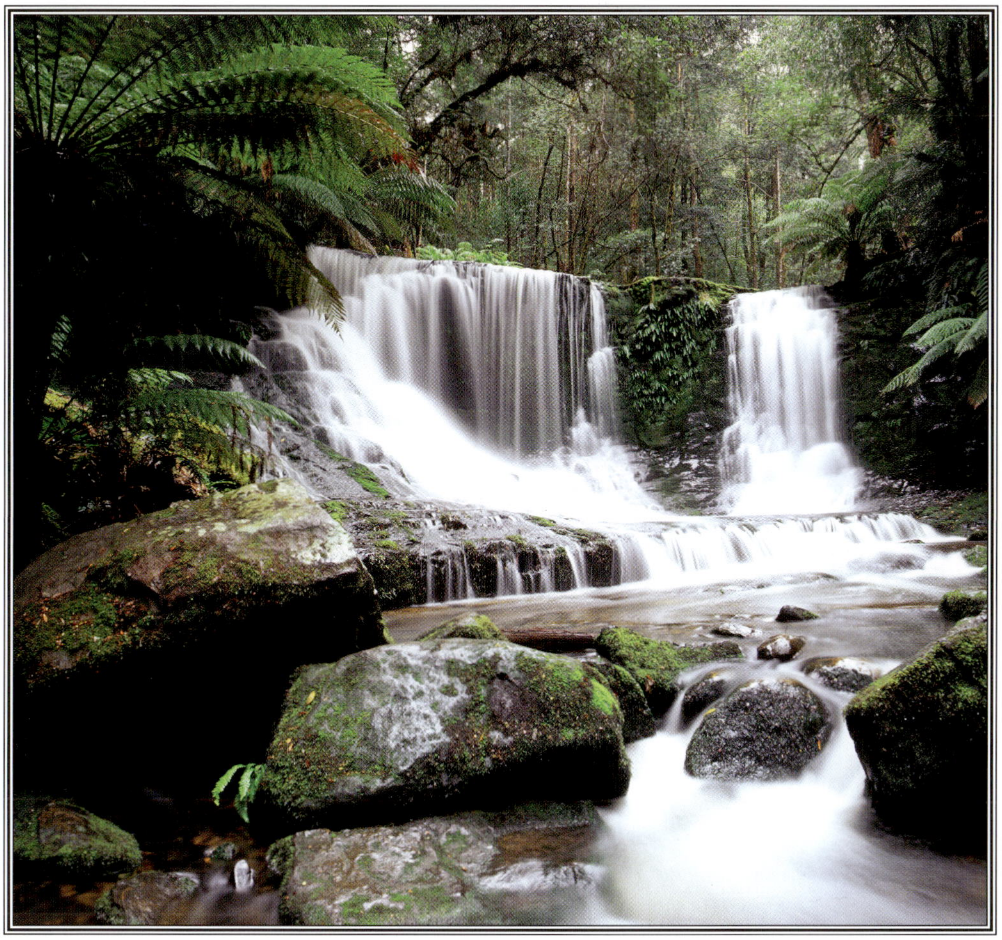

Mt. Field National Park

To the northwest of Hobart is Mt. Field National Park, Hobart's closest National Park. Lush green foliage lines the gentle walk to Russell Falls, where cascades of mountain water power over shelves of ancient rock.

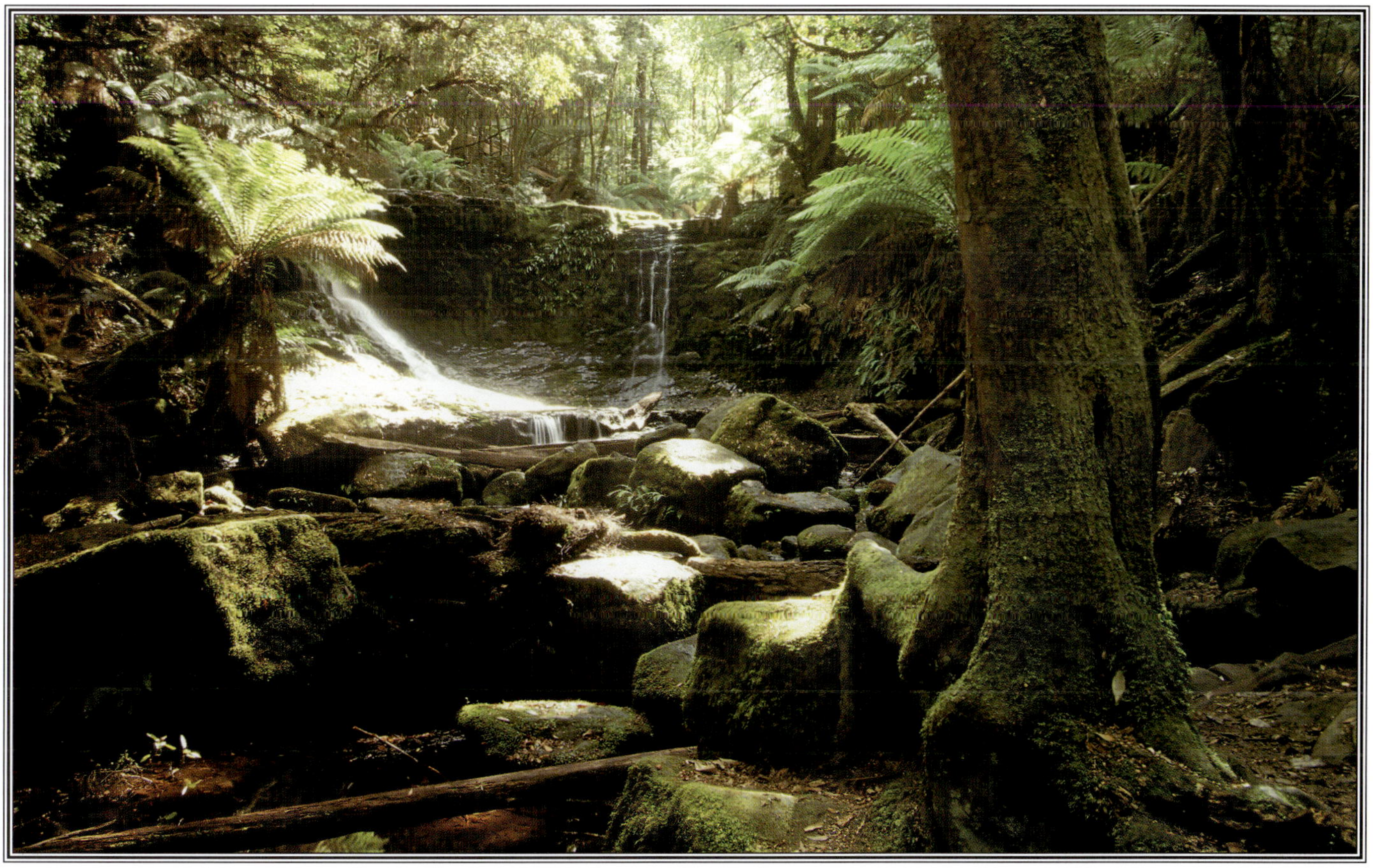

Top: *Horseshoe Falls running strong during winter*
Bottom: *The tranquil Horseshoe Falls during summer*

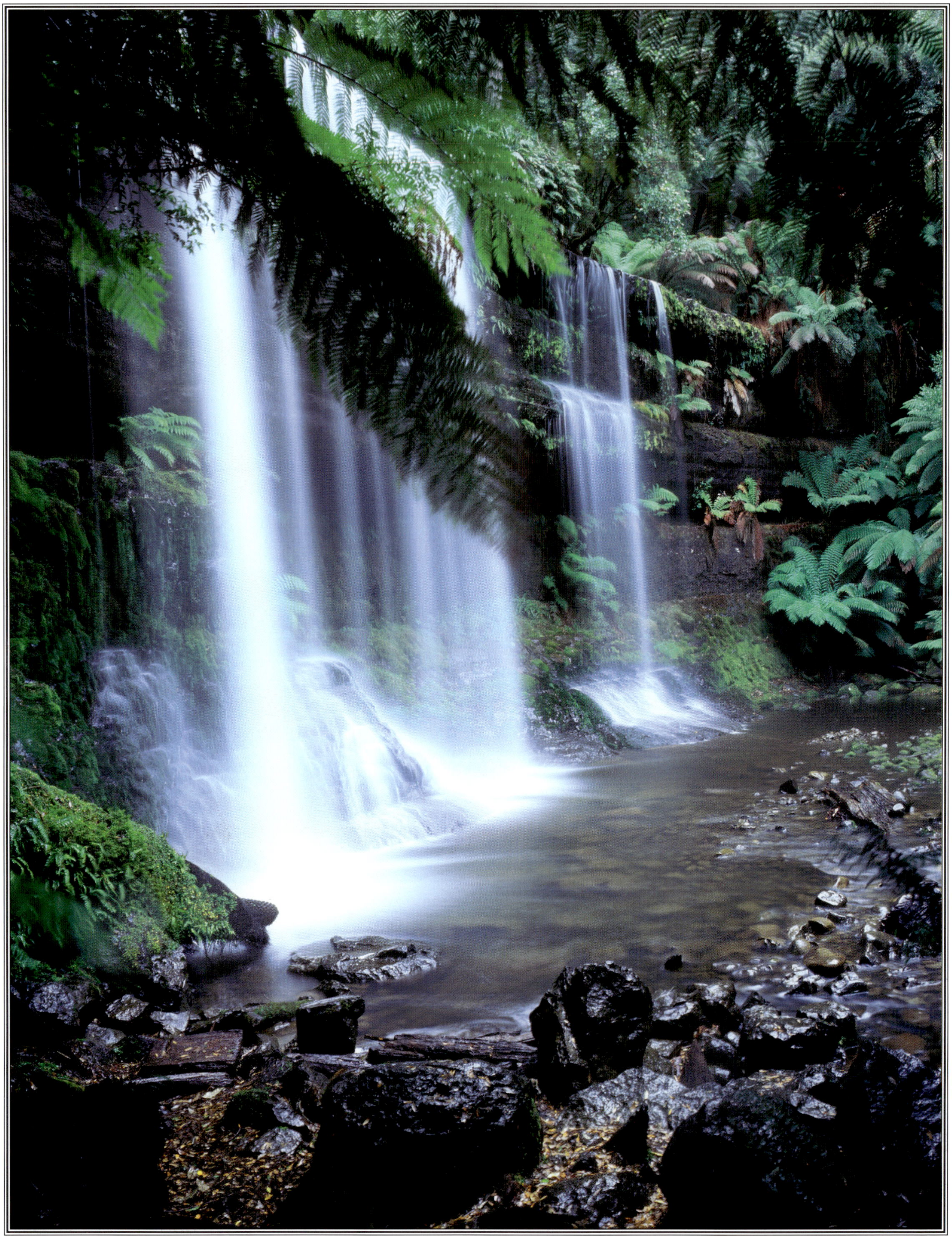

The might of Russell Falls

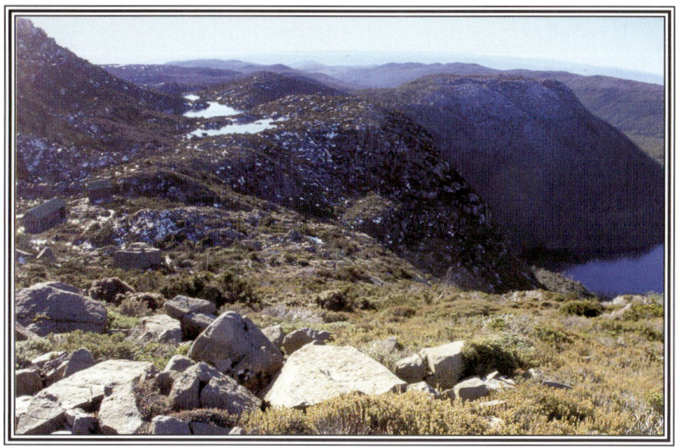

The Tarn Shelf

Located within Mt. Field National Park, the track around Lake Dobson provides an opportunity to walk to the Tarn Shelf, a series of smaller lakes, cradled on the plateau of a mountain.
The mirror-like surface of their cool waters provides perfect reflections of a spectacular mountain range, unless broken by the ripples of a mischievous platypus.

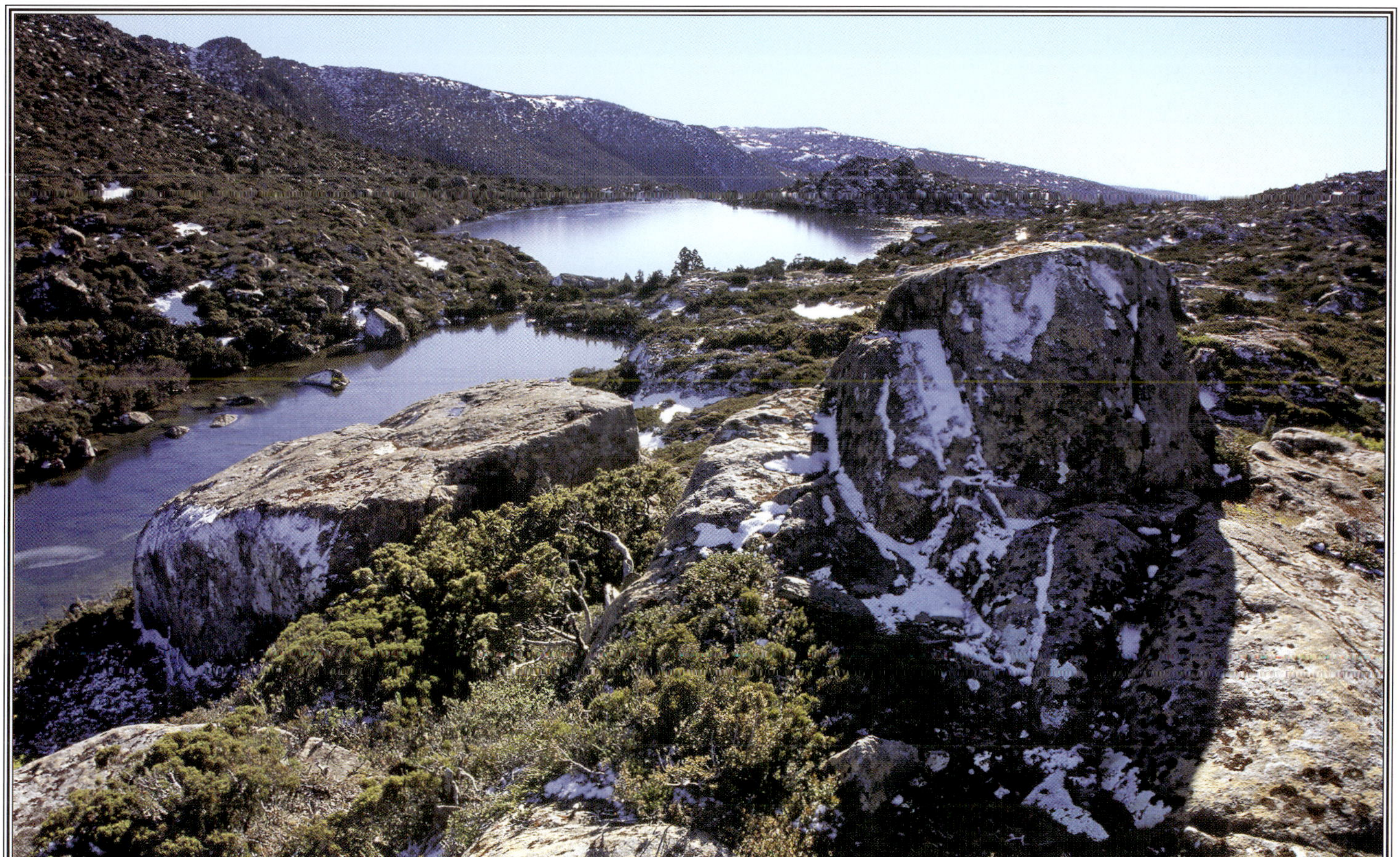

Top: *View to Lake Seal*
Bottom: *Still waters at The Tarn Shelf*

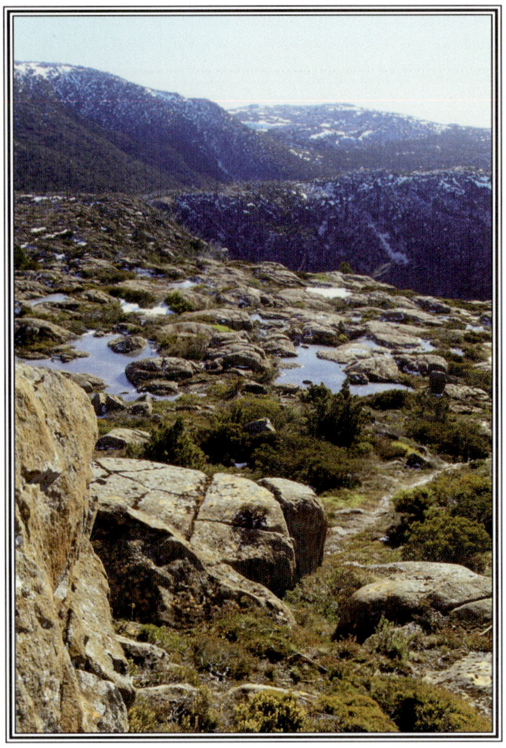

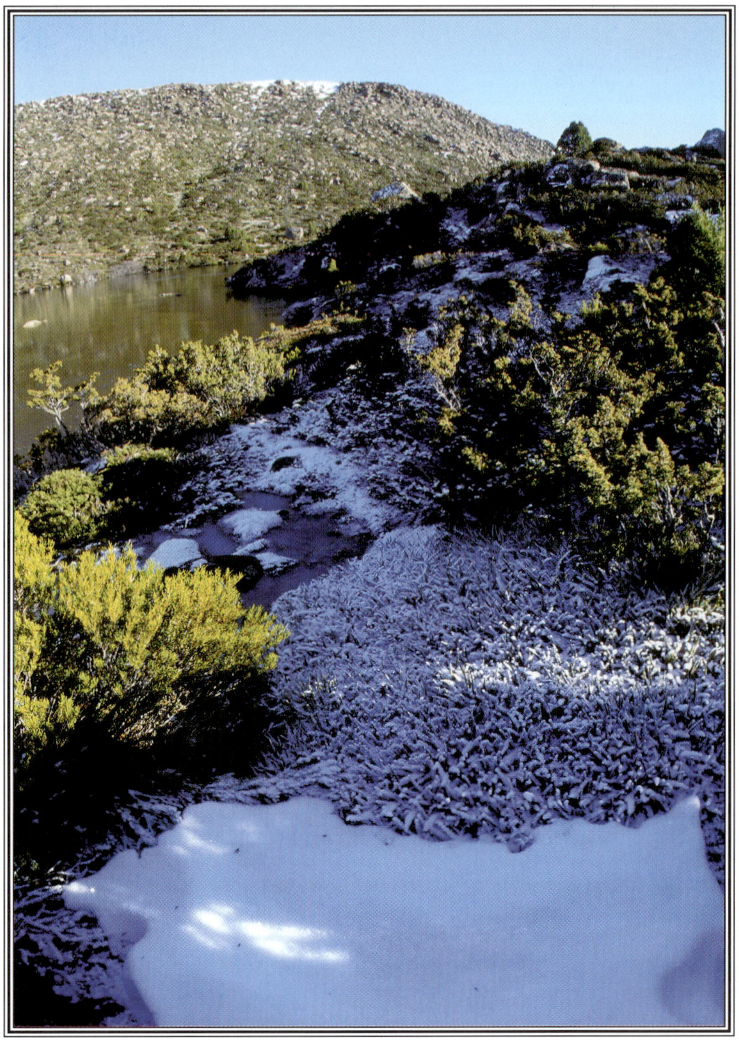

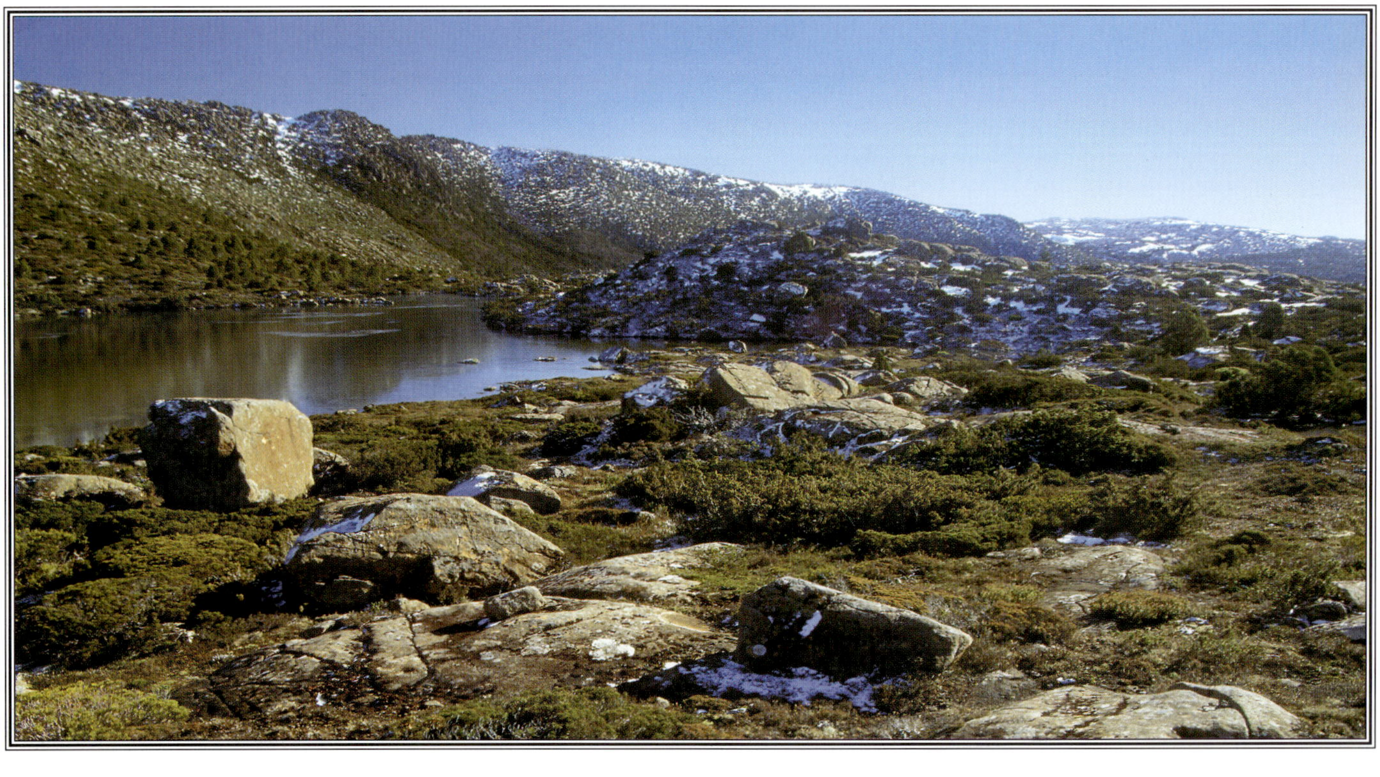

The Tarn Shelf, Mt. Field National Park

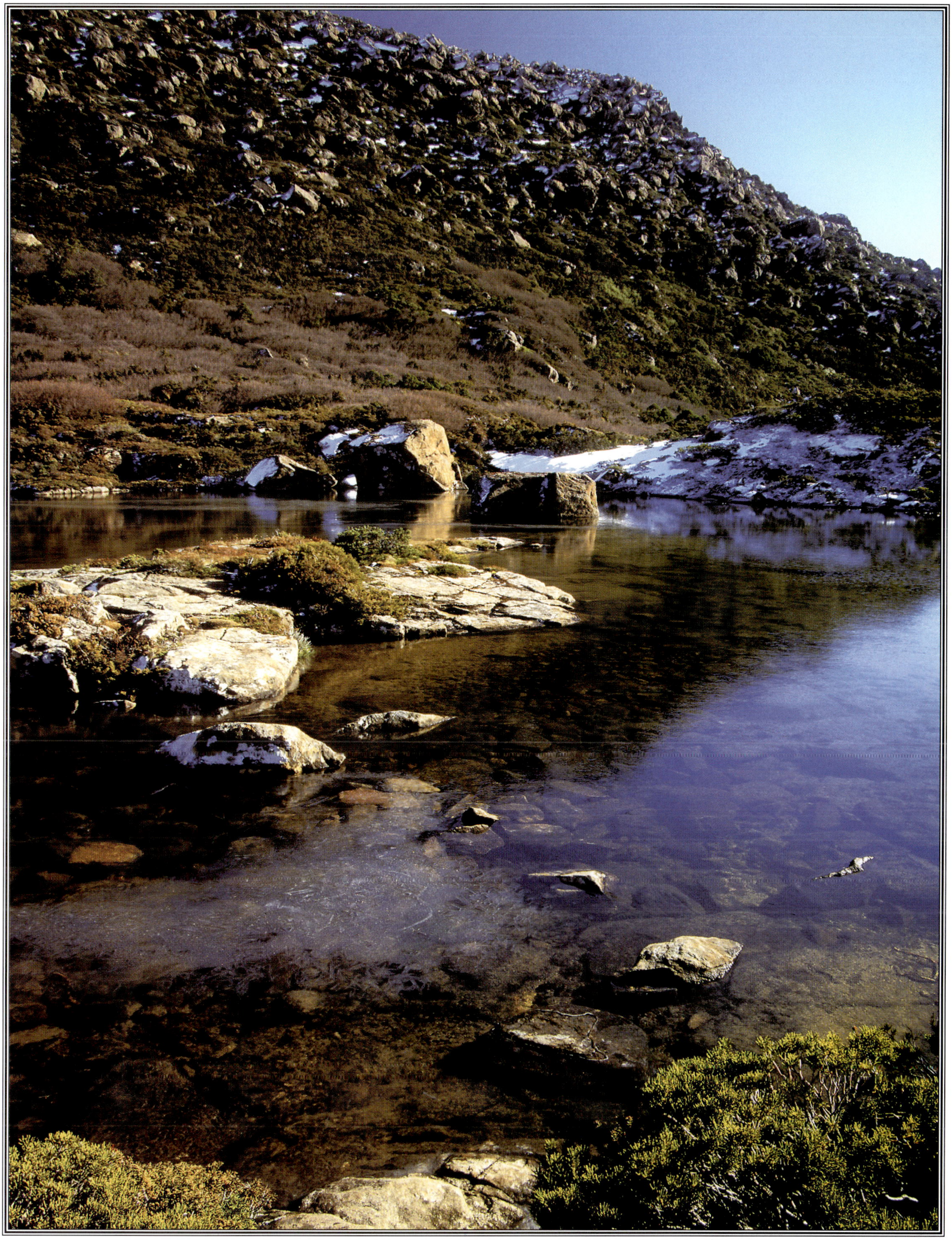

Frozen lakes at The Tarn Shelf

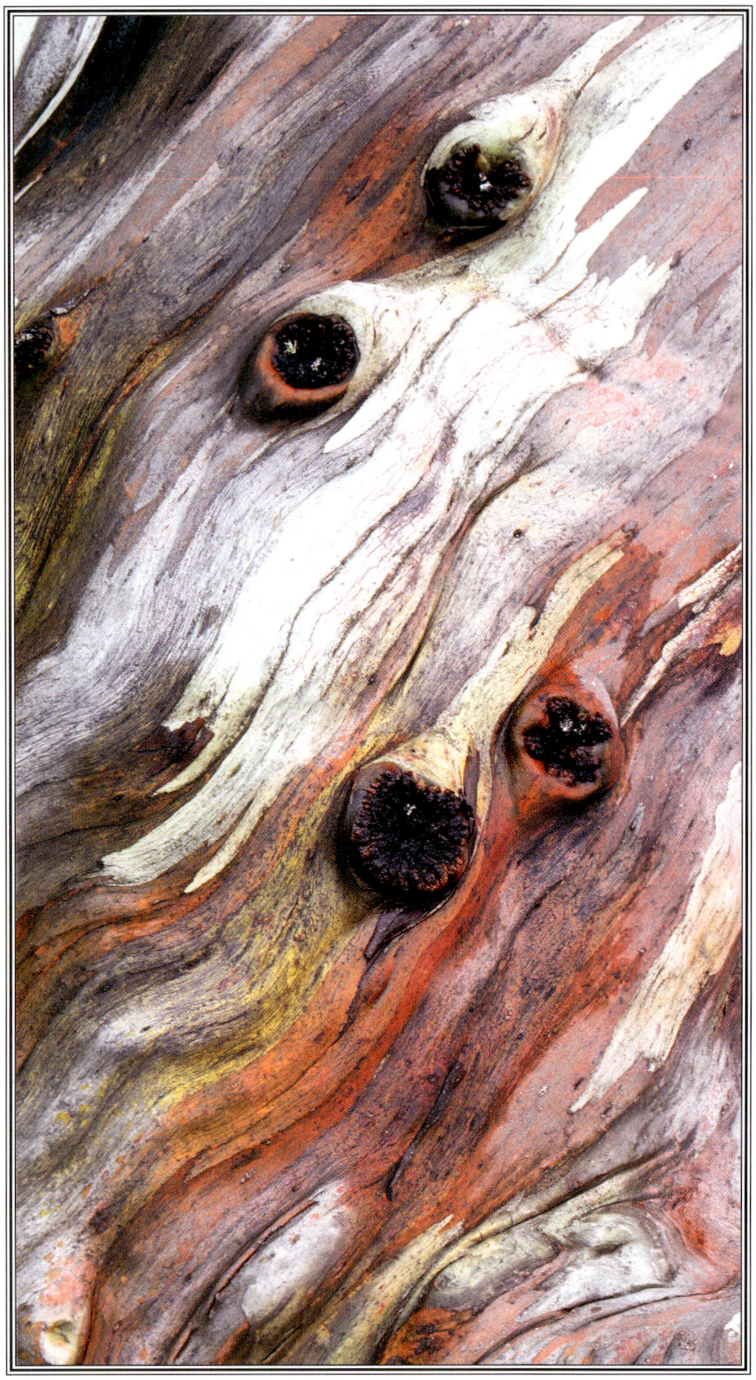

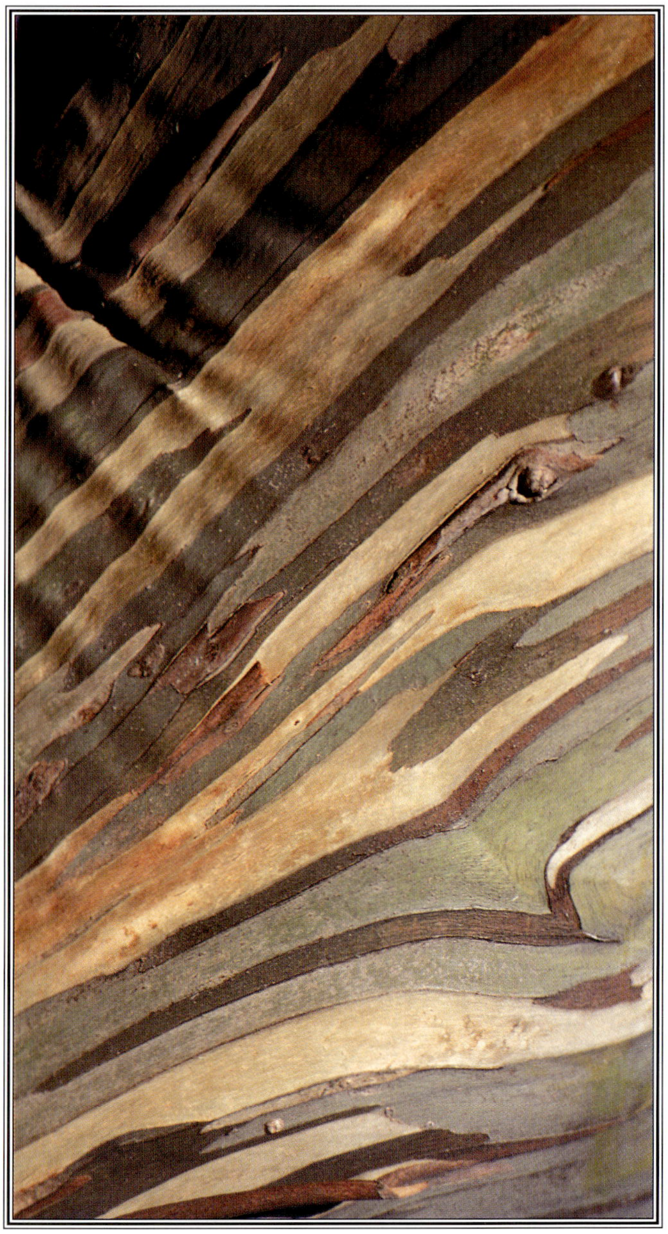

The colourful textures of nature, Snow Gum tree bark

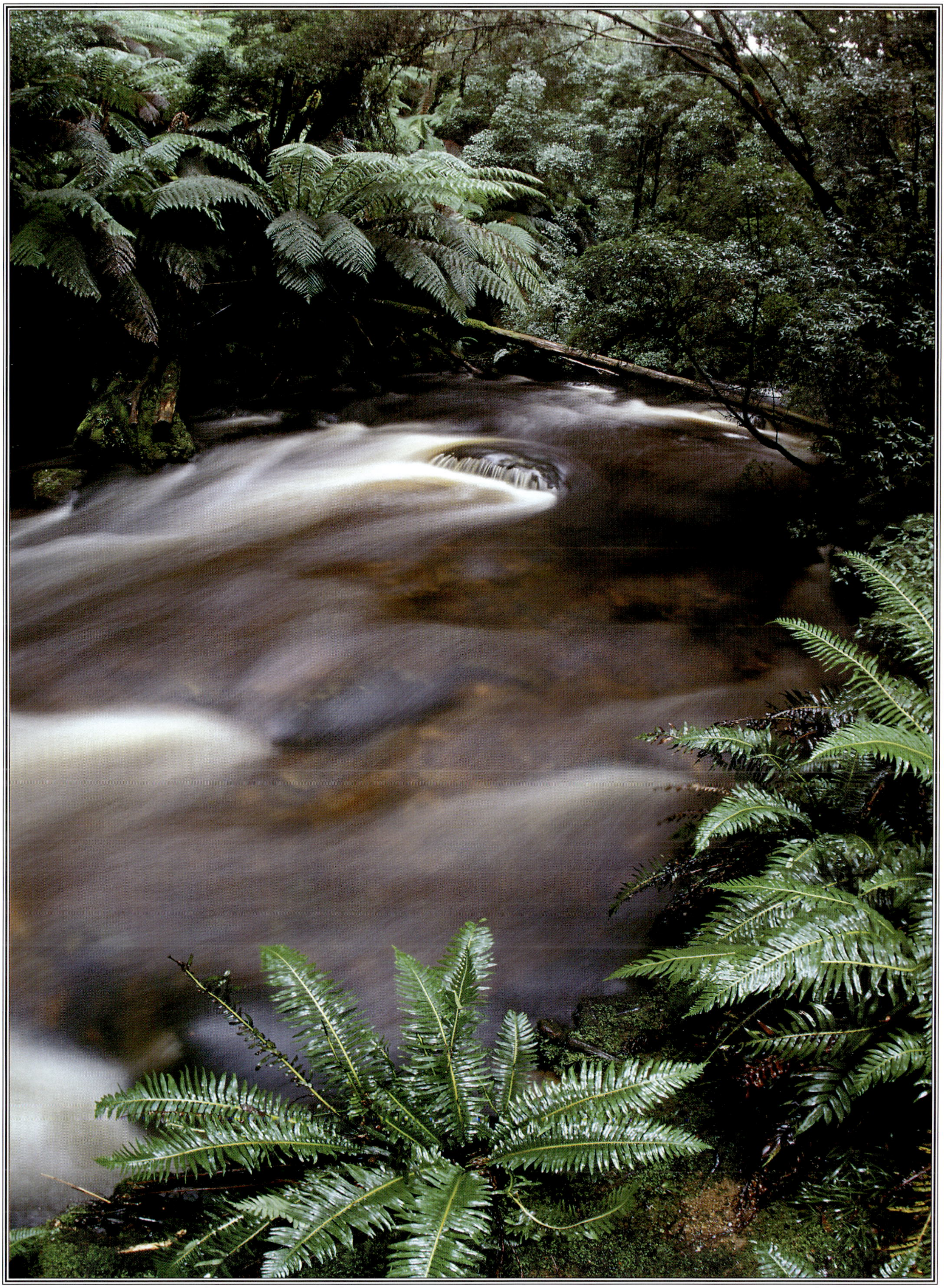

Bushwalking to Nelson Falls, near the Lyell highway

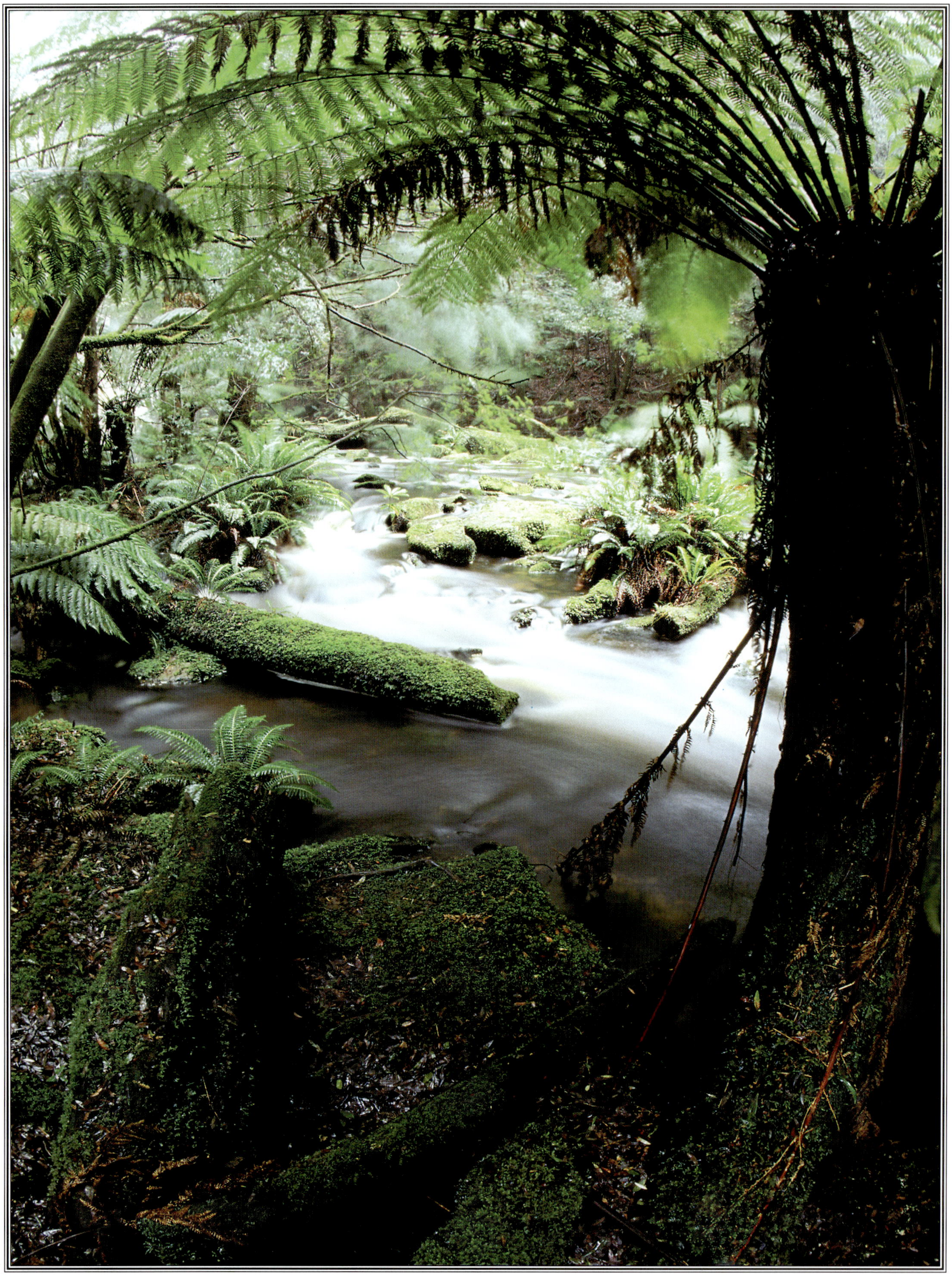

Bushwalking in Tasmania's west

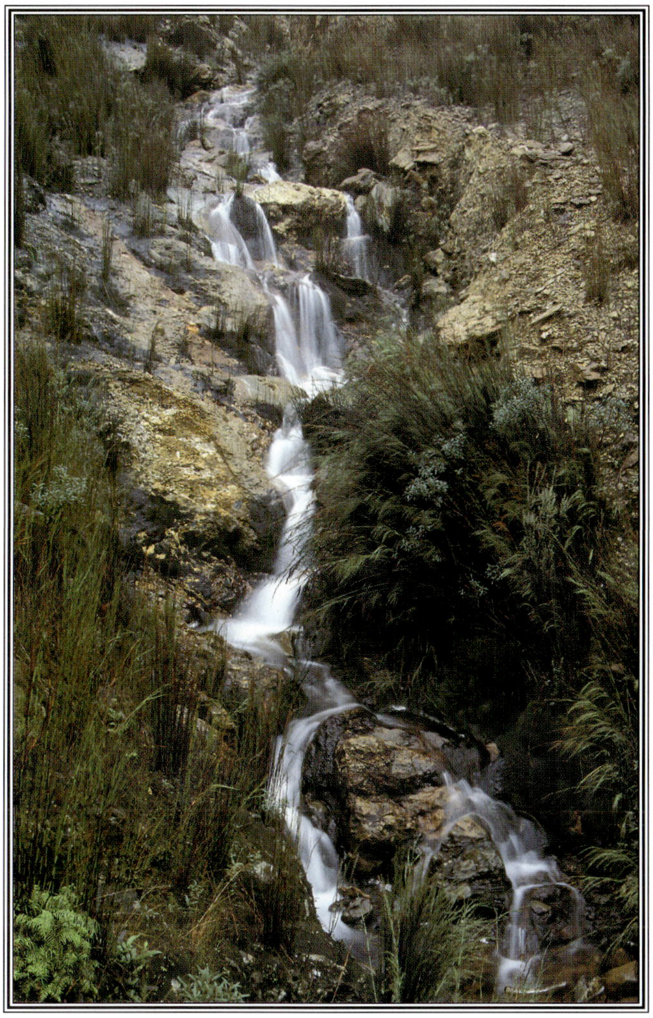

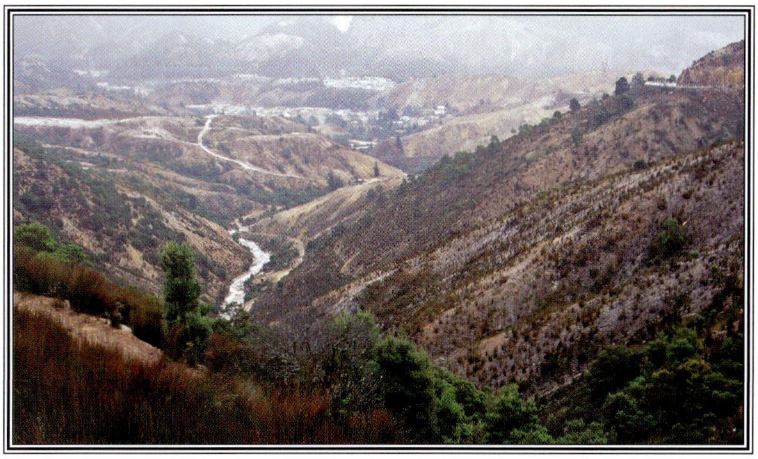

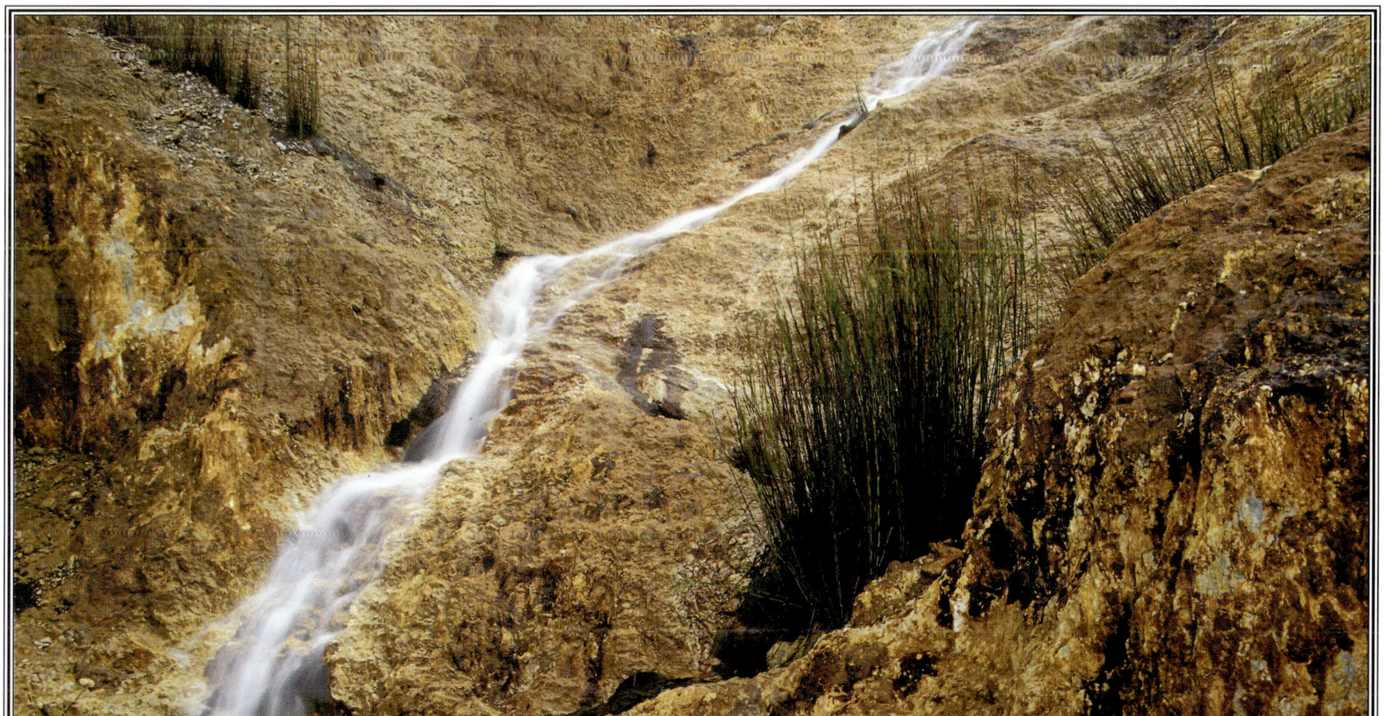

Top right: *The unique landscape of Queenstown*
Top left and bottom: *Waterfalls lining the Lyell Highway at Queenstown*

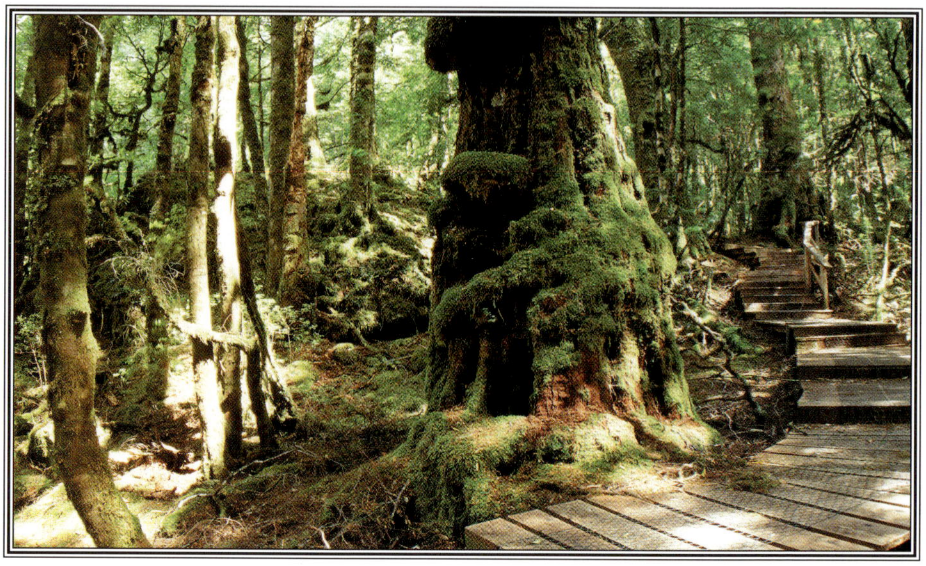

Mt. Wedge

Towering above the road to Strathgordon, Mt. Wedge stands proud, surrounded by the Sawback and Coronets mountain ranges, its peak provides unobstructed panoramic views of Tasmania's southwest.

Hike through forest tracks to the summit and gaze over the wilderness below; north to Lake Gordon, east to Mt. Field, south to Lake Pedder and west to the Coronets range.

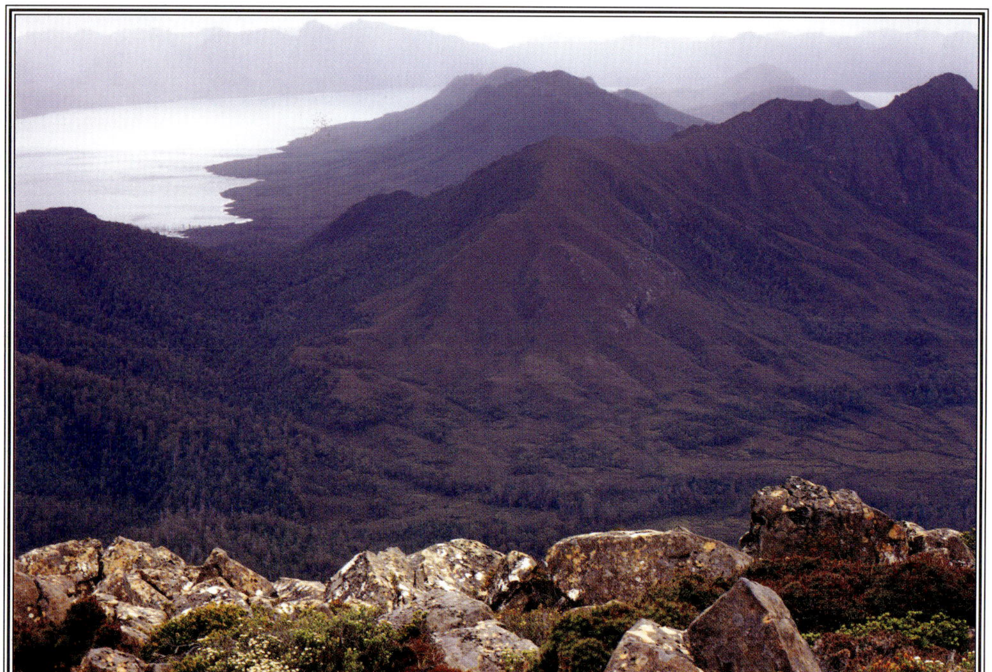

Top: *Bushwalking in the west*
Bottom: *View to Lake Pedder from Mt. Wedge*

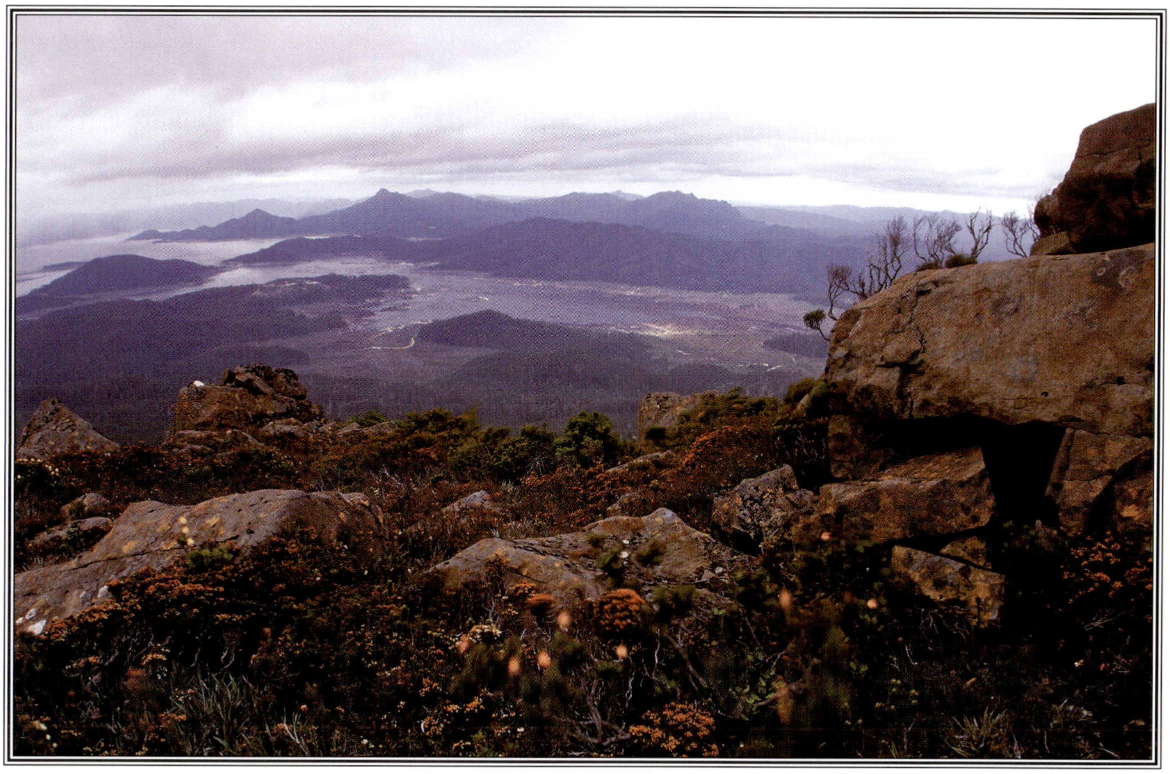

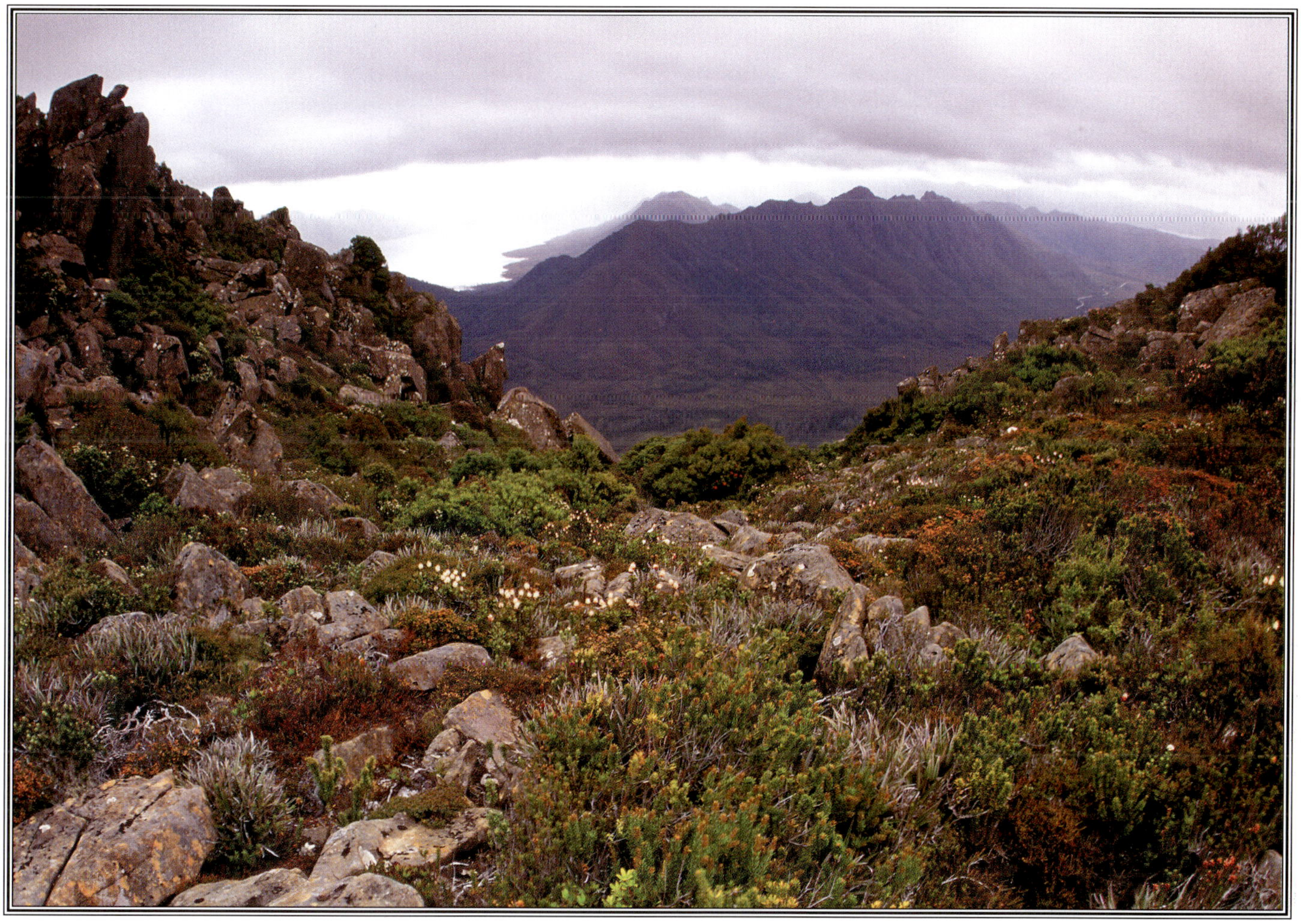

Top and bottom: *Views from Mt. Wedge*

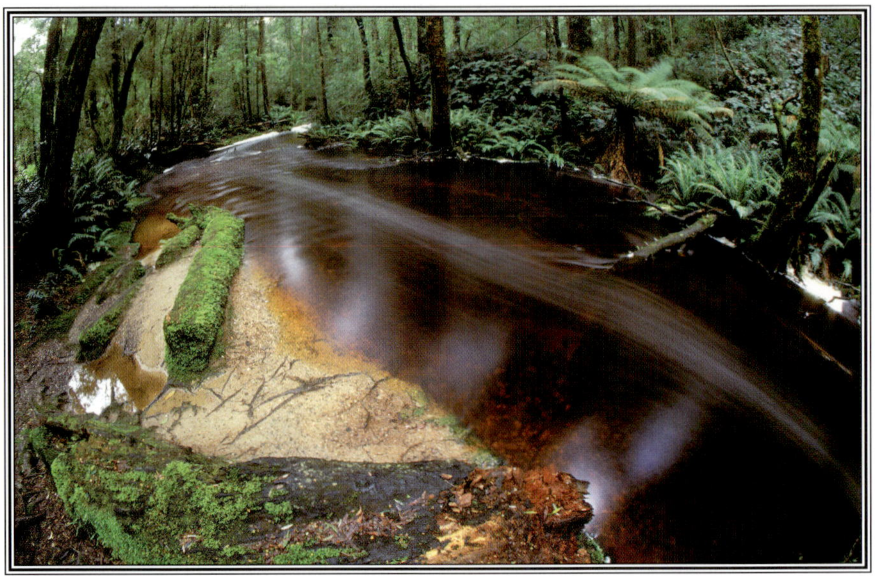

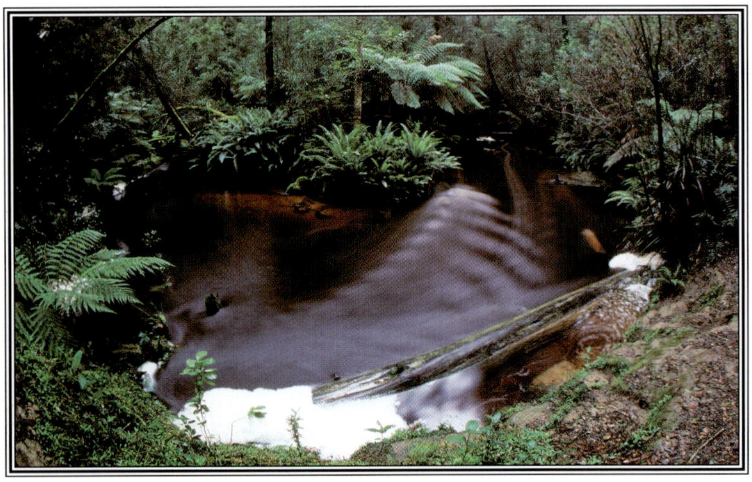

Hogarth Falls

These mighty falls are hidden near the west coast township of Strahan.
Stroll the track, along banks lined with fallen trees, submerged in the dark stained, tannin waters of a Tasmanian river.

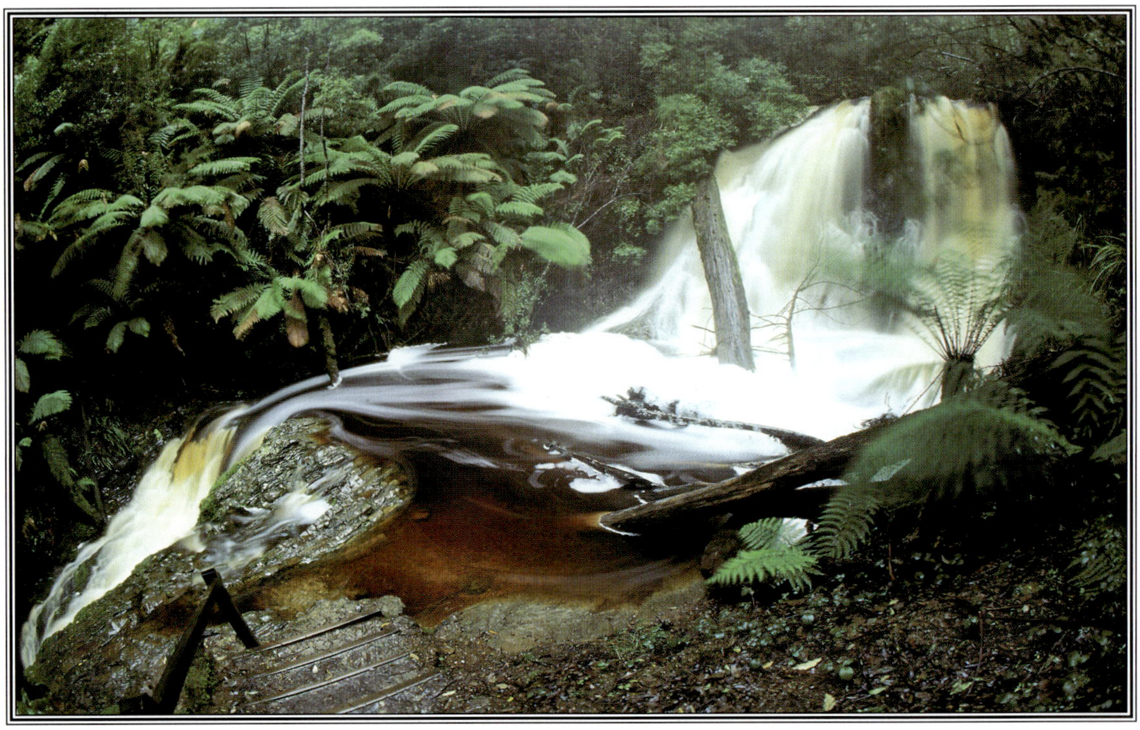

Top and centre: *Following the tannin waters*
Bottom: *Hogarth Falls*

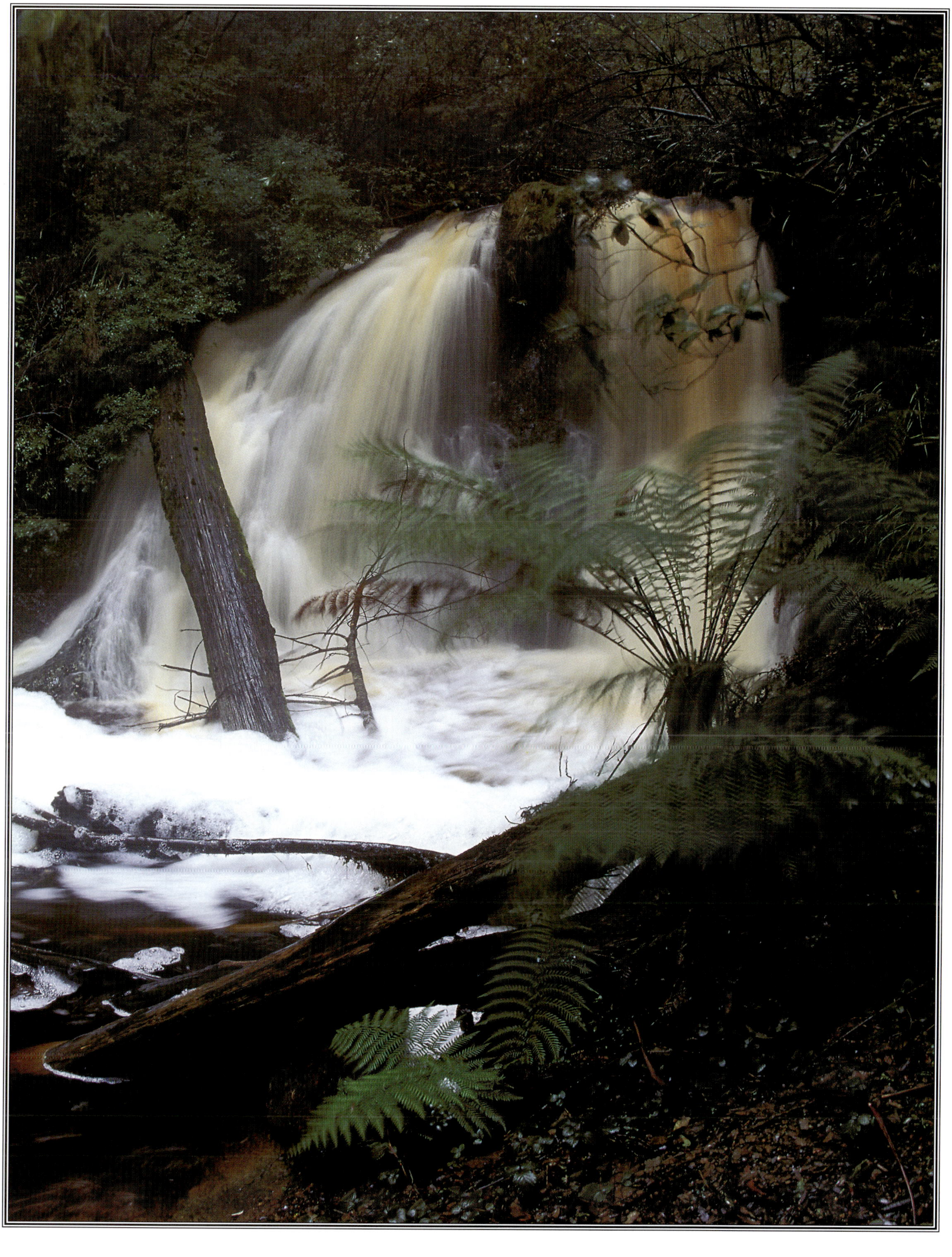

The power of Hogarth Falls

Ocean Beach

West of Strahan and to the north of Macquarie Harbour, is an area, simply named Ocean Beach, a stretch of sand that can only be described as a coastal wilderness.

One day battered by rolling ocean swells and windswept by the 'roaring forties', perfectly still and calm the next.

Ocean Beach is a spectacular sight at any time of day although sunsets should be considered its specialty.

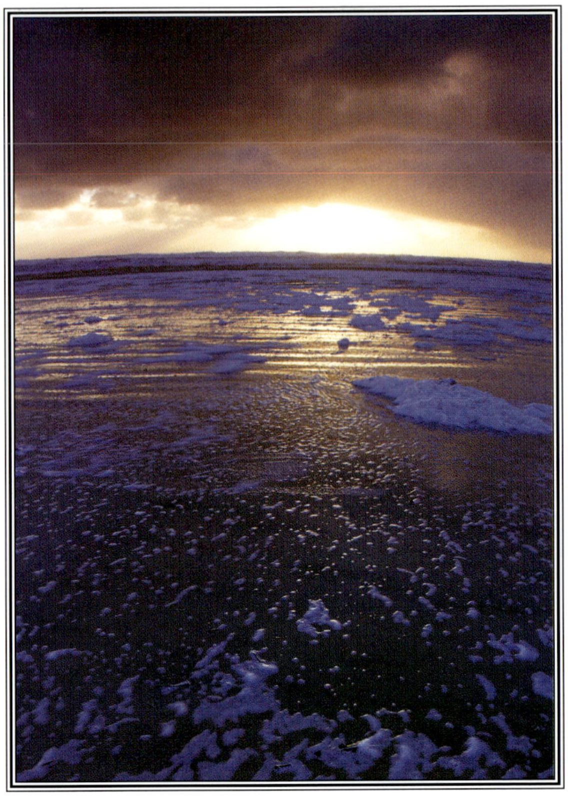

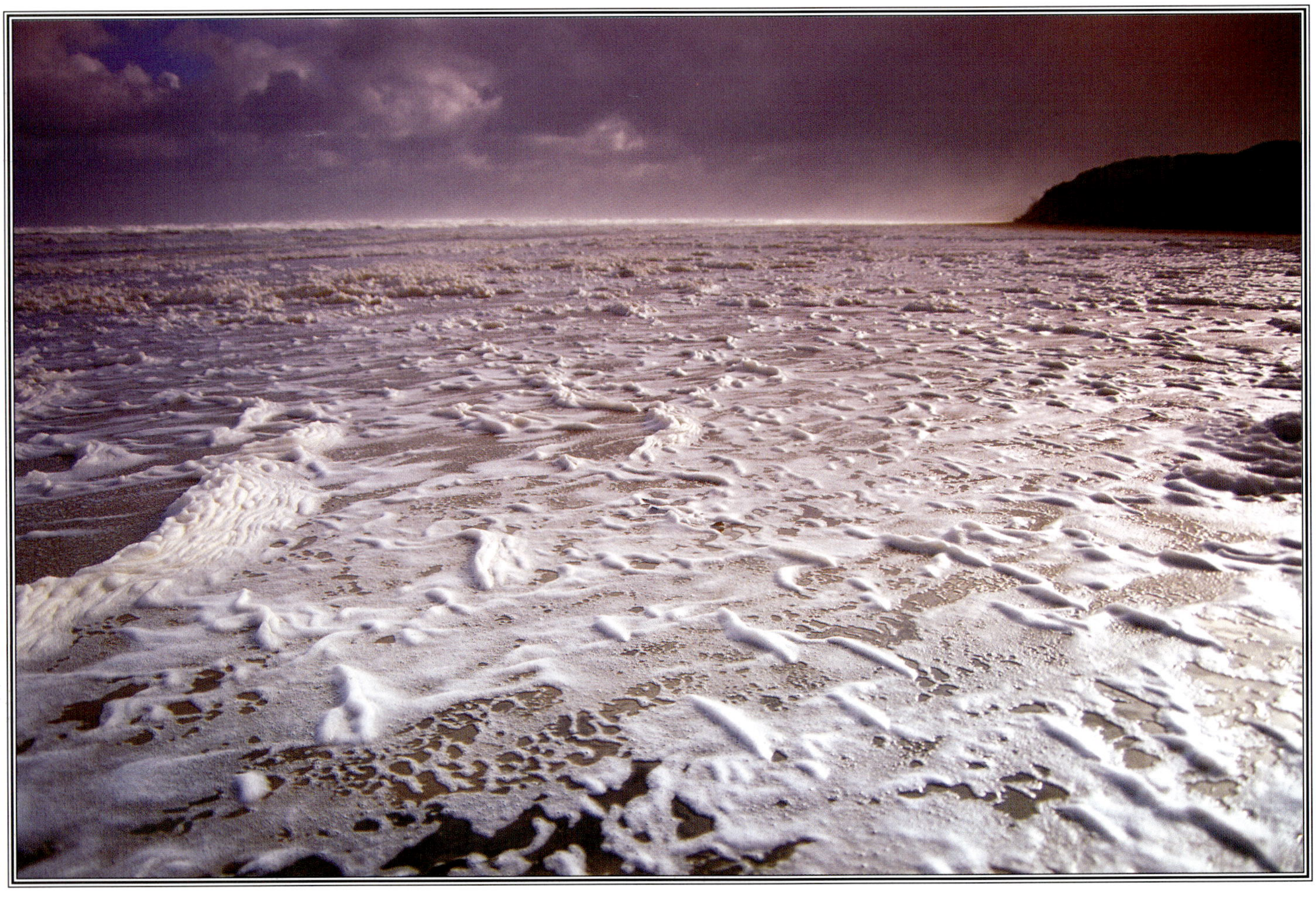

Top and bottom: *Ocean Beach following a storm*

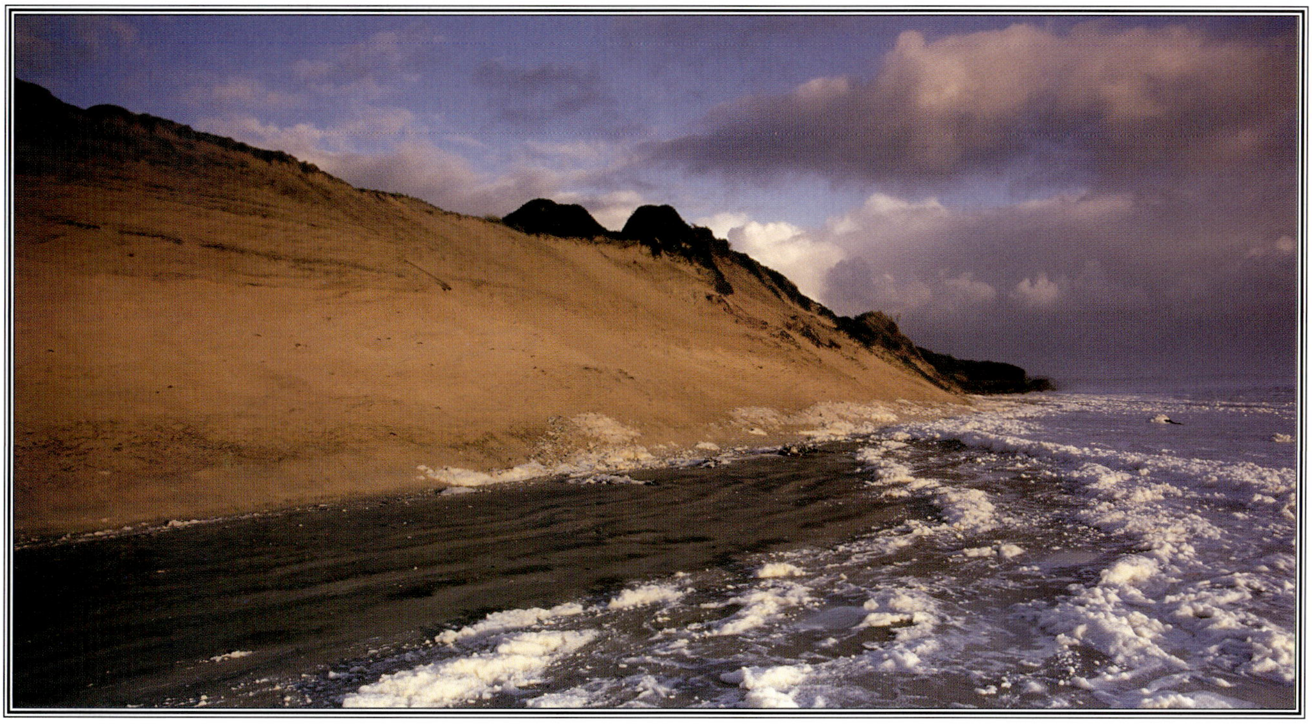

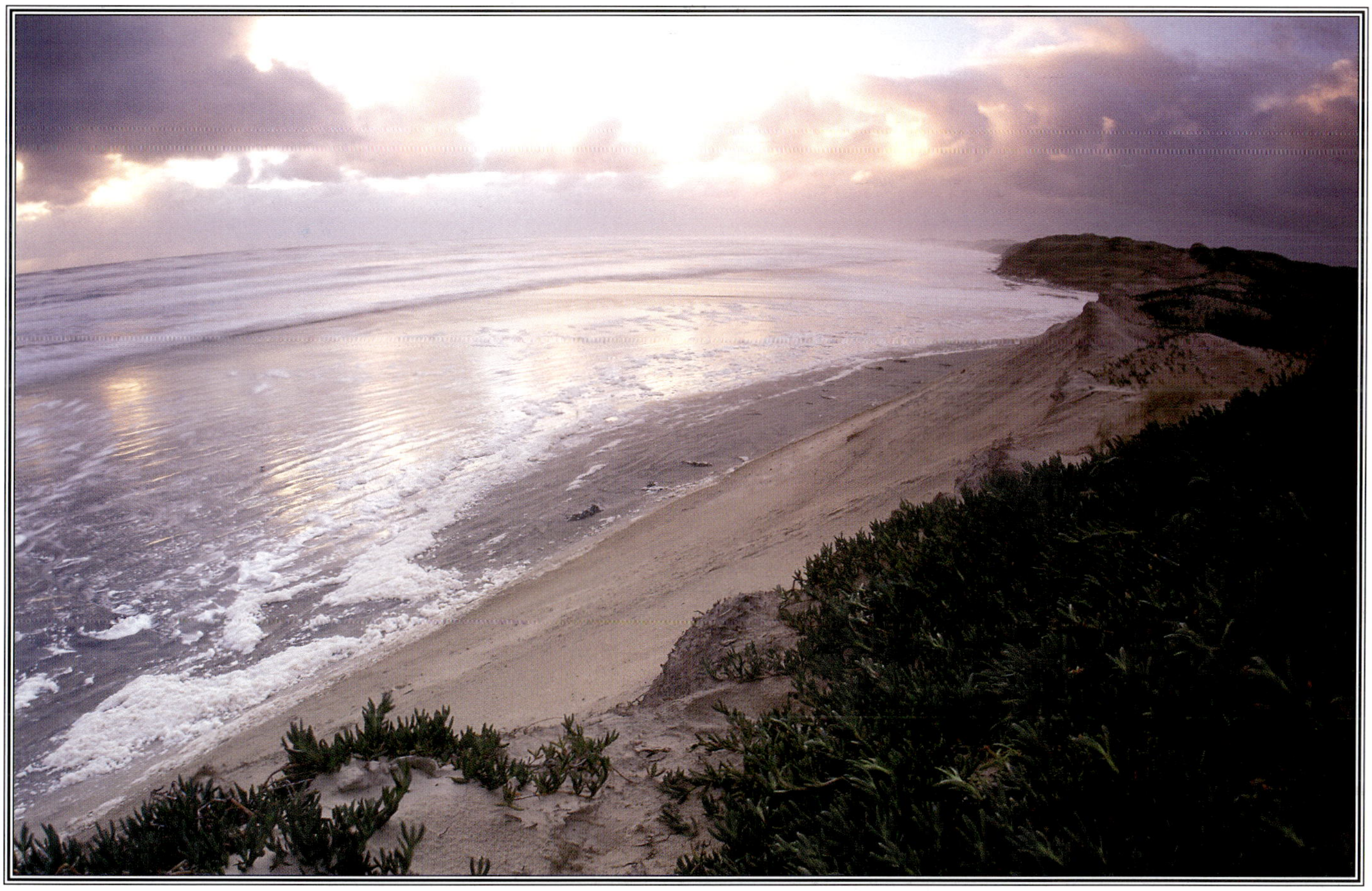

Top and bottom: *Sunset at Ocean Beach*

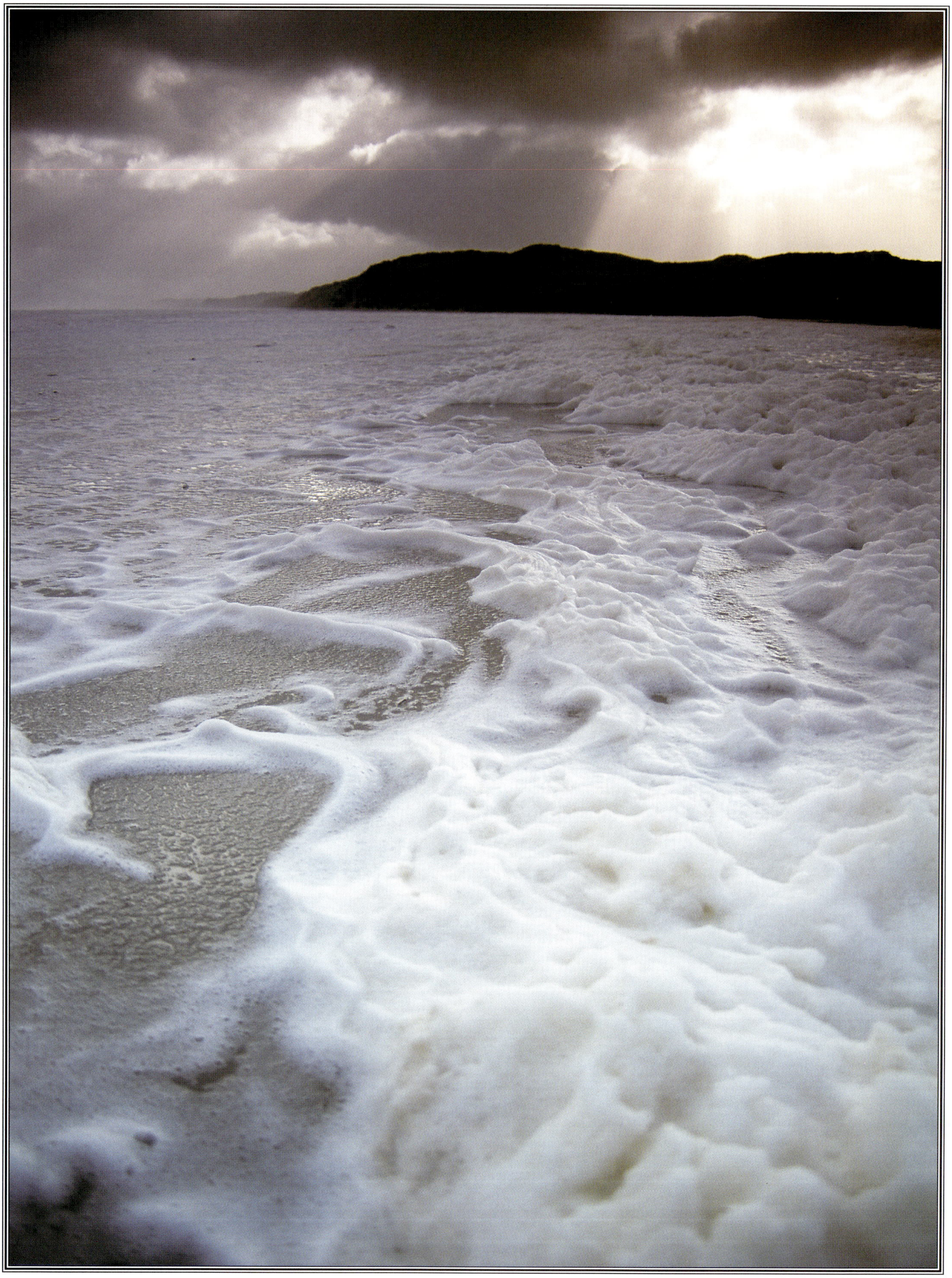

Ocean Beach - Strahan

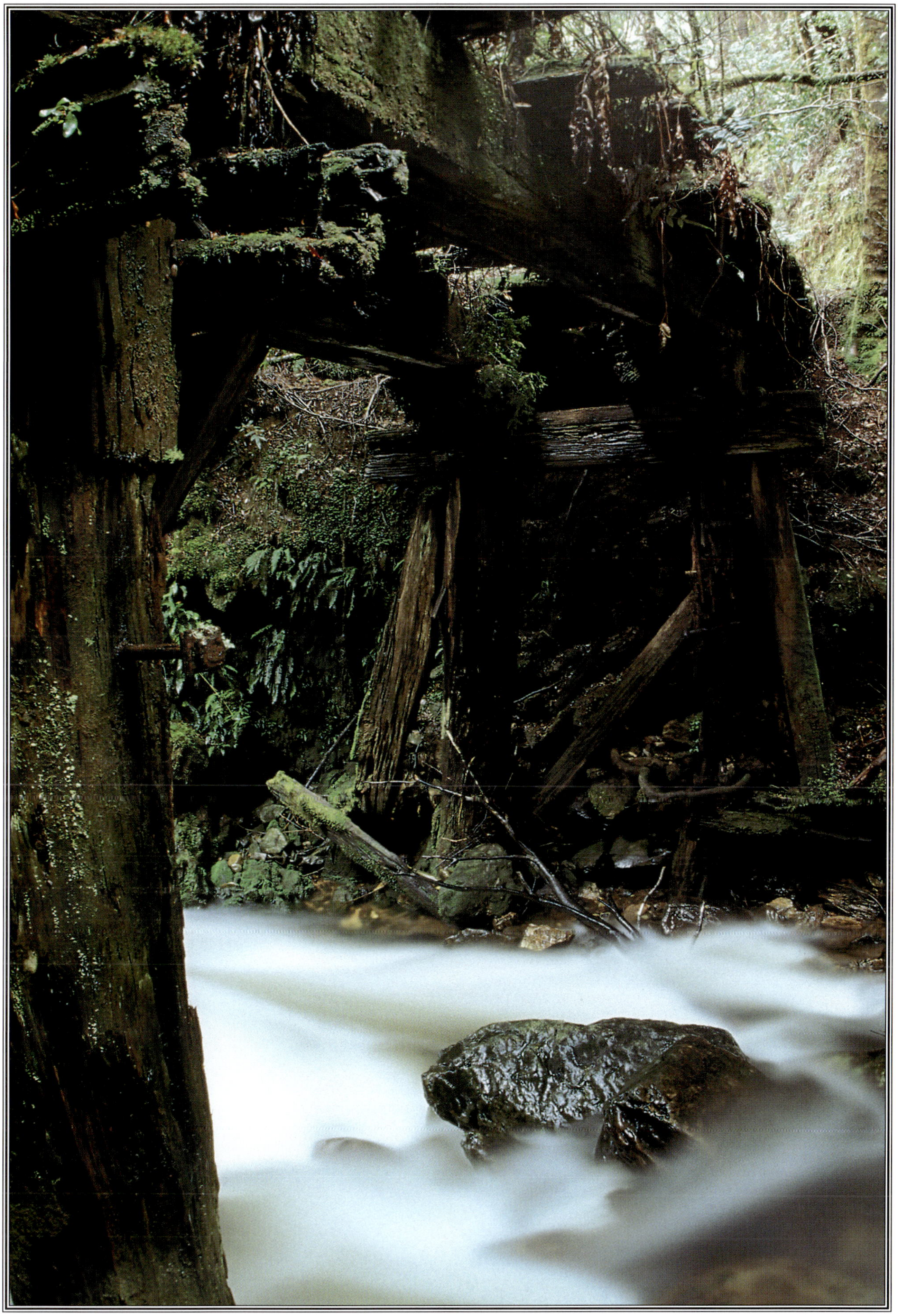

Disused mining rail bridge on the way to Montezuma Falls

Montezuma Falls

Located between the west coast towns of Rosebery and Zeehan, is Tasmania's tallest waterfall, Montezuma Falls.

Rediscover disused mine shafts and old rail bridges, on the hike to the one hundred metre high falls. Walk slowly over the narrow bridge, spanning the face of the falls and feel the mist of pure mountain water, spraying into cool forest air, whilst standing suspended above a lush forest valley.

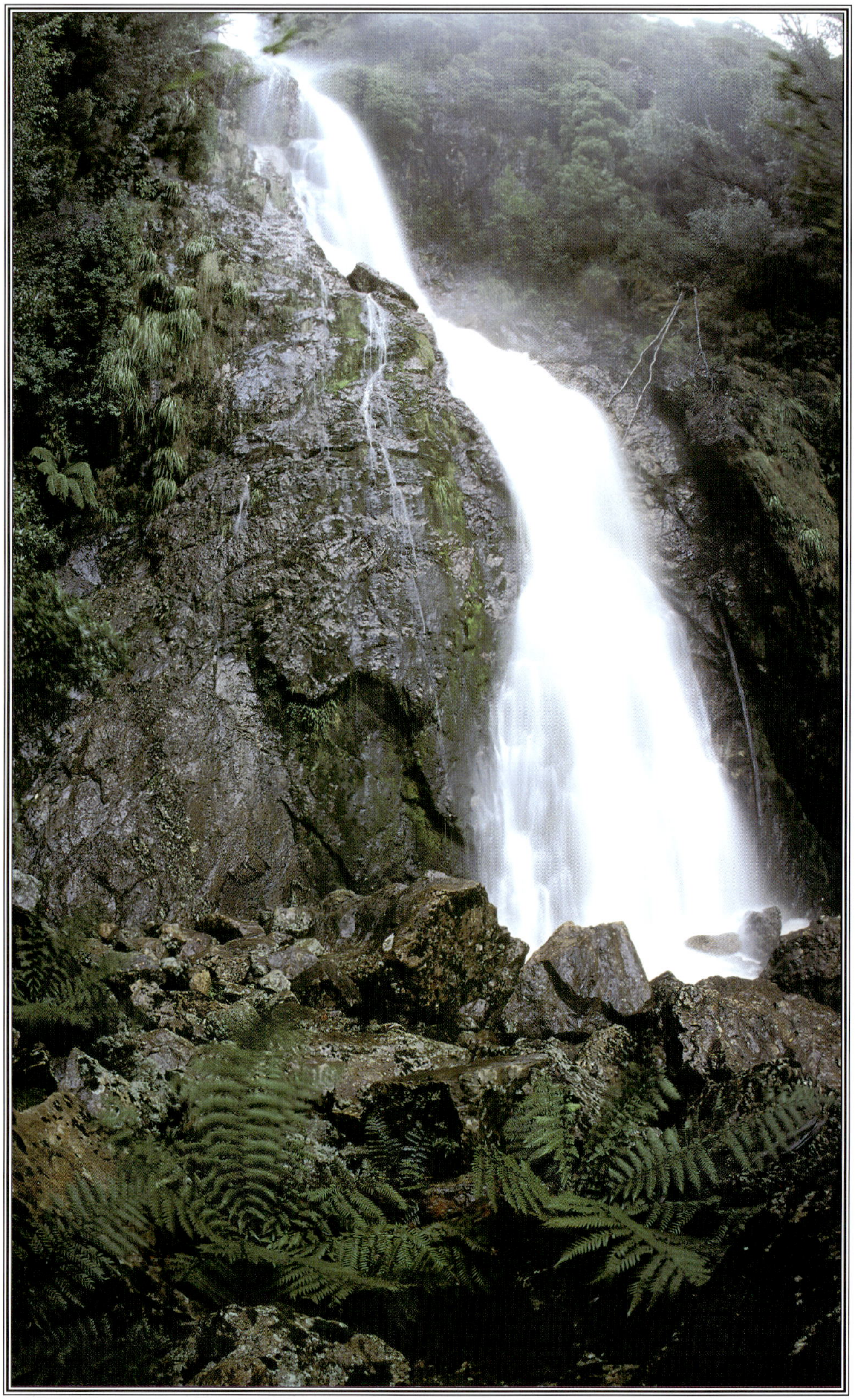

One hundred metres high - Tasmania's tallest falls

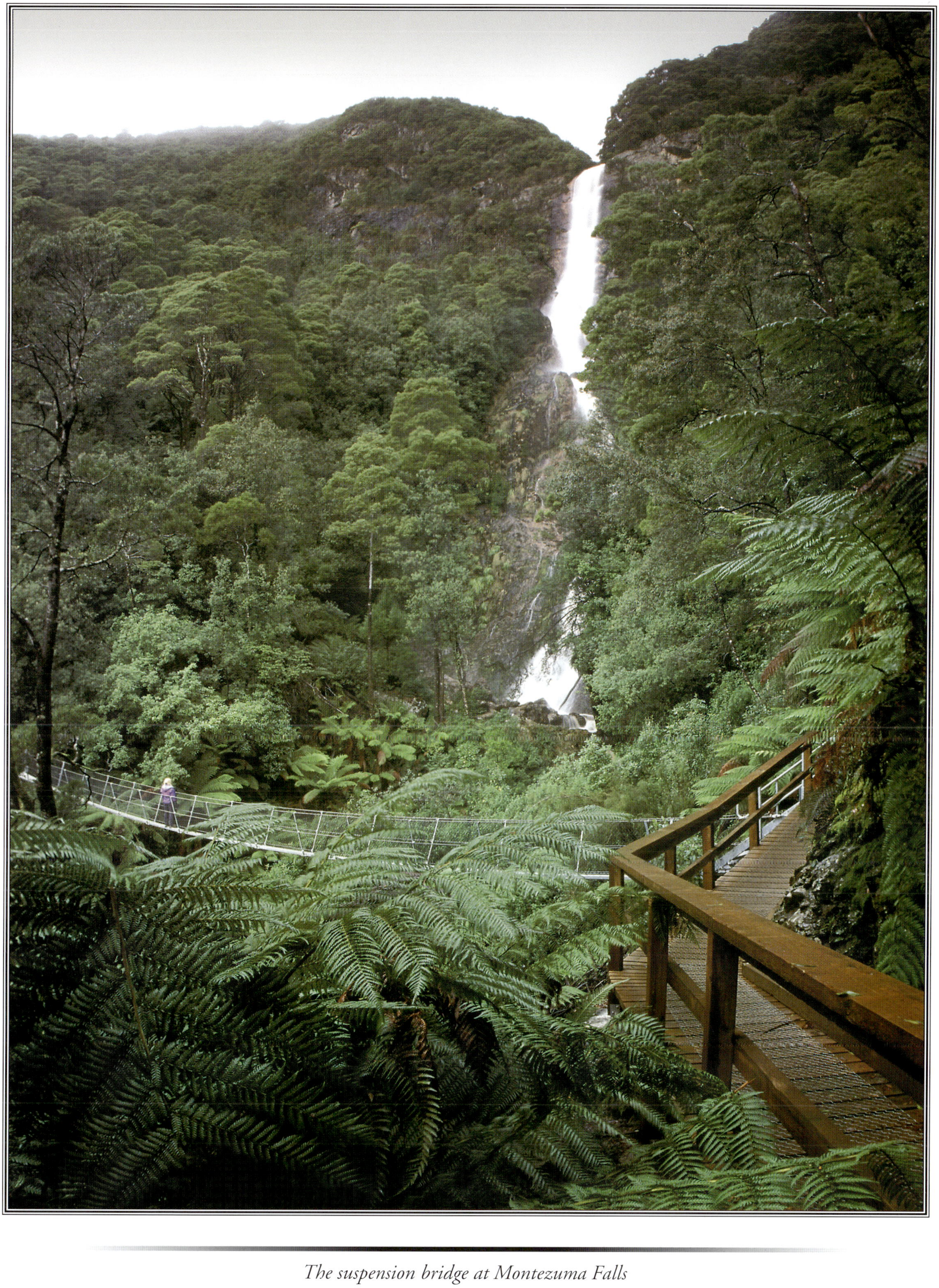

The suspension bridge at Montezuma Falls

Cradle Mountain

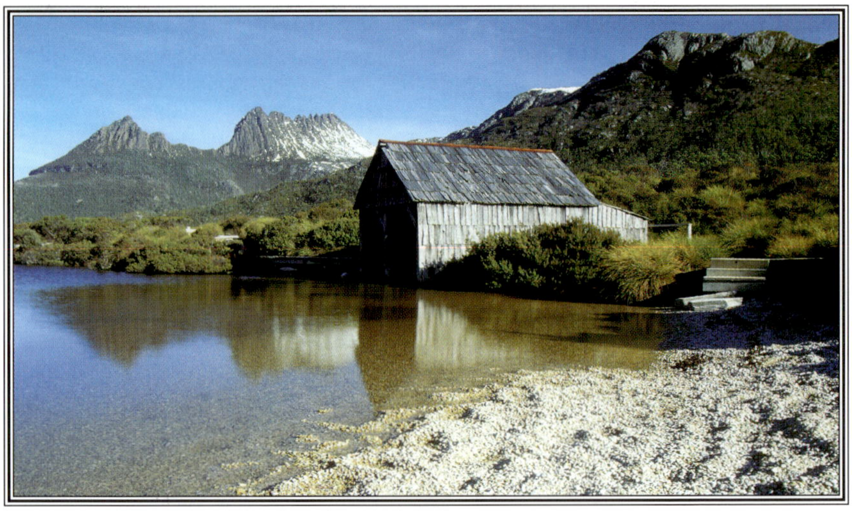

In one of the best-known national park areas of Tasmania, the Cradle Mountain-Lake St. Clare National Park towers the iconic Cradle Mountain.

Take an easy stroll around the calm waters of Dove Lake or tackle a more adventurous hike across the face of the mountain.
Observe the dramatics of Cradle Mountain changing colour at first light; the cool purple of dawn melts into a warm orange glow as the sun sheds its first rays of light on the mountaintops.

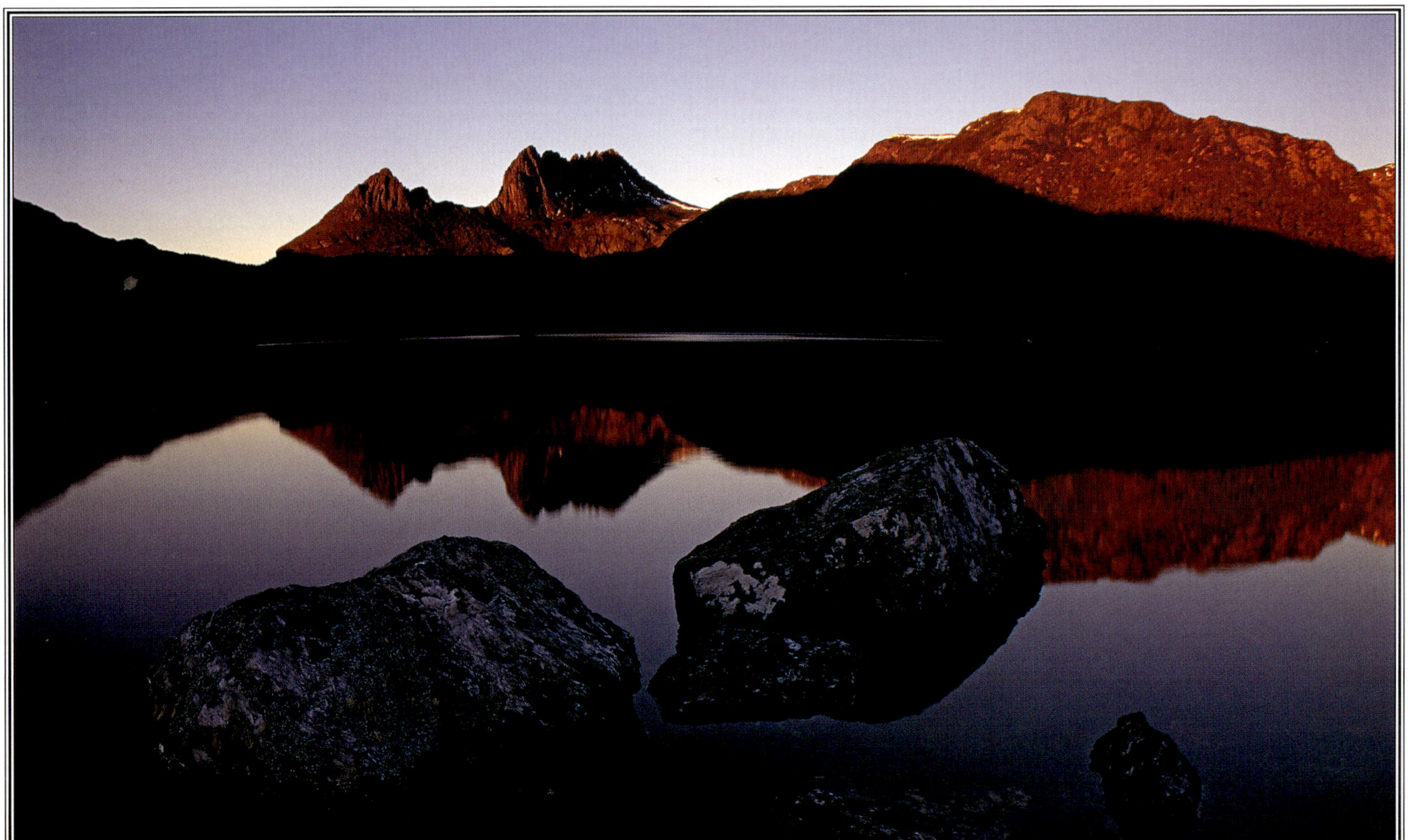

Top: *The boat shed on the banks of Dove Lake*
Bottom: *The first rays of light on Cradle Mountain*

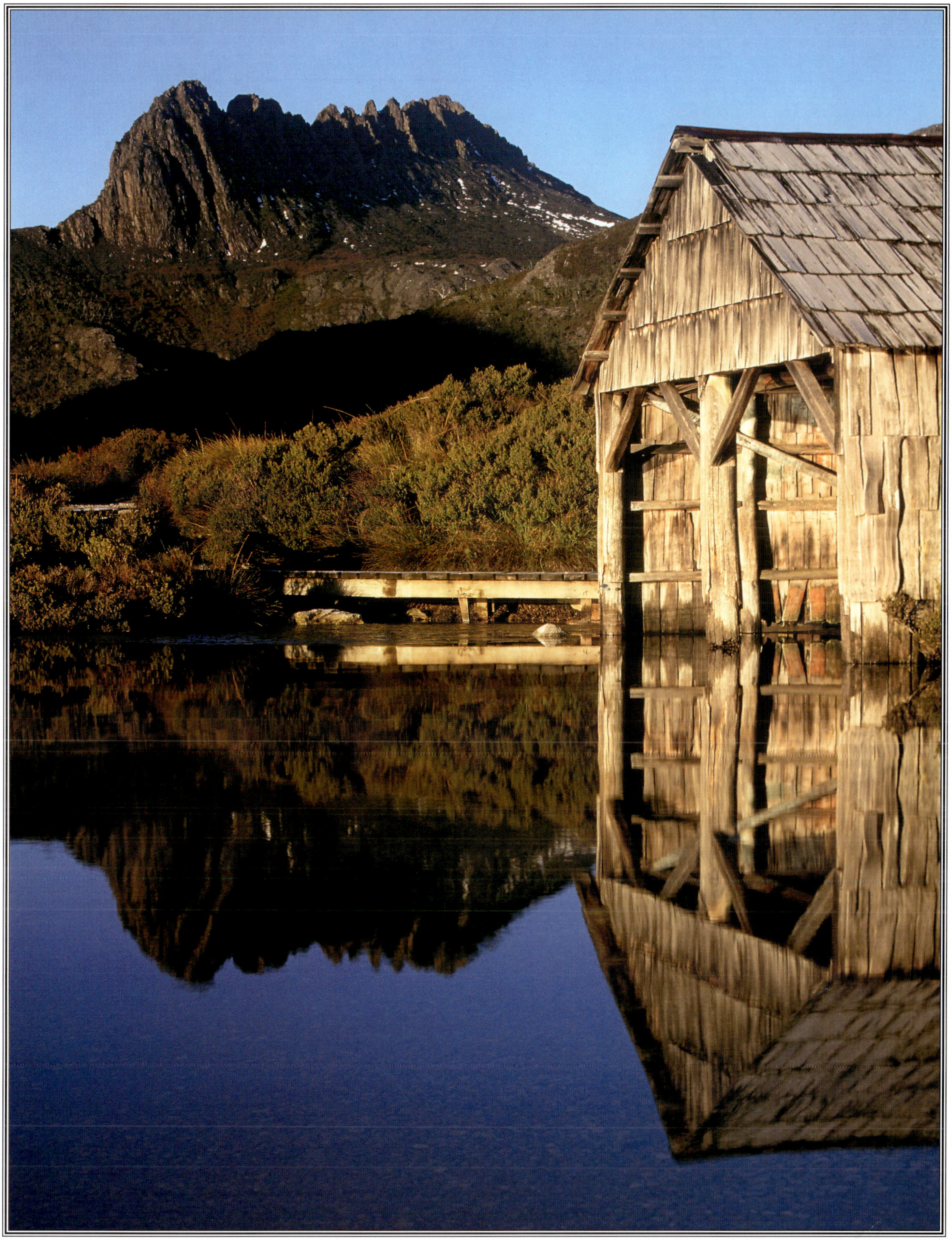

Reflections of the boat shed in the cool waters of Dove Lake

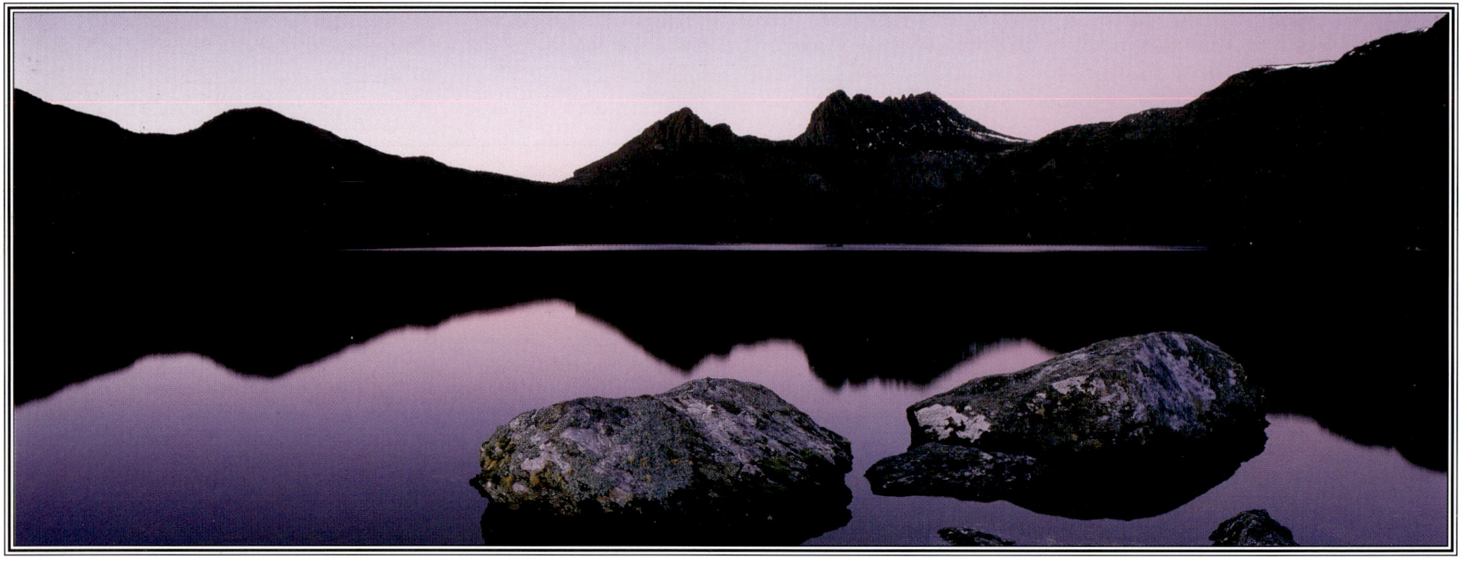

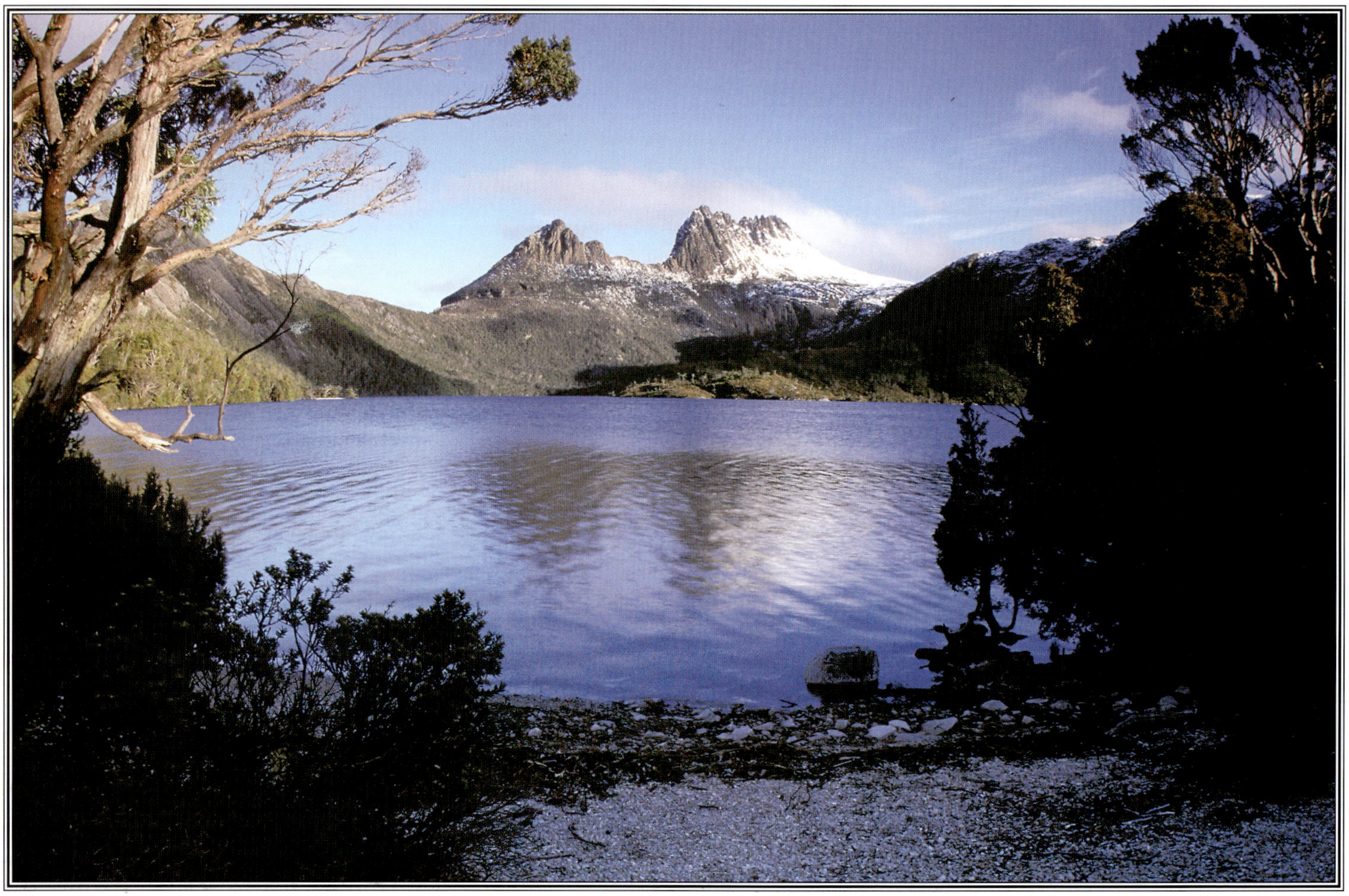

Top: *Dawn colours*
Bottom: *A pebble beach on the walk around Dove Lake*

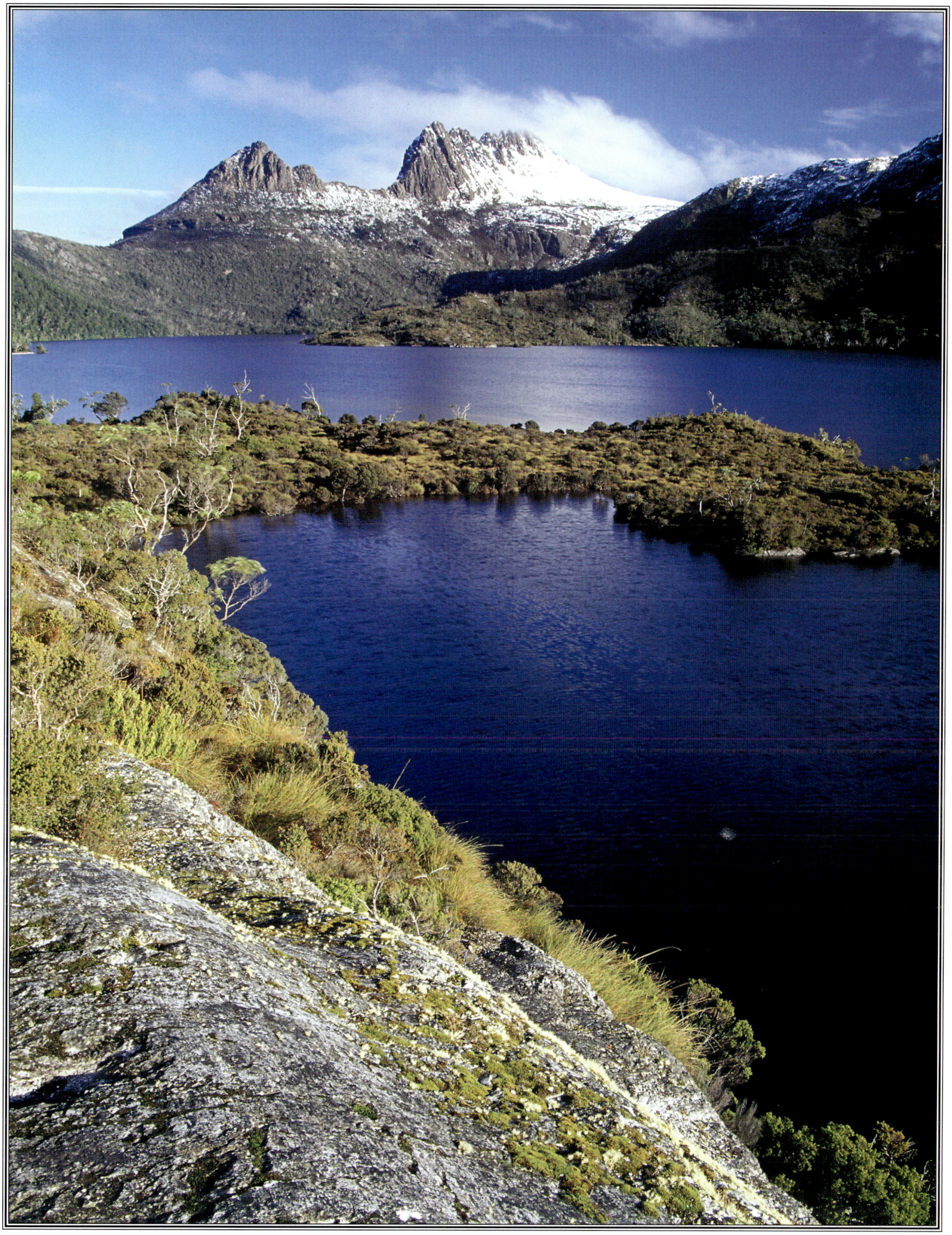

Snow on the peaks of Cradle Mountain viewed from Marble Rock

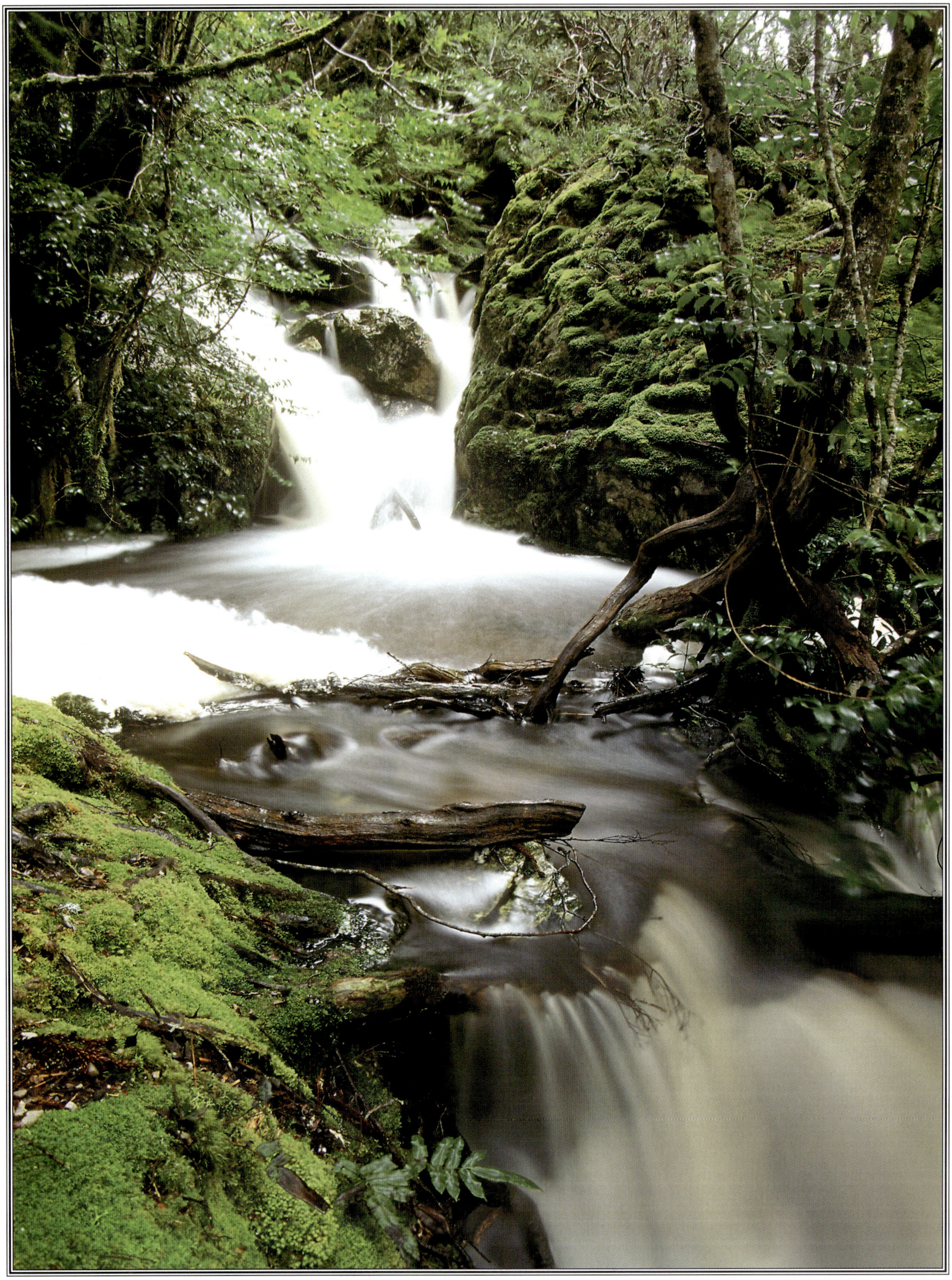

Crater Falls found on one of the many bushwalks within the National Park

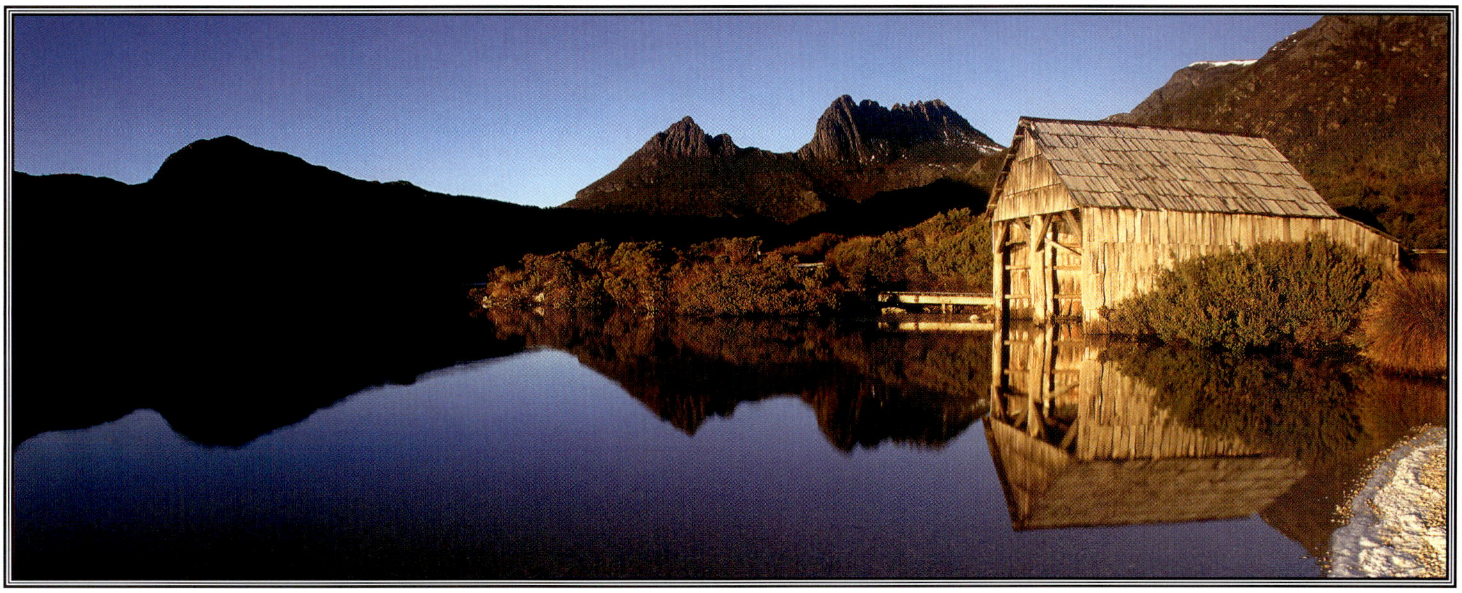

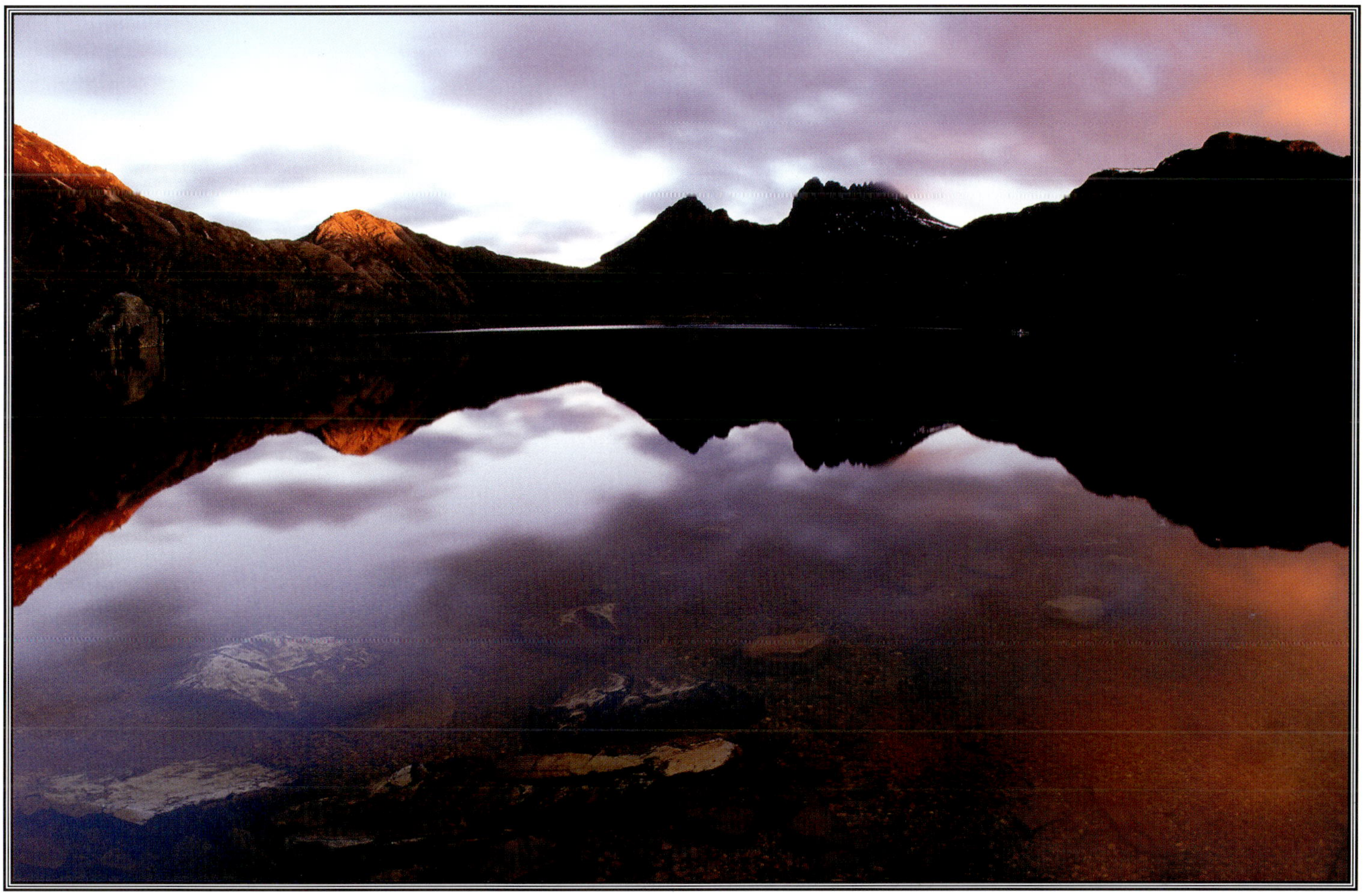

***Top:** Dove Lake track passes the boat shed*
***Bottom:** Sunset colours reflected in the lake*

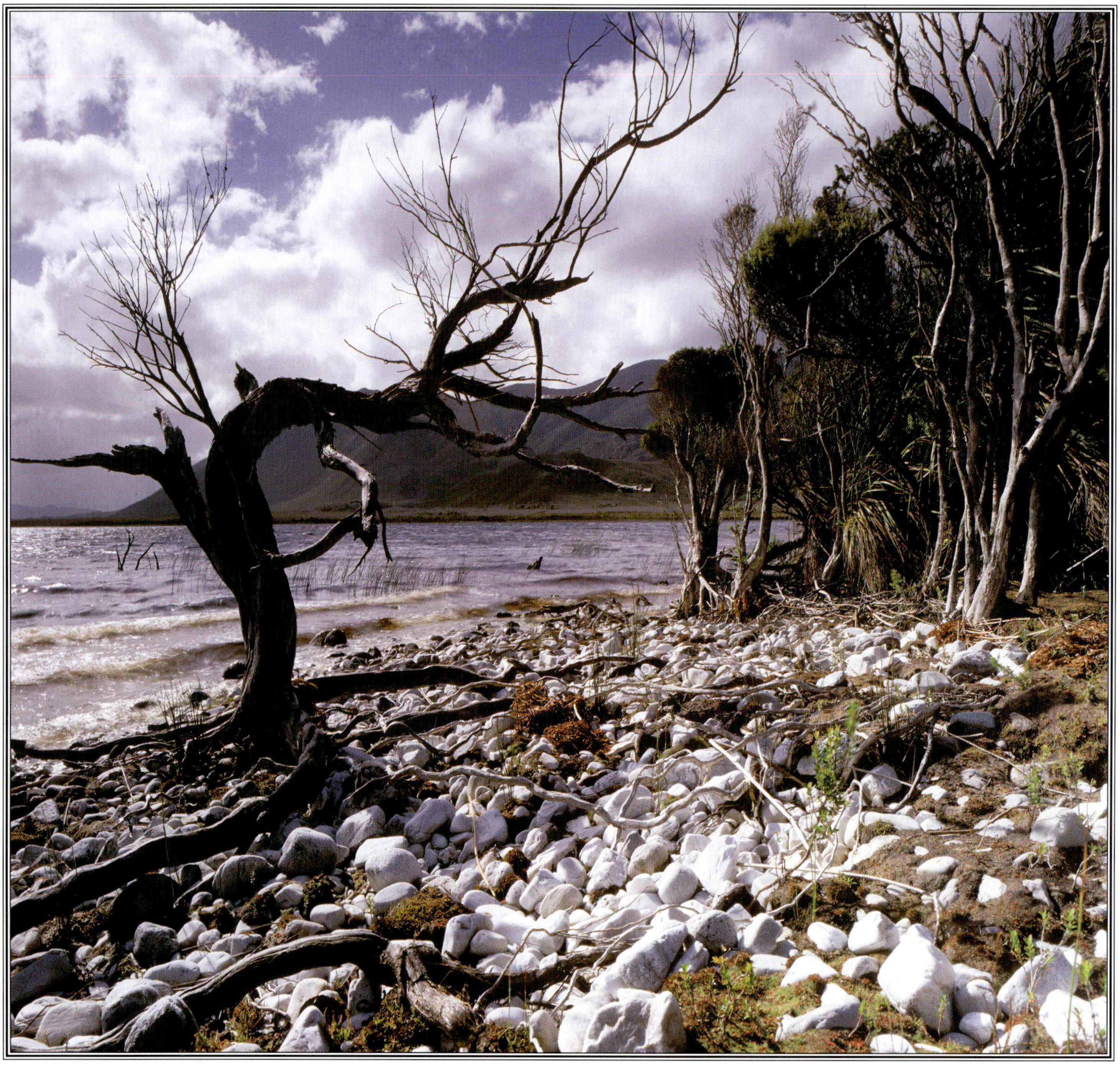

Twisted tree on the banks of Freney Lagoon

Cox Bight

Deep within the wilderness of Tasmania's Southwest National Park, lies Cox Bight, a coastal seascape that really has to be seen, to be believed.

Although shadowed by the New Harbour Range, Cox Bight is subject to the wildest of untamed elements. Such dynamic weather patterns cause vast swirls of cloud shapes to paint their patterns in a sky that simply ignites into an explosion of colours at the end of another day in paradise.

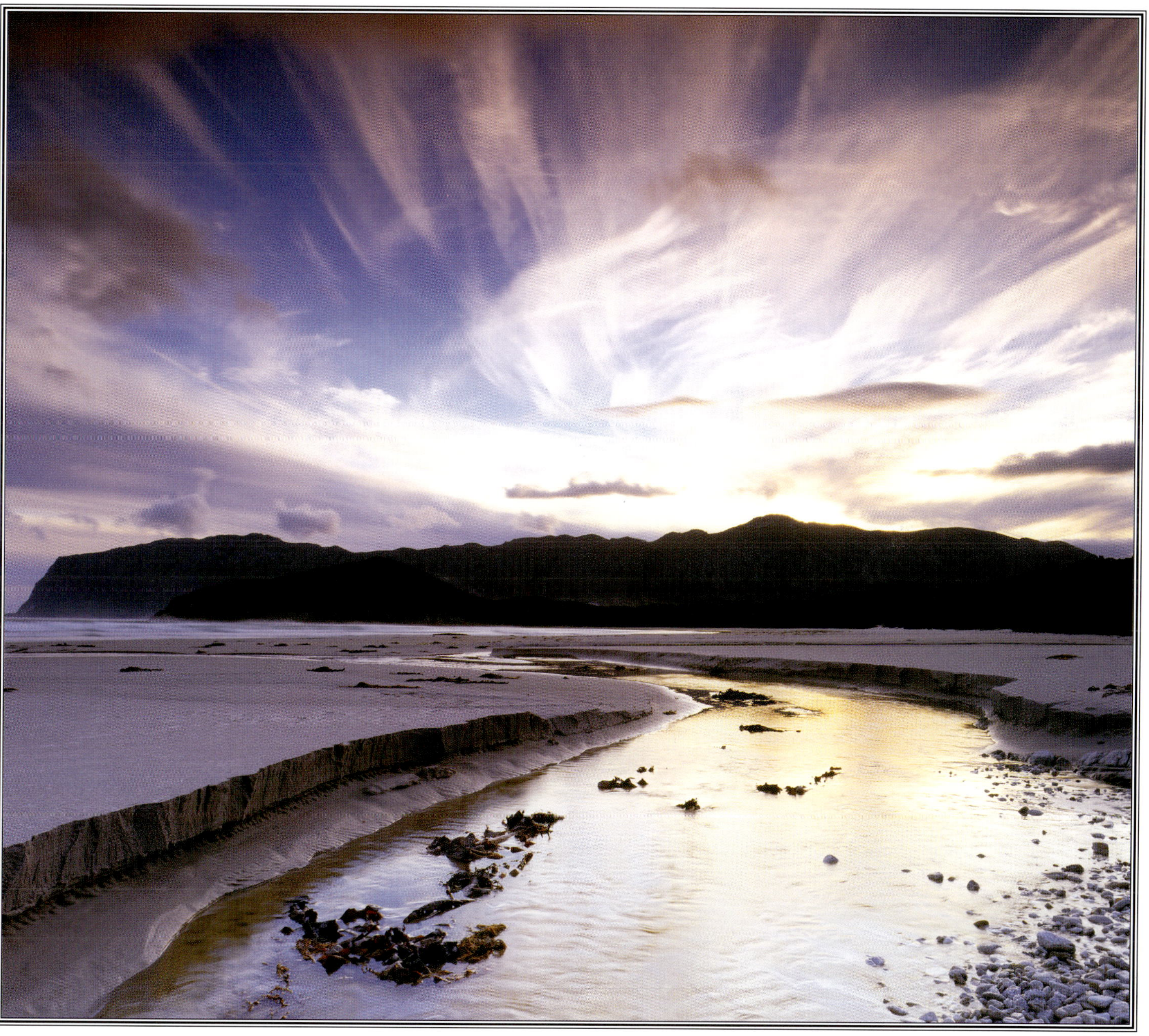

Sunset over New Harbour Range - Cox Bight beach

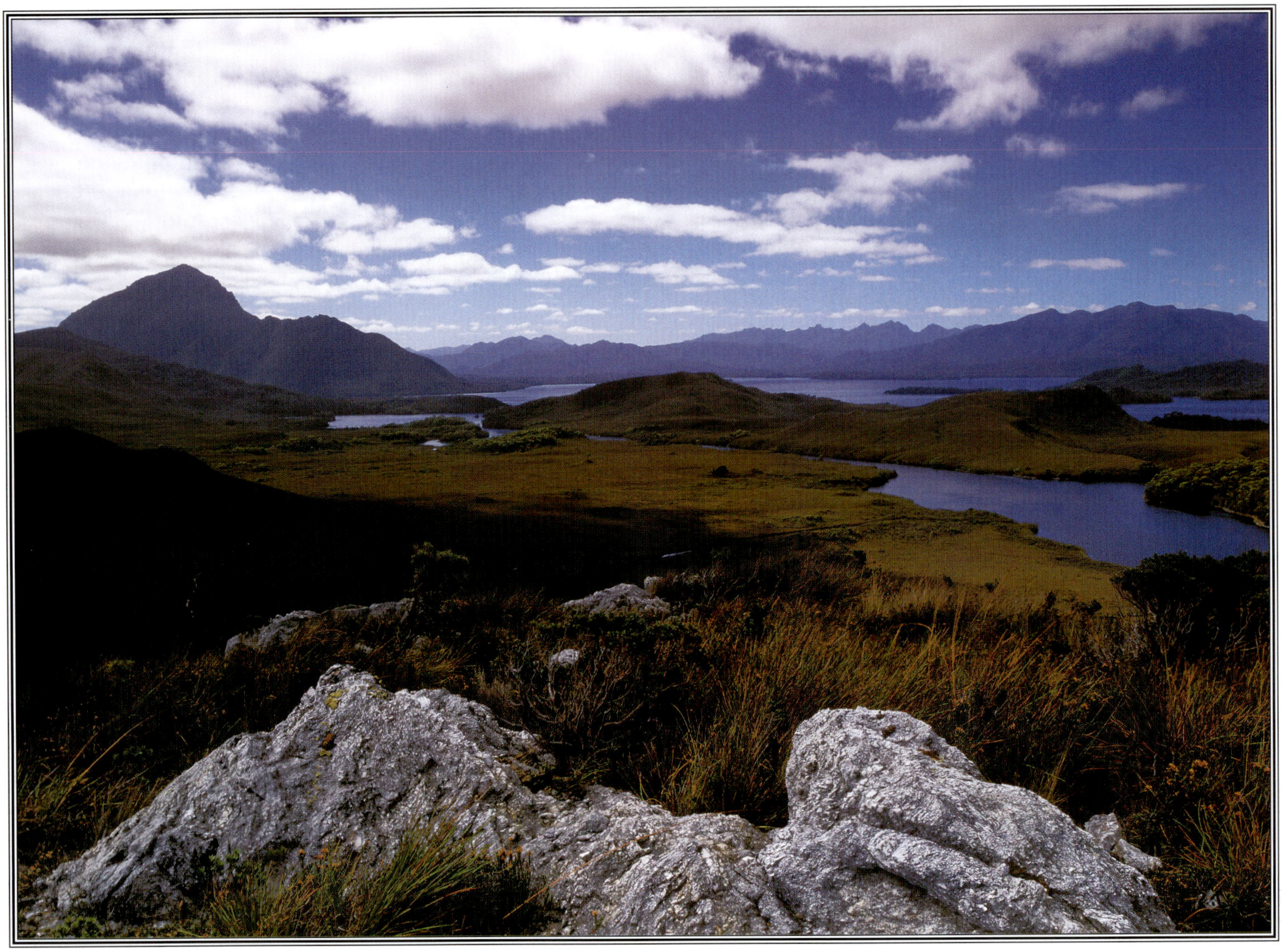

Melaleuca

On the southern tip of Bathurst Harbour is Melaleuca. Equipped with an airstrip, it is an ideal location from which to explore, north to Port Davey, or south to the South West Cape.

Tall, craggy mountains rise above sweeping button-grass plains and provide an elevation from which the entire southwest can be viewed.

The remote beauty of Tasmania's southwest region is a testament to the importance of protecting, and responsibly managing, wilderness environments within Australia. We must make sure that their unspoiled magnificence will remain so, and can be witnessed by all who choose to look, today and in the future.

View to Bathurst Harbour

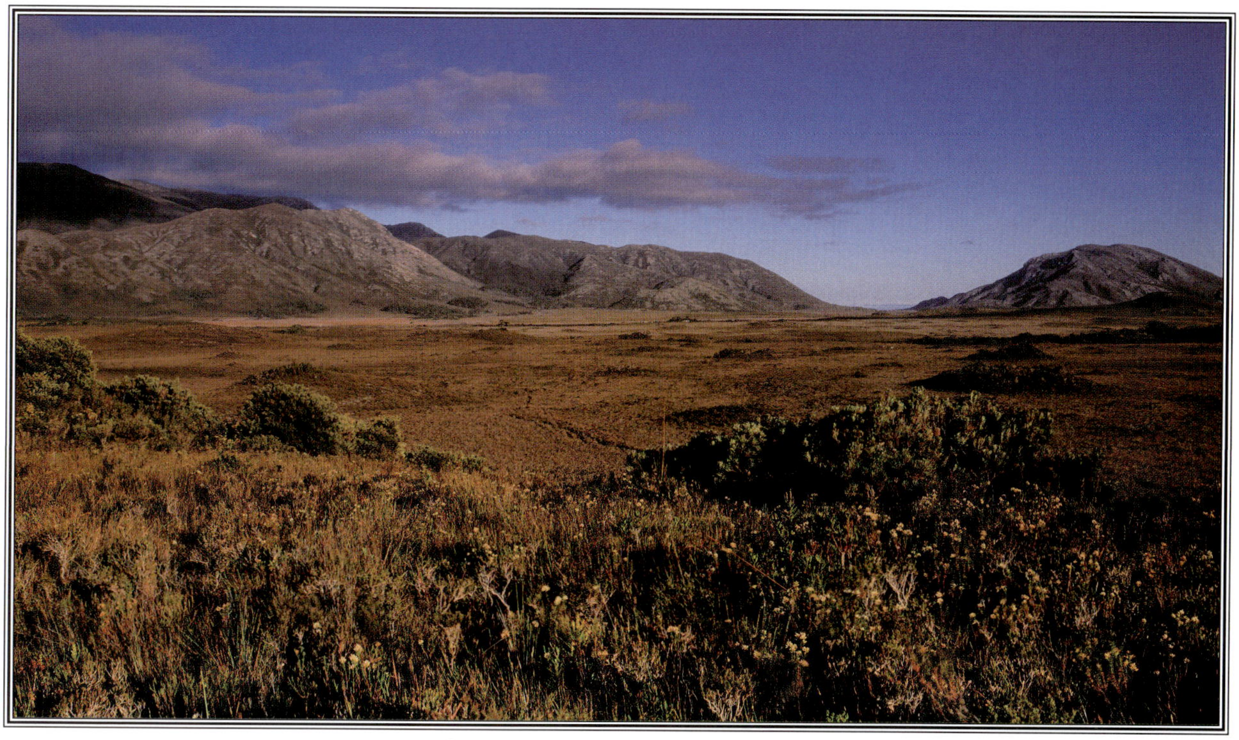

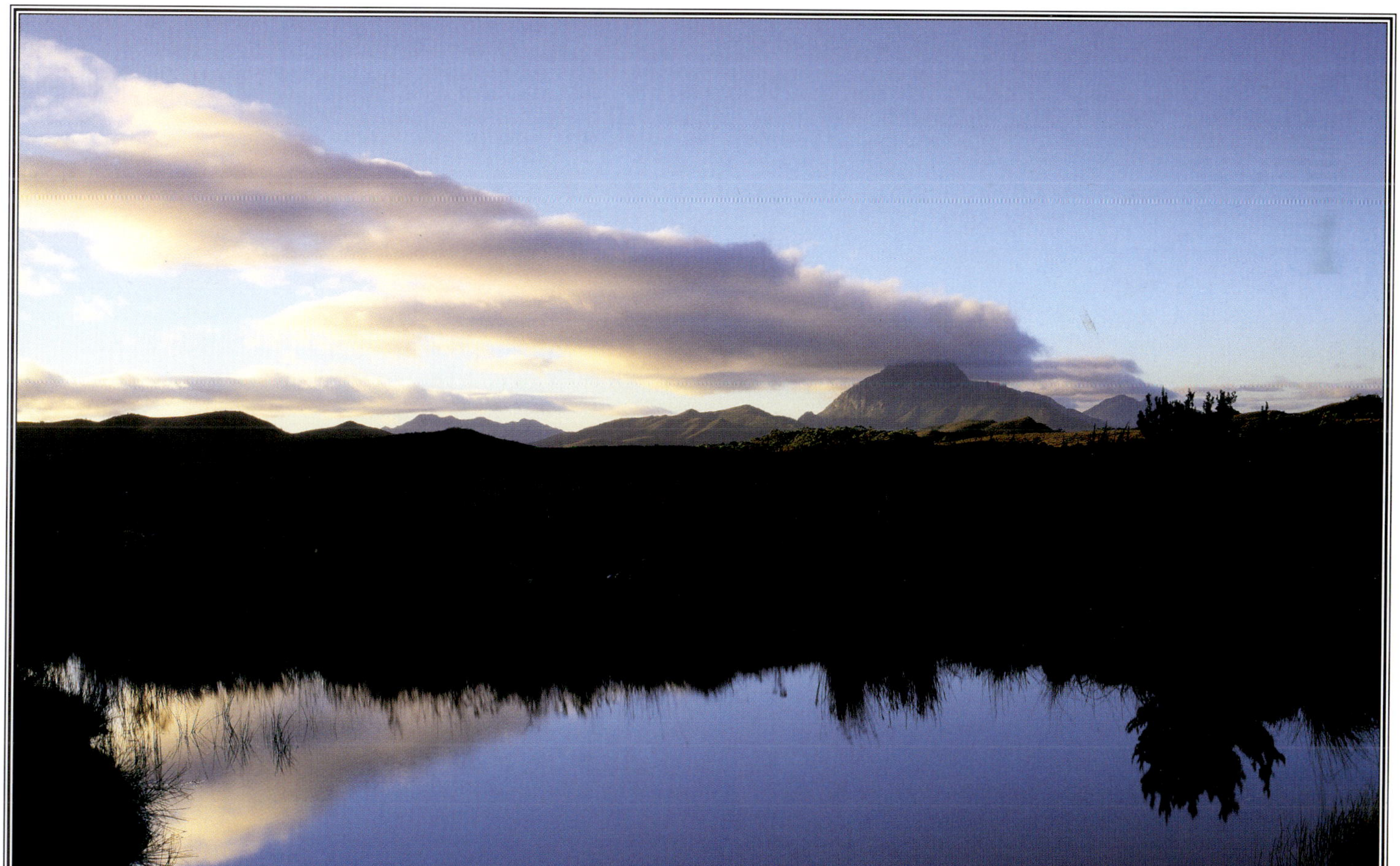

Top: *View to Cox Bight from Melaleuca*
Bottom: *Mt. Rugby reflected in a creek at sunset*

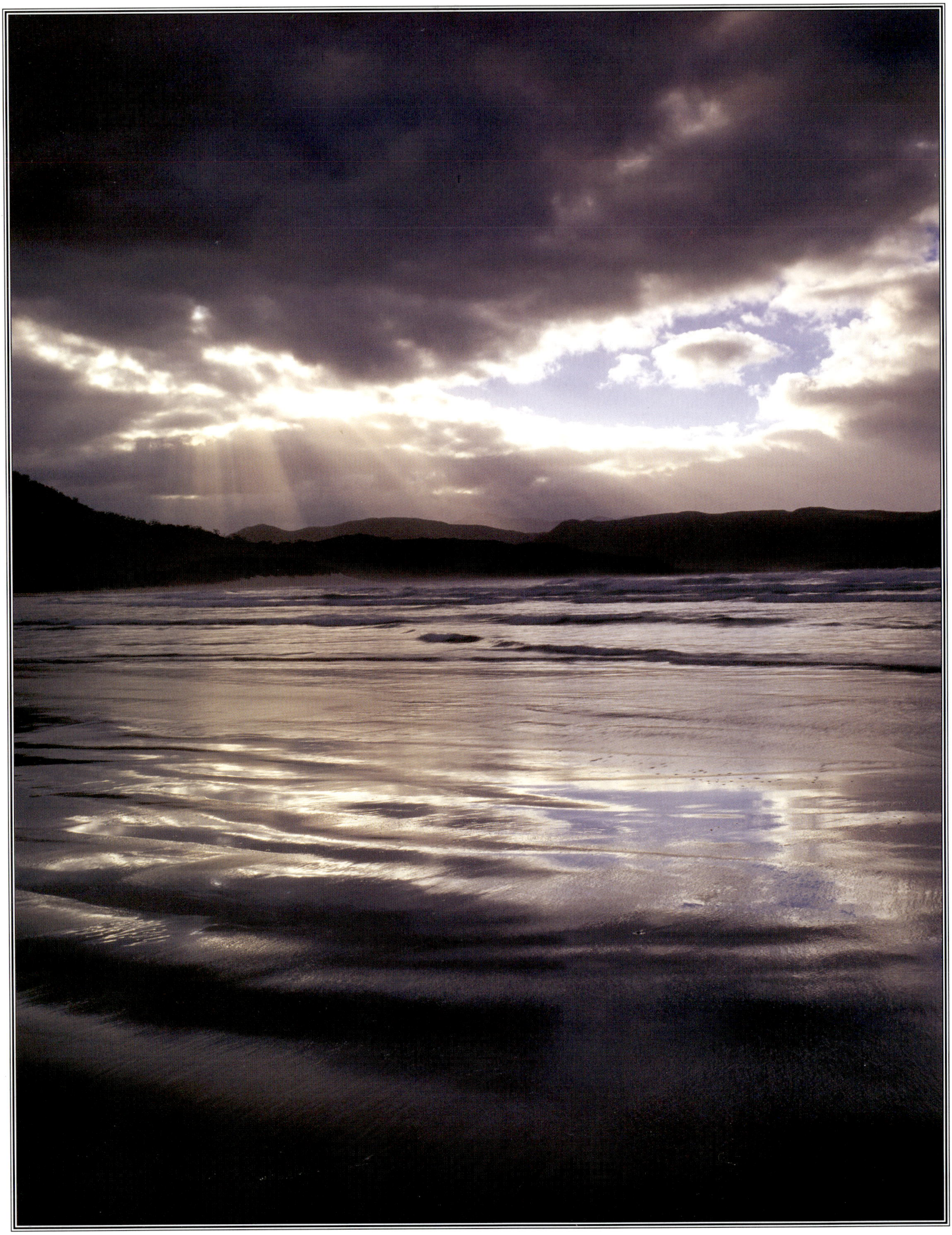

Sunrise breaking through the clouds at Cox Bight

LES NOUVELLES AVENTURES DE

CUBITUS

D'APRÈS DUPA

UN CHIEN PEUT EN CACHER UN AUTRE

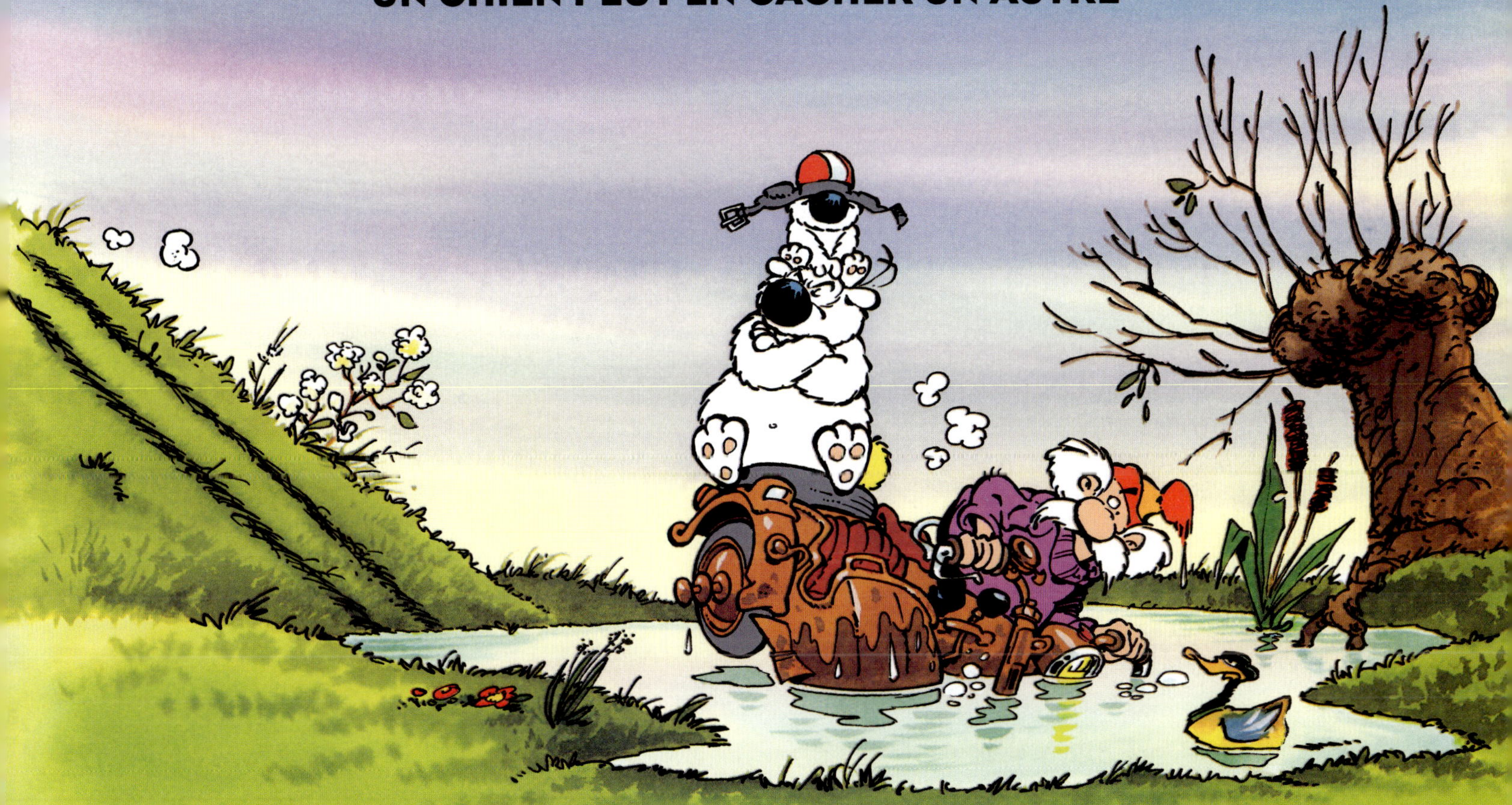

Scénario : Pierre Aucaigne & Michel Rodrigue

Dessin : Michel Rodrigue

Couleurs : Marcy

LE LOMBARD

Un grand merci à Bruno et Vincent ainsi qu'à Jean-Yves et Marc de nous laisser "croquer" leurs talents...

Première édition

D/2006/0086/280
ISBN 2-80362-187-8

Dépôt légal : septembre 2006
Imprimé en Belgique par Fleurus BD Land

LES EDITIONS DU LOMBARD
7, AVENUE PAUL-HENRI SPAAK - 1060 BRUXELLES - BELGIQUE

www.lelombard.com
l'internet des 7 à 77 ans

VERRES GROSSISSANTS

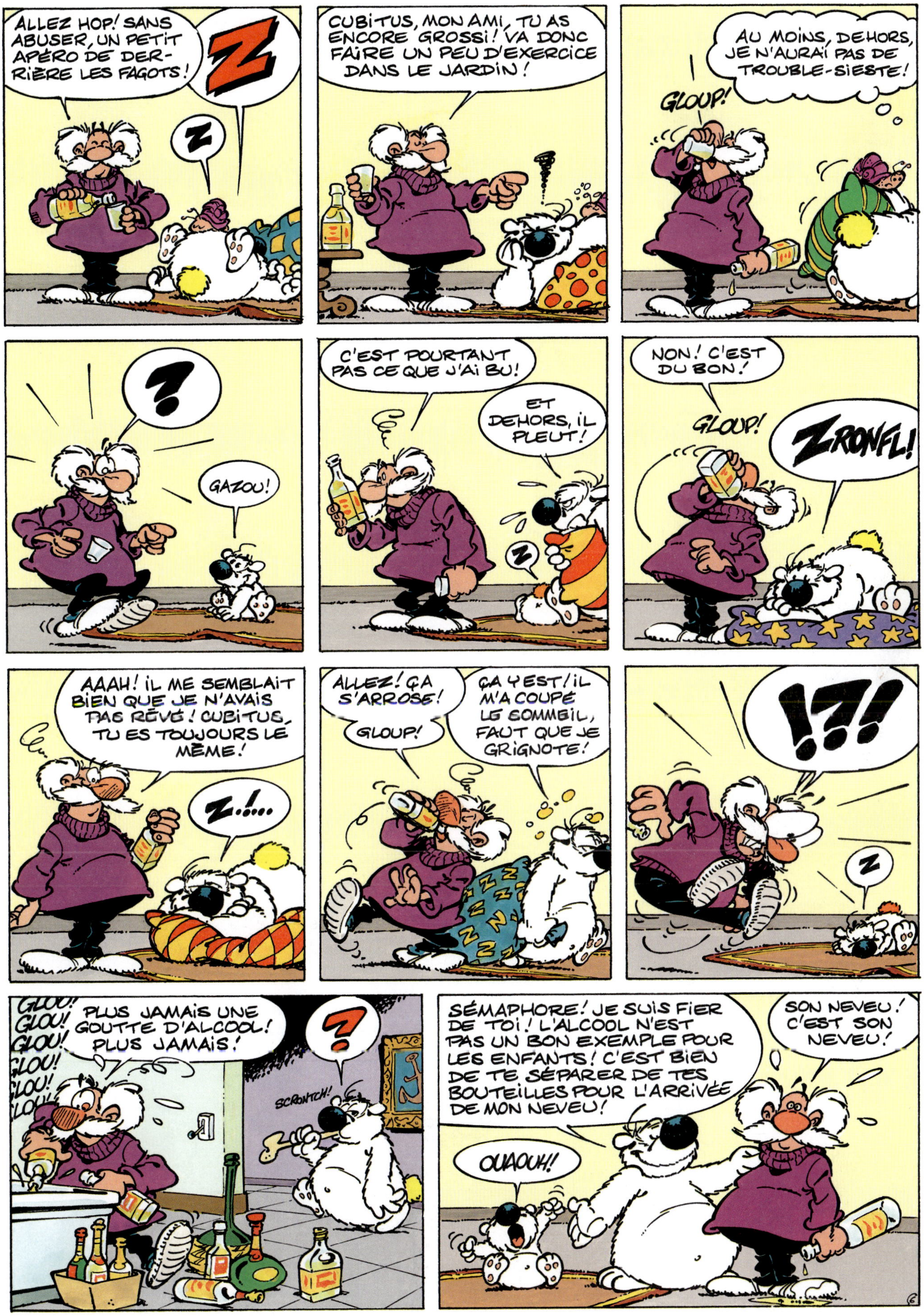

SUR LA TOUCHE

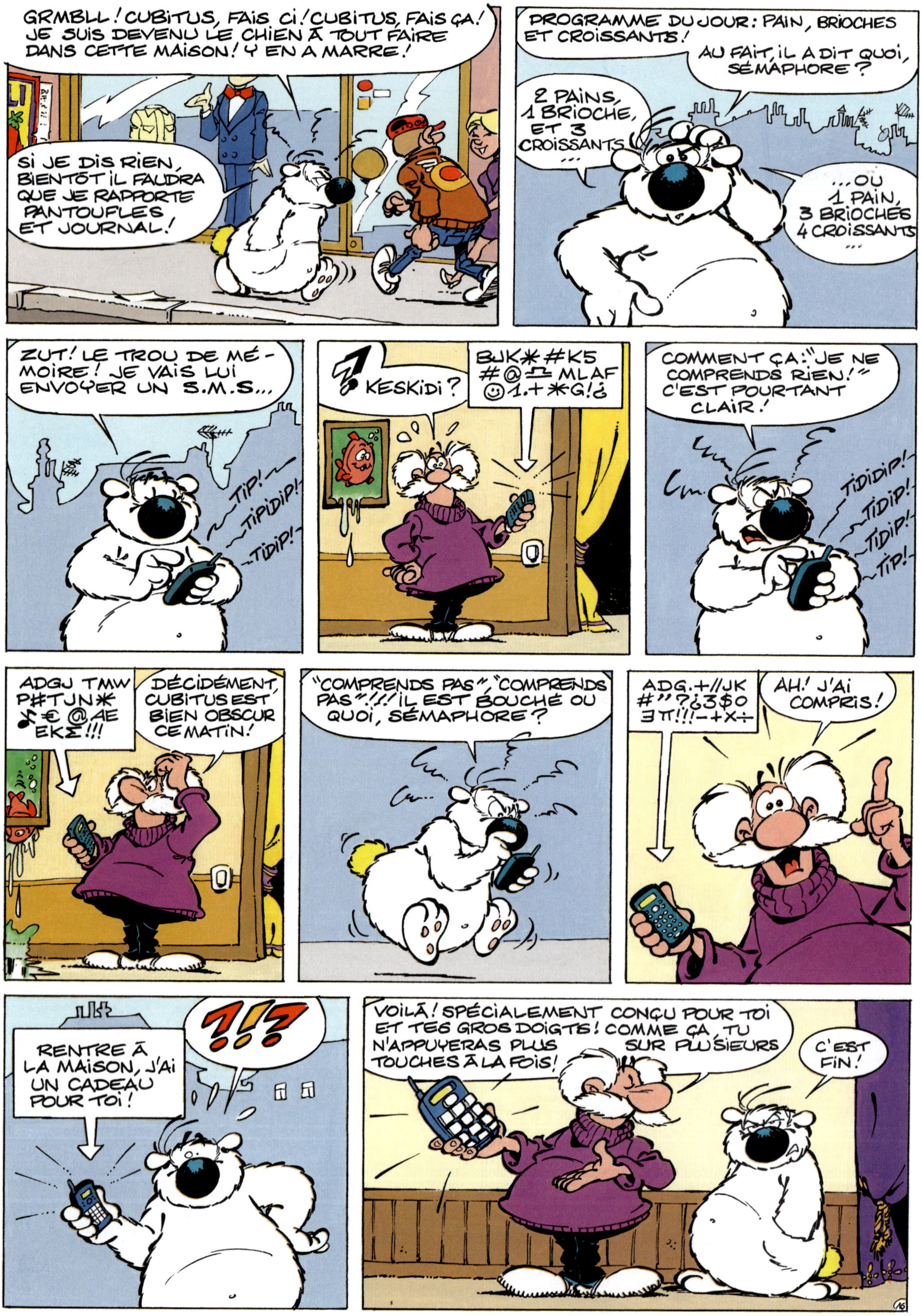

TRIONS MES FRÈRES

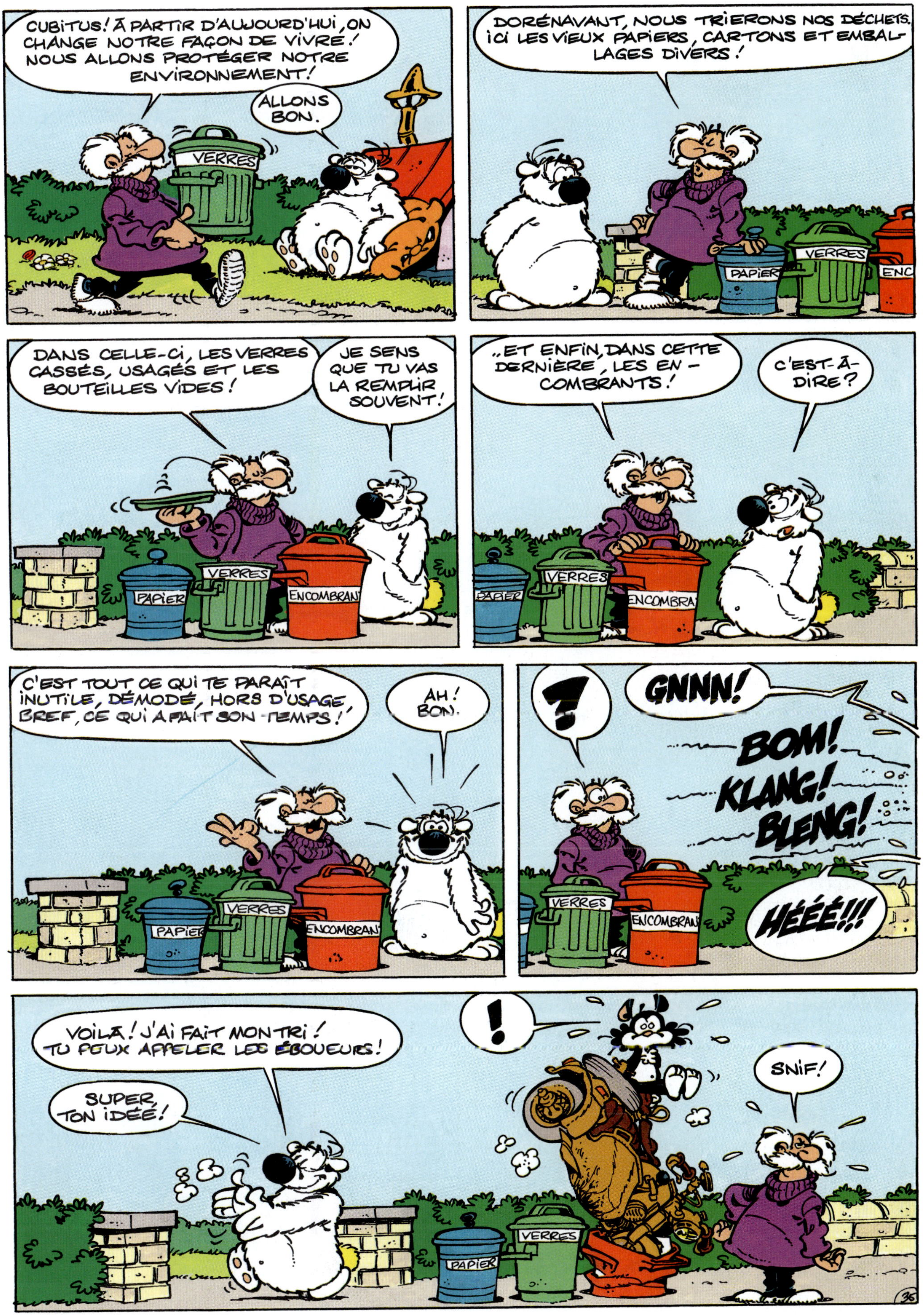

PETITE MISE AU POING

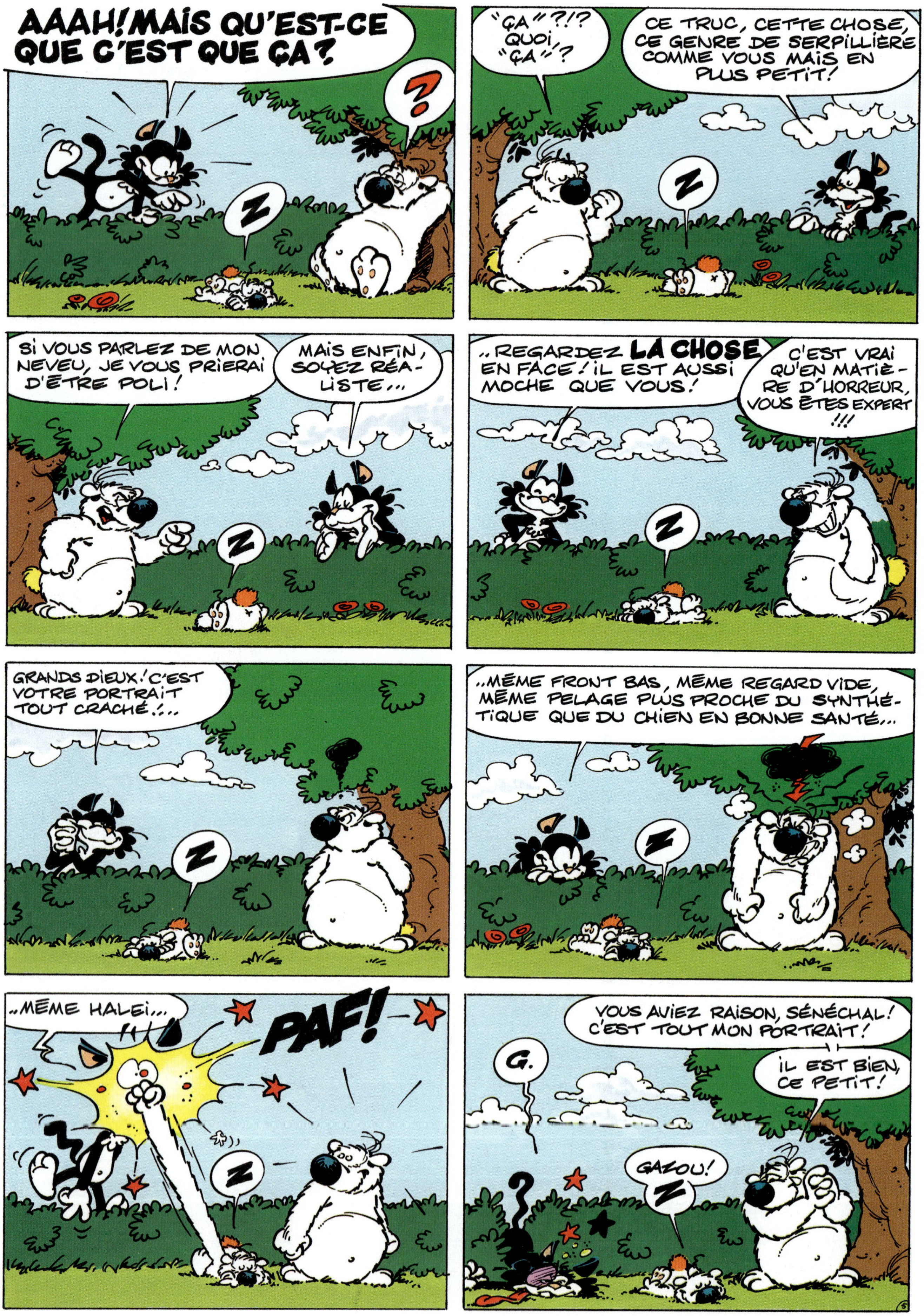

INDIEN AVERTI EN VAUT DEUX

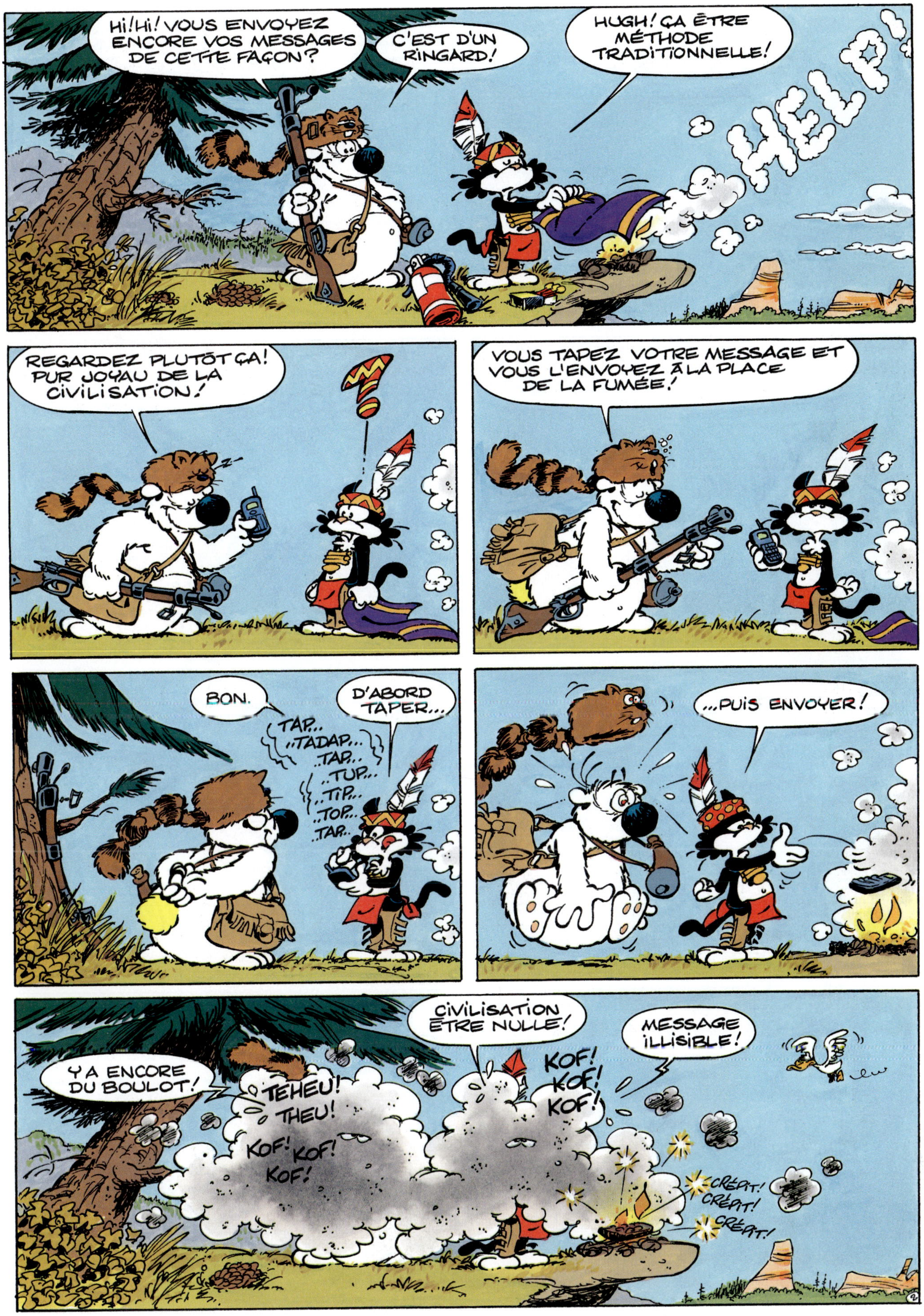

LA GUERRE DES FRITES N'AURA PAS LIEU

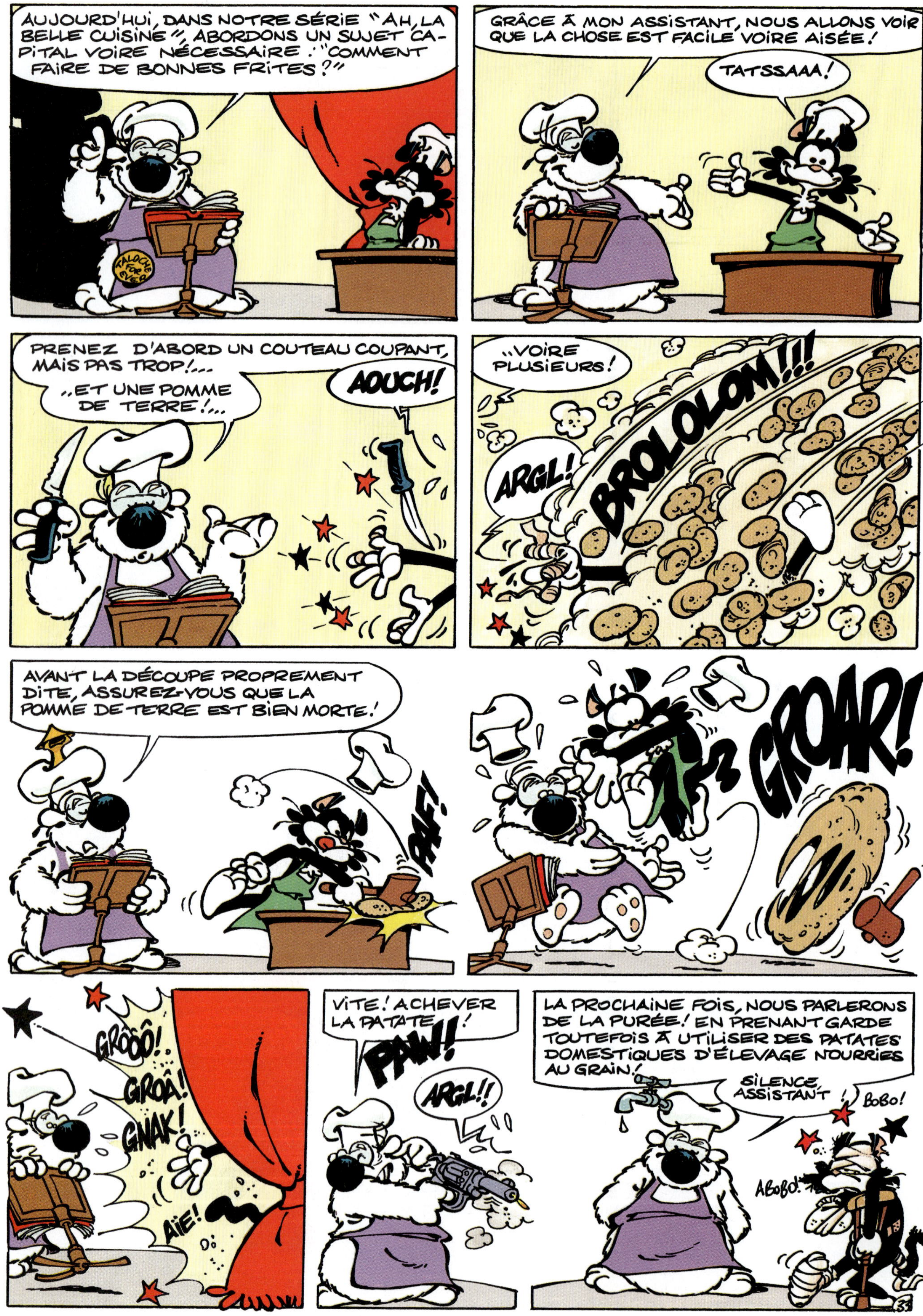

LA FUITE DANS LES IDÉES

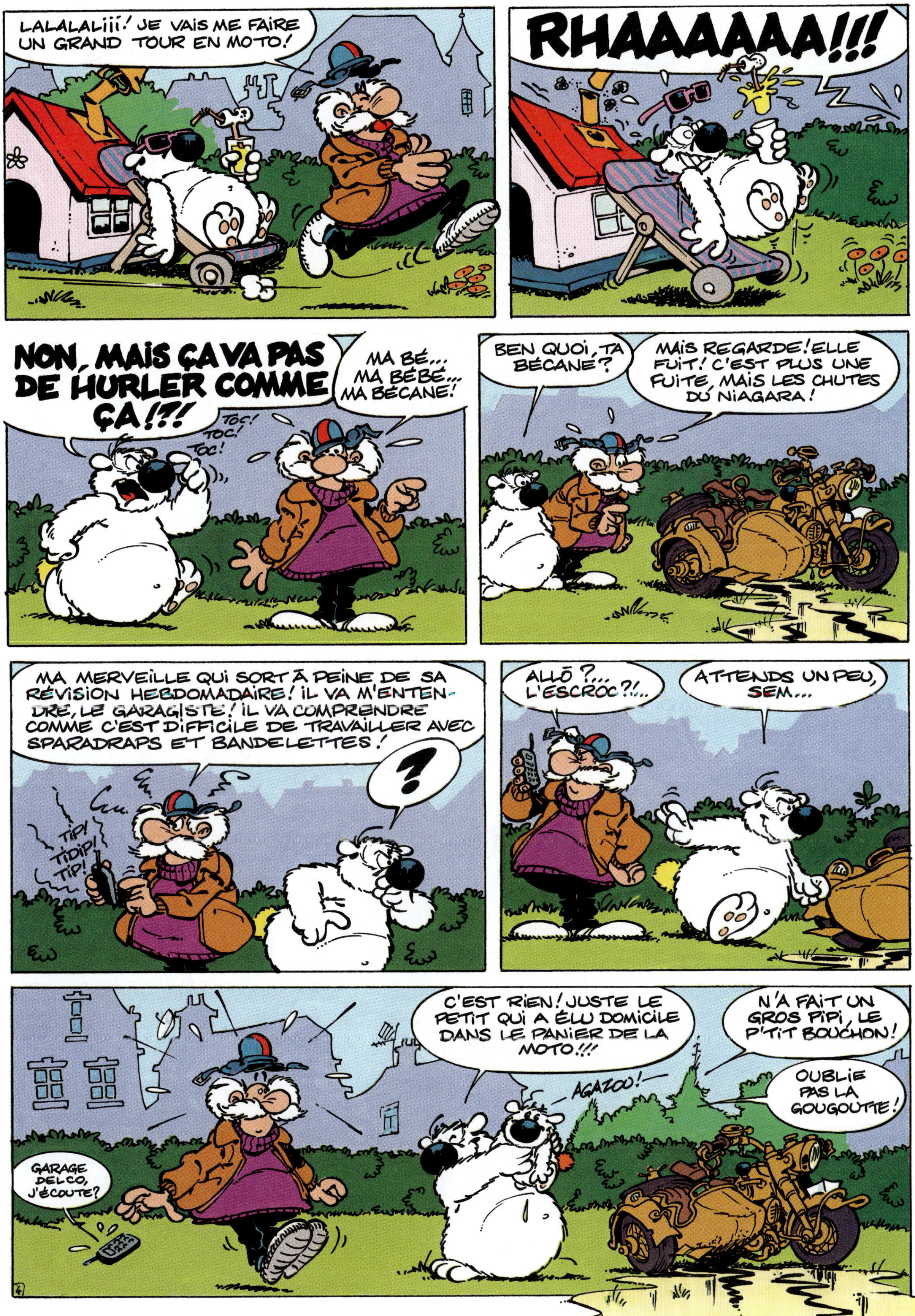

RÈGLEMENT DE CONTE

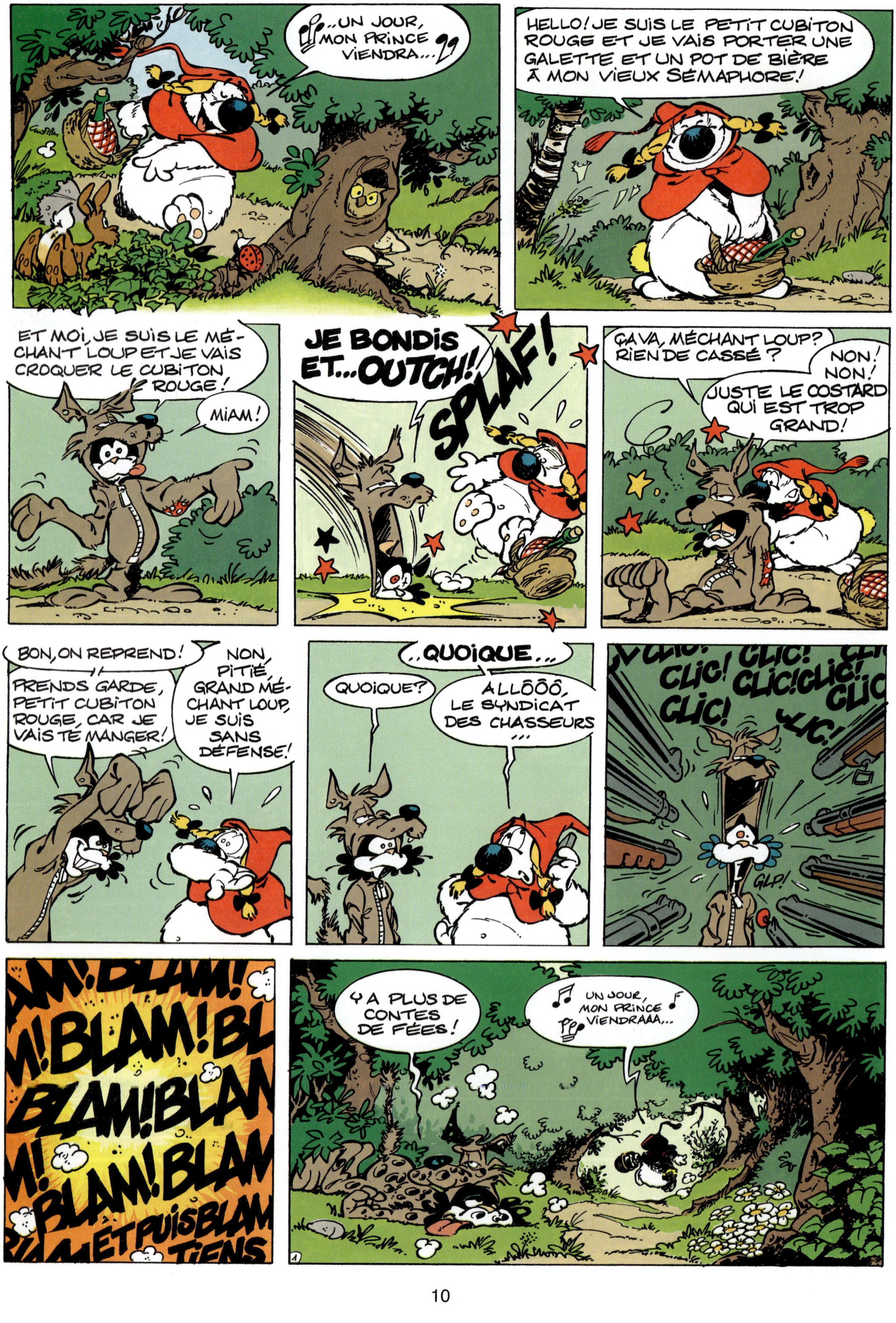

UN MAUX POUR UN AUTRE

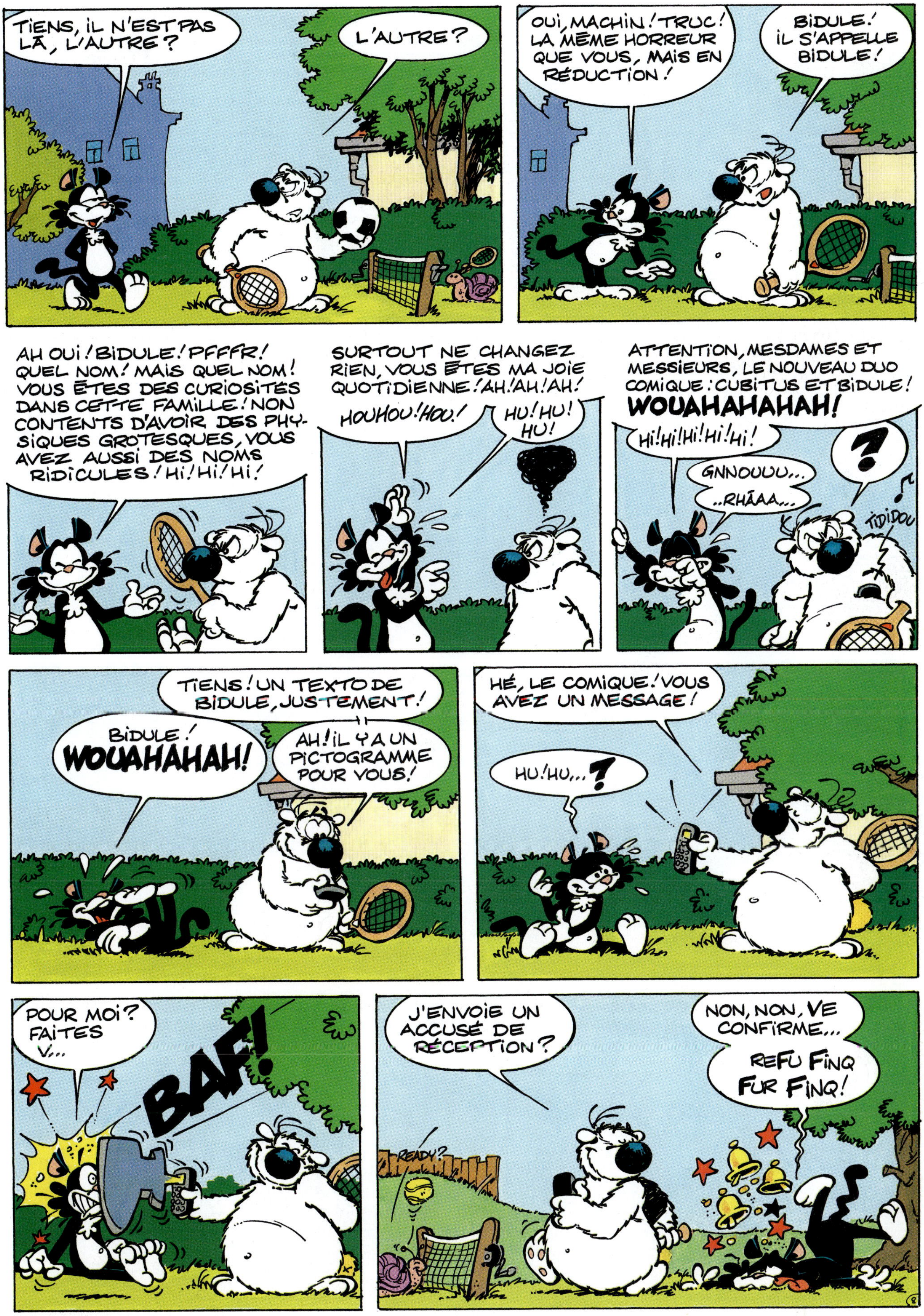

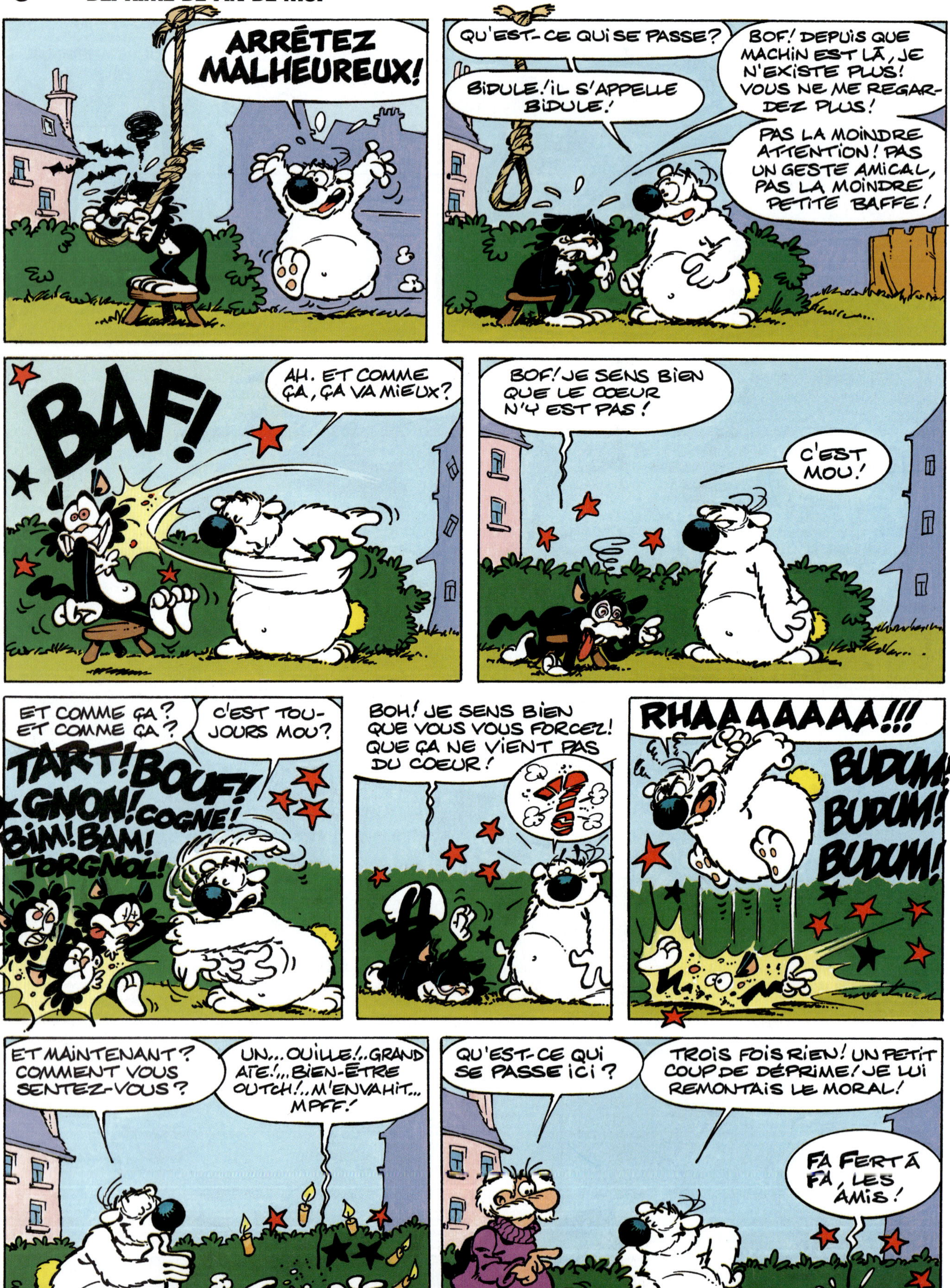
ARRÊTEZ MALHEUREUX!
QU'EST-CE QUI SE PASSE?
BIDULE! IL S'APPELLE BIDULE!
BOF! DEPUIS QUE MACHIN EST LÀ, JE N'EXISTE PLUS! VOUS NE ME REGARDEZ PLUS!
PAS LA MOINDRE ATTENTION! PAS UN GESTE AMICAL, PAS LA MOINDRE PETITE BAFFE!
BAF!
AH. ET COMME ÇA, ÇA VA MIEUX?
BOF! JE SENS BIEN QUE LE COEUR N'Y EST PAS!
C'EST MOU!
ET COMME ÇA? ET COMME ÇA?
C'EST TOUJOURS MOU?
TART! BOUF! GNON! COGNE! BIM! BAM! TORGNOL!
BOH! JE SENS BIEN QUE VOUS VOUS FORCEZ! QUE ÇA NE VIENT PAS DU COEUR!
RHAAAAAAA!!!
BUDUM! BUDUM! BUDUM!
ET MAINTENANT? COMMENT VOUS SENTEZ-VOUS?
UN... OUILLE!.. GRAND AÏE!.. BIEN-ÊTRE OUTCH!.. M'ENVAHIT... MPFF!
QU'EST-CE QUI SE PASSE ICI?
TROIS FOIS RIEN! UN PETIT COUP DE DÉPRIME! JE LUI REMONTAIS LE MORAL!
FA FERT À FA, LES AMIS!

UNE CASE EN MOINS

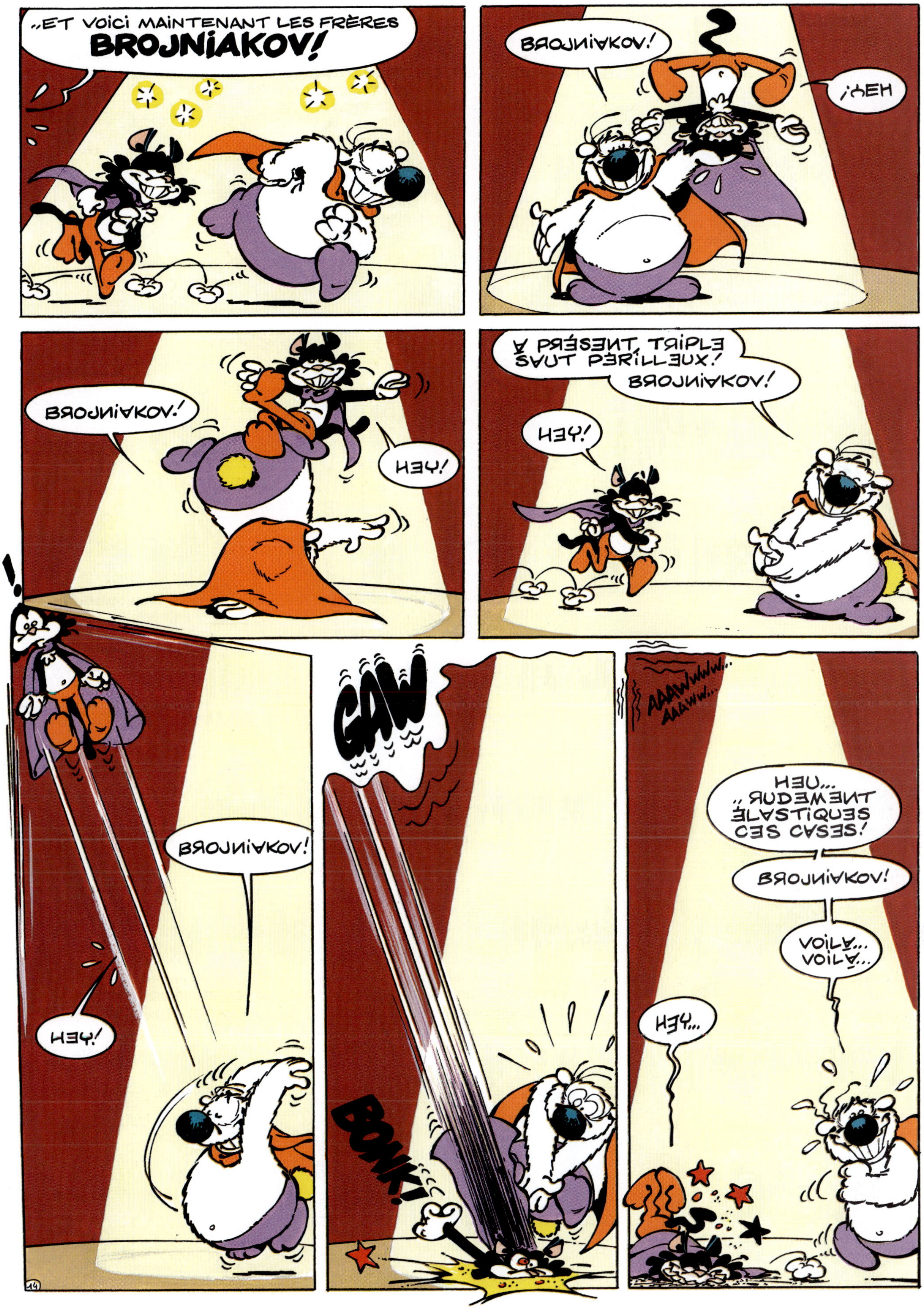

PLUS DURE SERA LA CHUTE

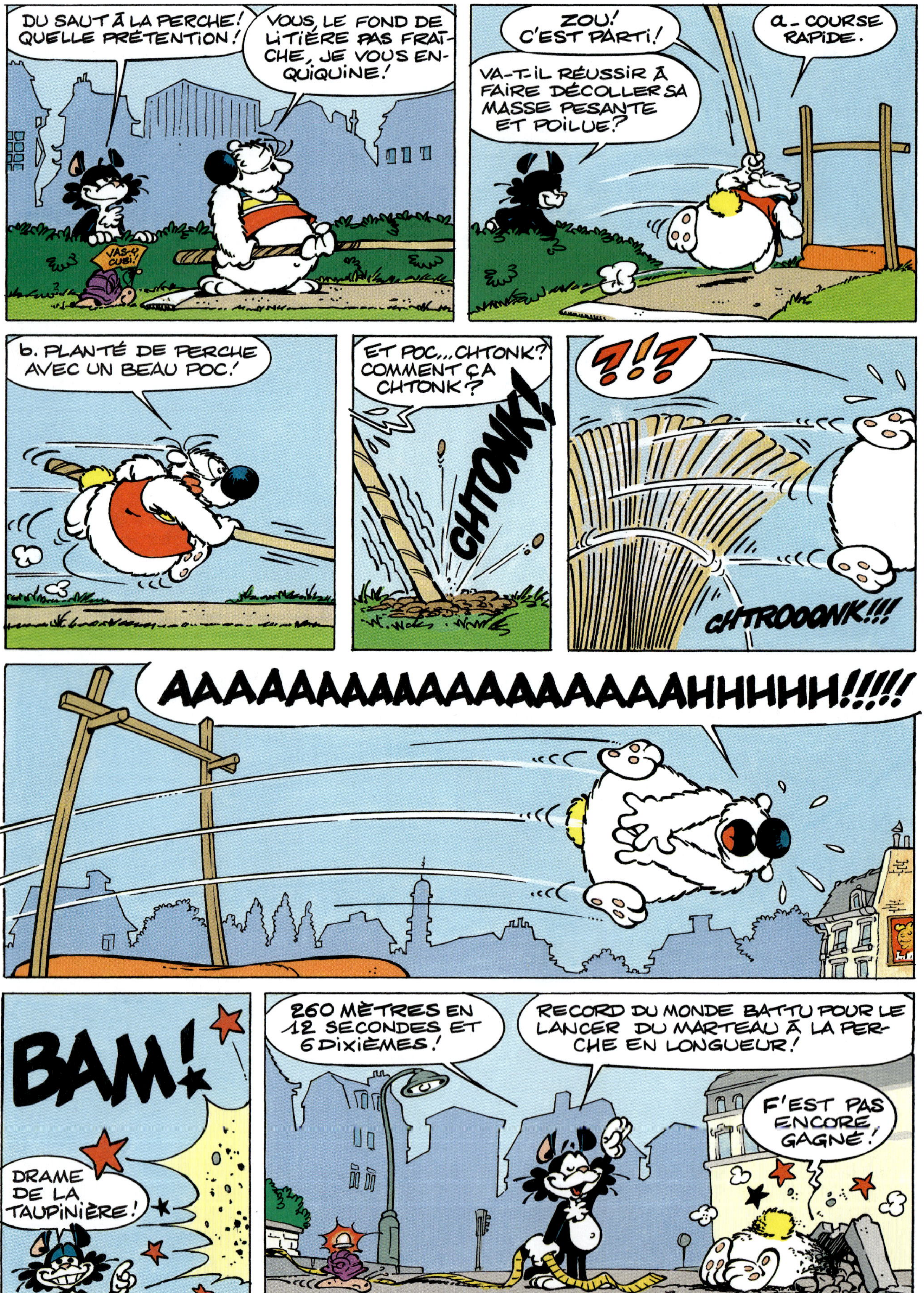

FAIS COUCOU À LA DAME

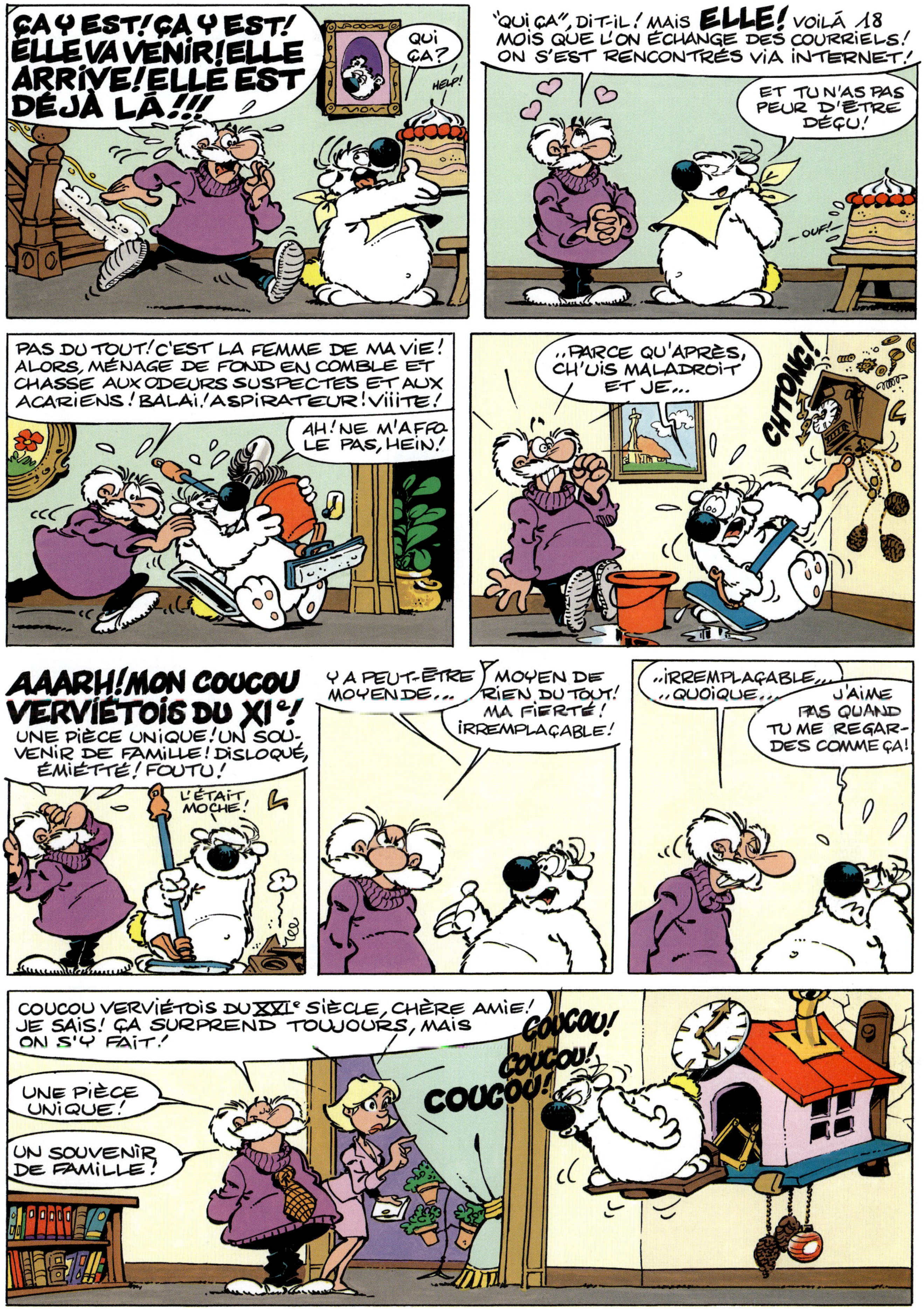

ON A TOUJOURS BESOIN D'UN PAPY-SITTER

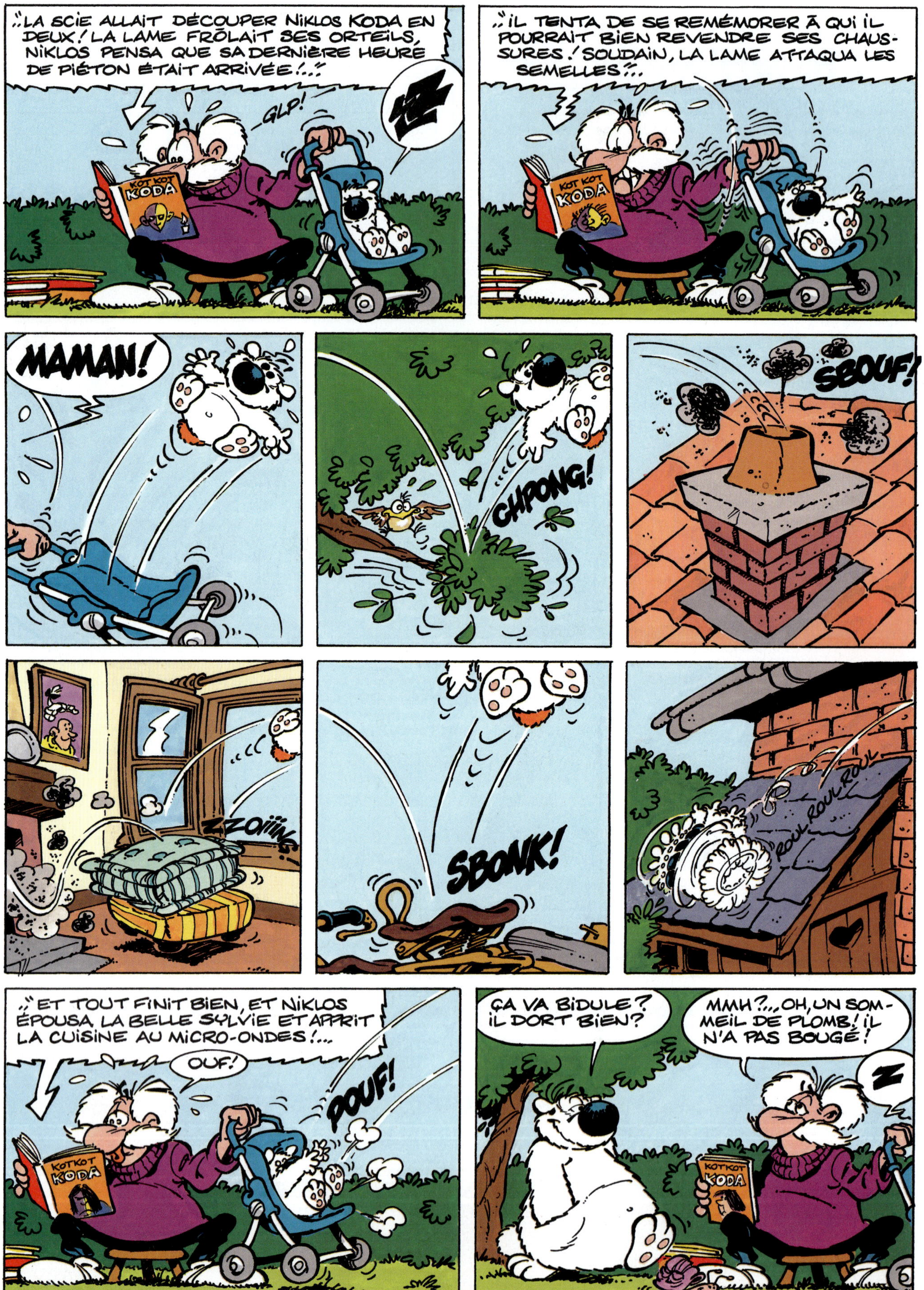

QUAND ON AIME, ON COMPTE

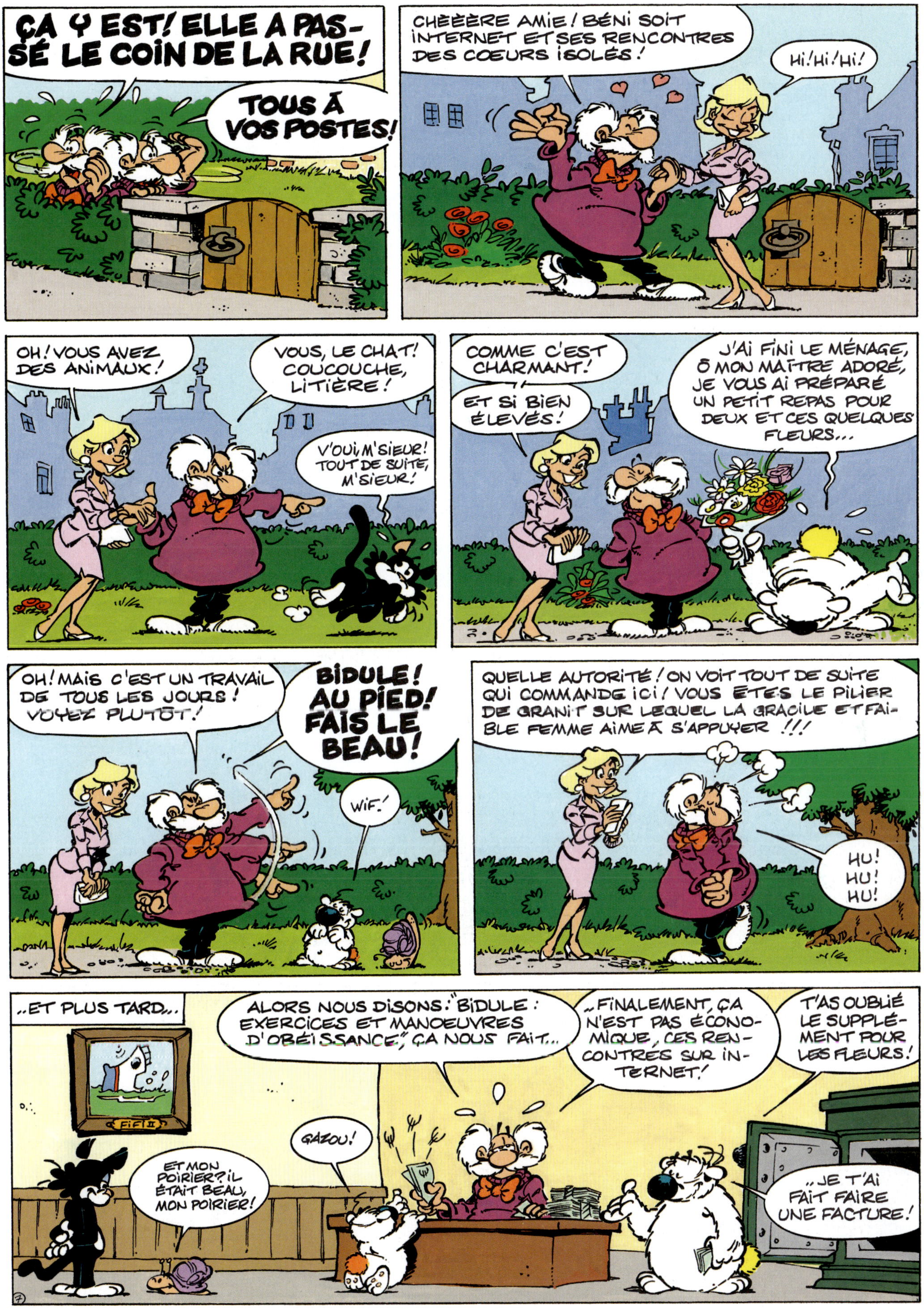

SOLITUDE, QUAND TU NOUS TIENS...

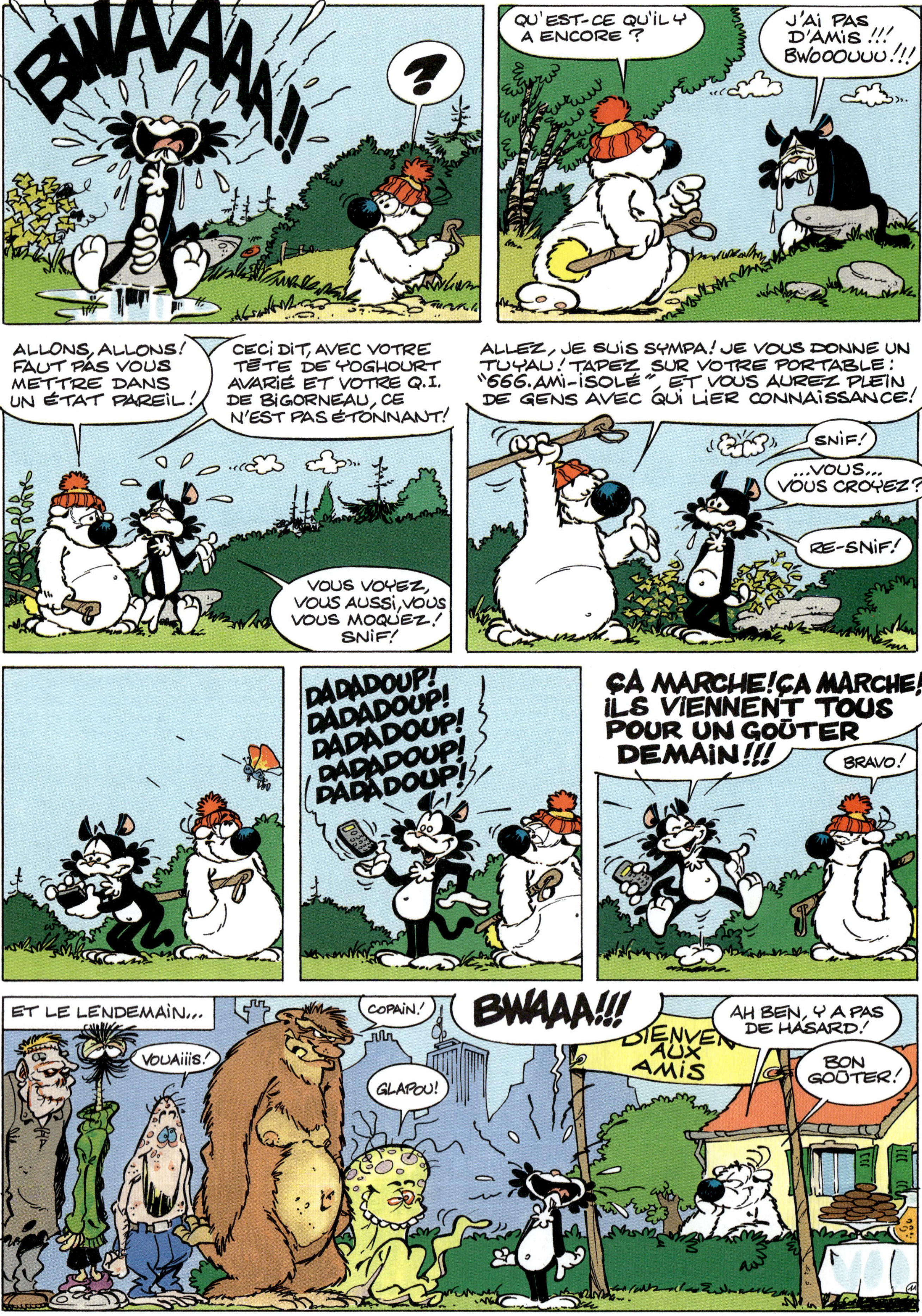

LE FUTUR DU PROGRÈS A DE L'AVENIR

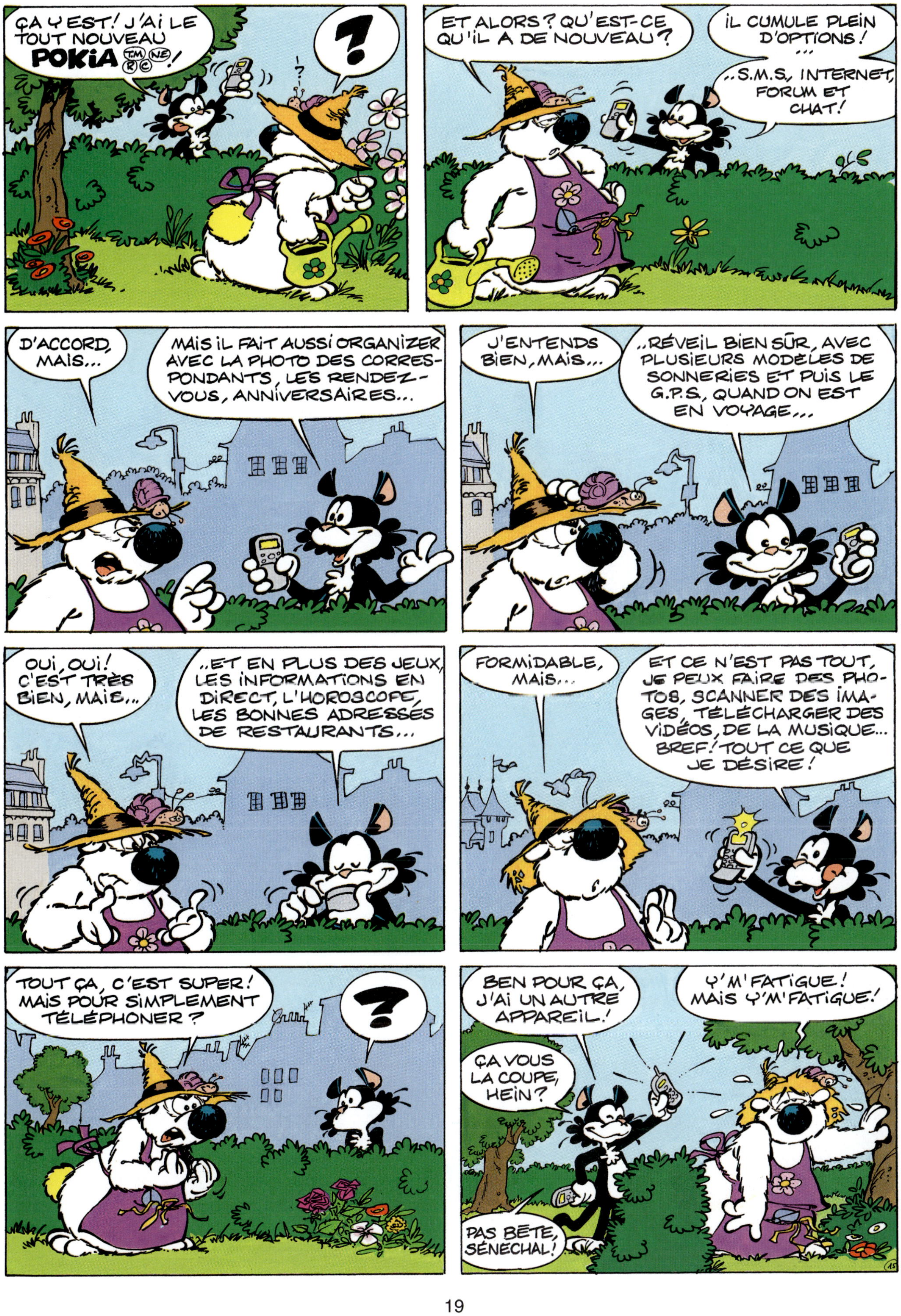

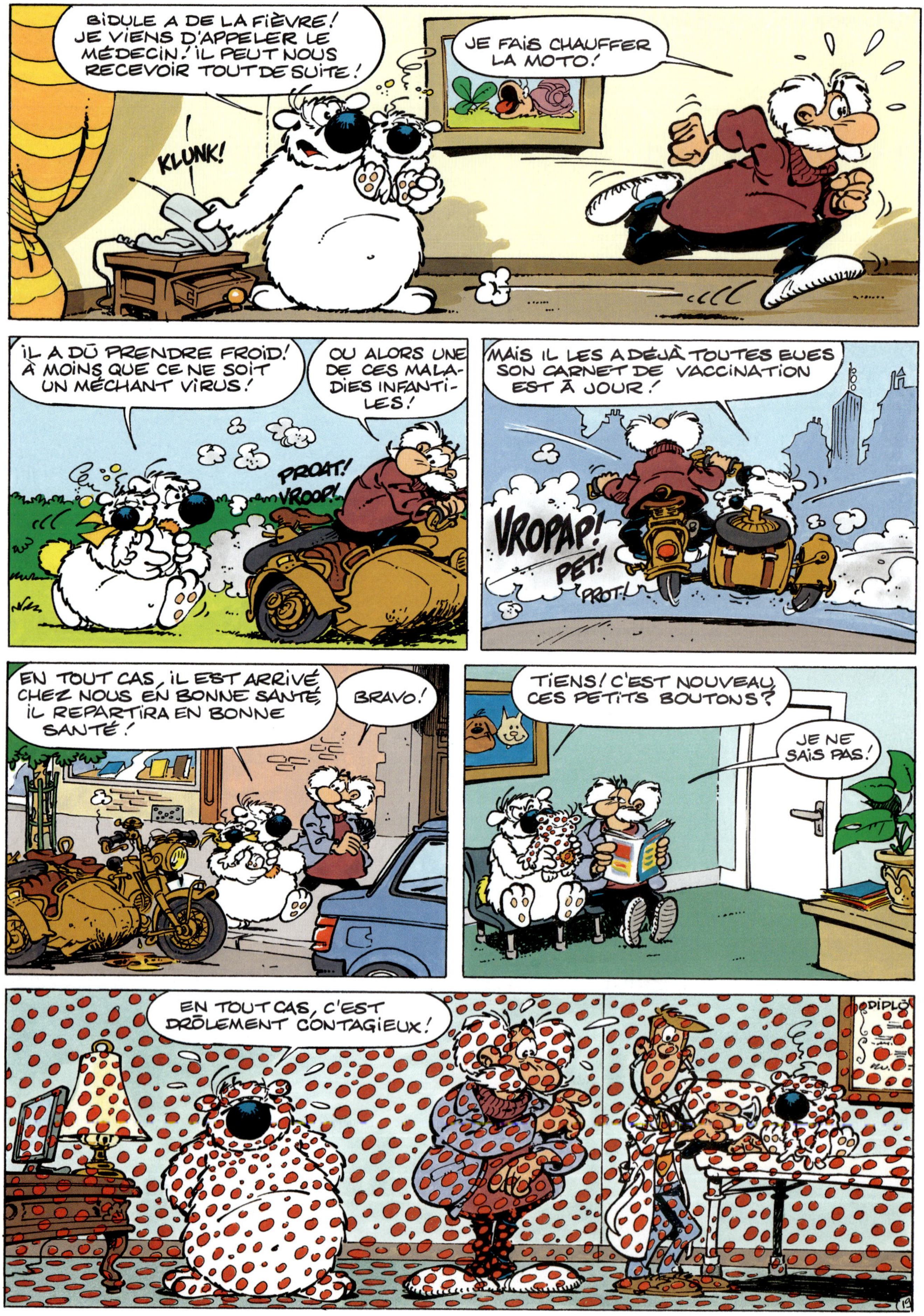
BIDULE A DE LA FIÈVRE! JE VIENS D'APPELER LE MÉDECIN! IL PEUT NOUS RECEVOIR TOUT DE SUITE!
KLUNK!
JE FAIS CHAUFFER LA MOTO!
IL A DÛ PRENDRE FROID! À MOINS QUE CE NE SOIT UN MÉCHANT VIRUS!
OU ALORS UNE DE CES MALADIES INFANTILES!
PROAT! VROOP!
MAIS IL LES A DÉJÀ TOUTES EUES SON CARNET DE VACCINATION EST À JOUR!
VROPAP! PET! PROT!
EN TOUT CAS, IL EST ARRIVÉ CHEZ NOUS EN BONNE SANTÉ, IL REPARTIRA EN BONNE SANTÉ!
BRAVO!
TIENS! C'EST NOUVEAU CES PETITS BOUTONS?
JE NE SAIS PAS!
EN TOUT CAS, C'EST DRÔLEMENT CONTAGIEUX!
DIPLÔ

LAISSE FAIRE...

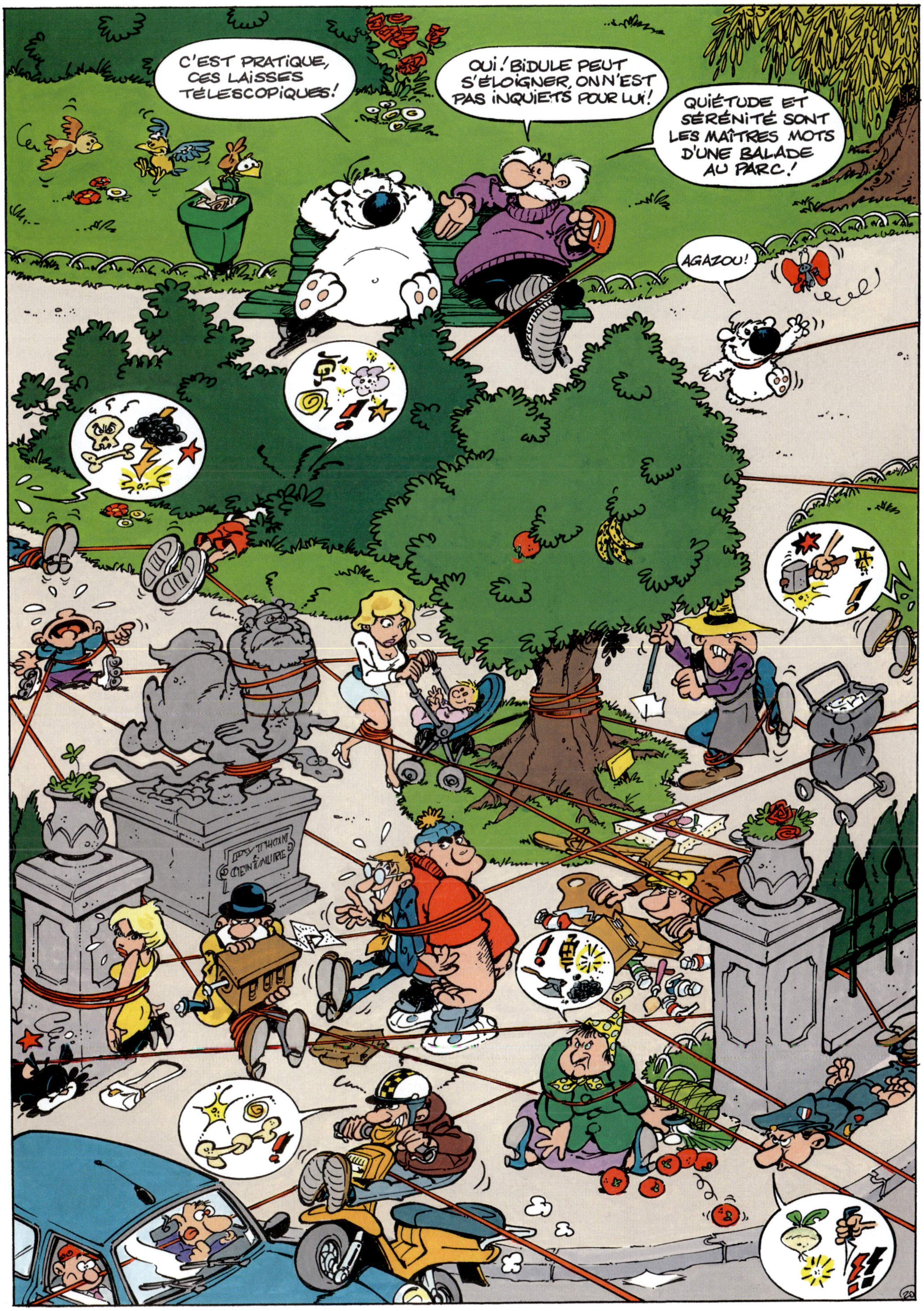

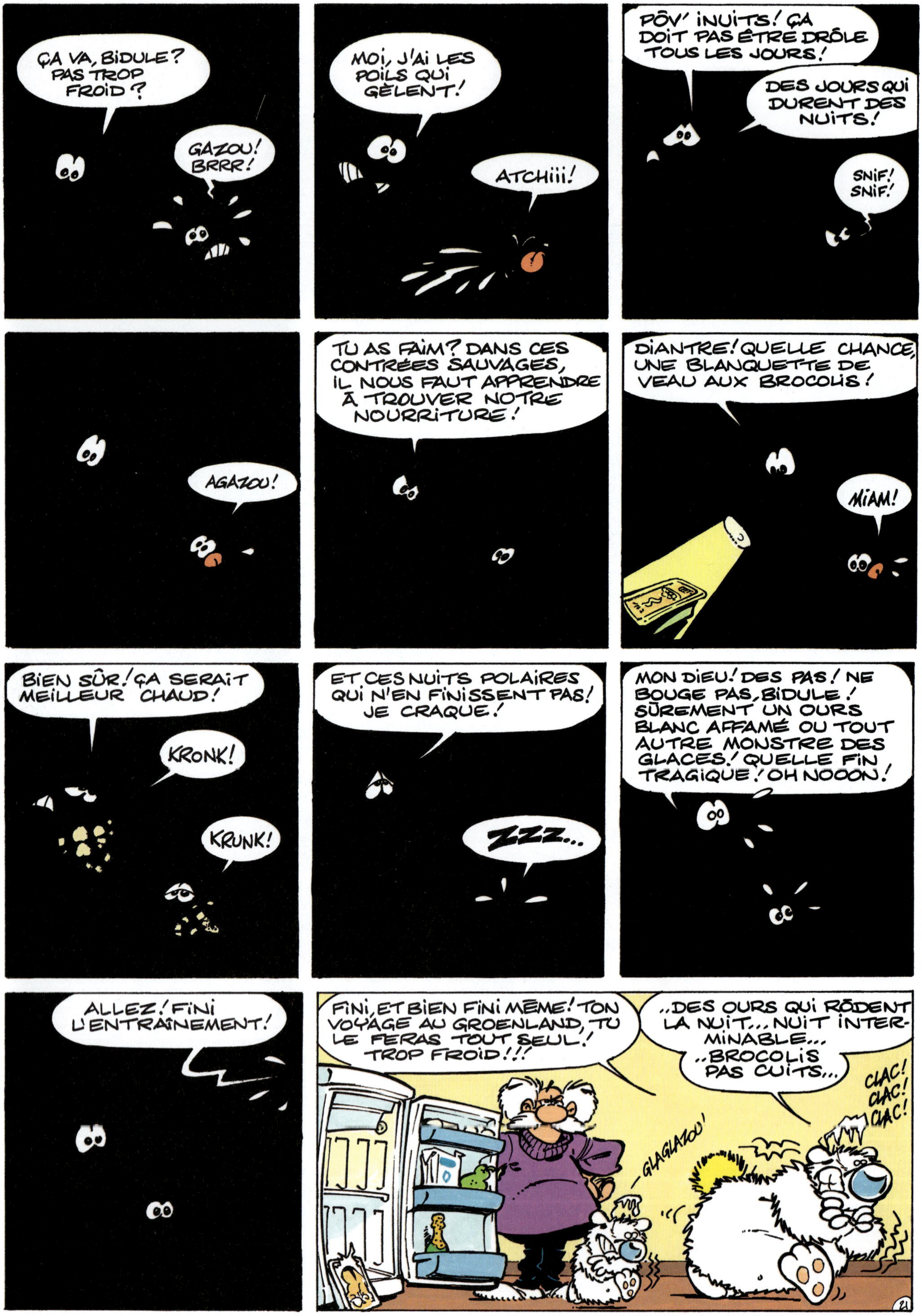
ÇA VA, BIDULE? PAS TROP FROID?
GAZOU! BRRR!
MOI, J'AI LES POILS QUI GÈLENT!
ATCHIII!
PÔV' INUITS! ÇA DOIT PAS ÊTRE DRÔLE TOUS LES JOURS!
DES JOURS QUI DURENT DES NUITS!
SNIF! SNIF!
AGAZOU!
TU AS FAIM? DANS CES CONTRÉES SAUVAGES, IL NOUS FAUT APPRENDRE À TROUVER NOTRE NOURRITURE!
DIANTRE! QUELLE CHANCE, UNE BLANQUETTE DE VEAU AUX BROCOLIS!
MIAM!
BIEN SÛR! ÇA SERAIT MEILLEUR CHAUD!
KRONK!
KRUNK!
ET CES NUITS POLAIRES QUI N'EN FINISSENT PAS! JE CRAQUE!
ZZZ...
MON DIEU! DES PAS! NE BOUGE PAS, BIDULE! SÛREMENT UN OURS BLANC AFFAMÉ OU TOUT AUTRE MONSTRE DES GLACES! QUELLE FIN TRAGIQUE! OH NOOON!
ALLEZ! FINI L'ENTRAÎNEMENT!
FINI, ET BIEN FINI MÊME! TON VOYAGE AU GROENLAND, TU LE FERAS TOUT SEUL! TROP FROID!!!
..DES OURS QUI RÔDENT LA NUIT... NUIT INTERMINABLE... ..BROCOLIS PAS CUITS...
CLAC! CLAC! CLAC!
GLAGLAGLAZOU!

PETIT CREUX POUR UNE GRANDE FIN

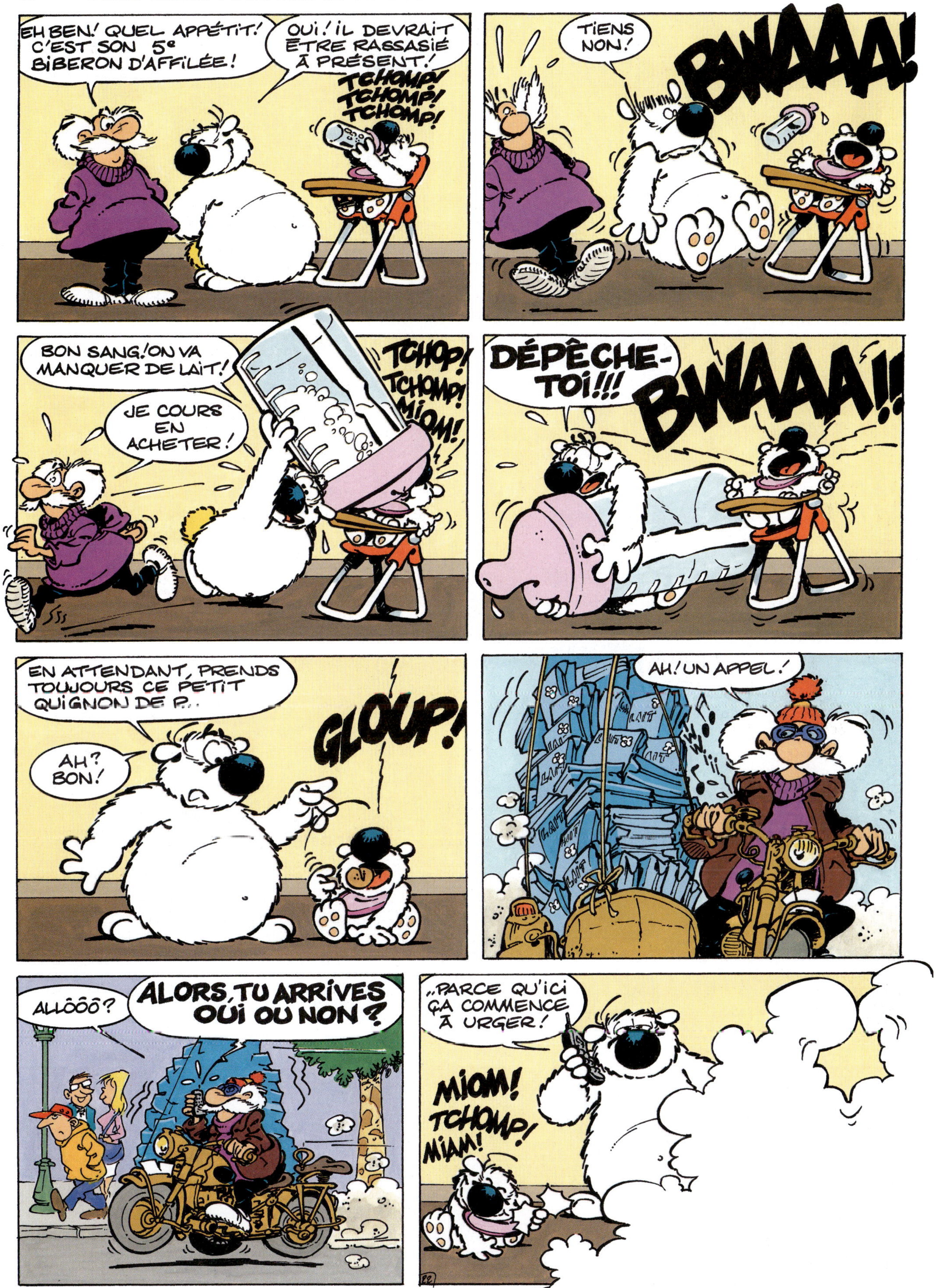

CE SOIR LES SOURDS DÎNENT !!!

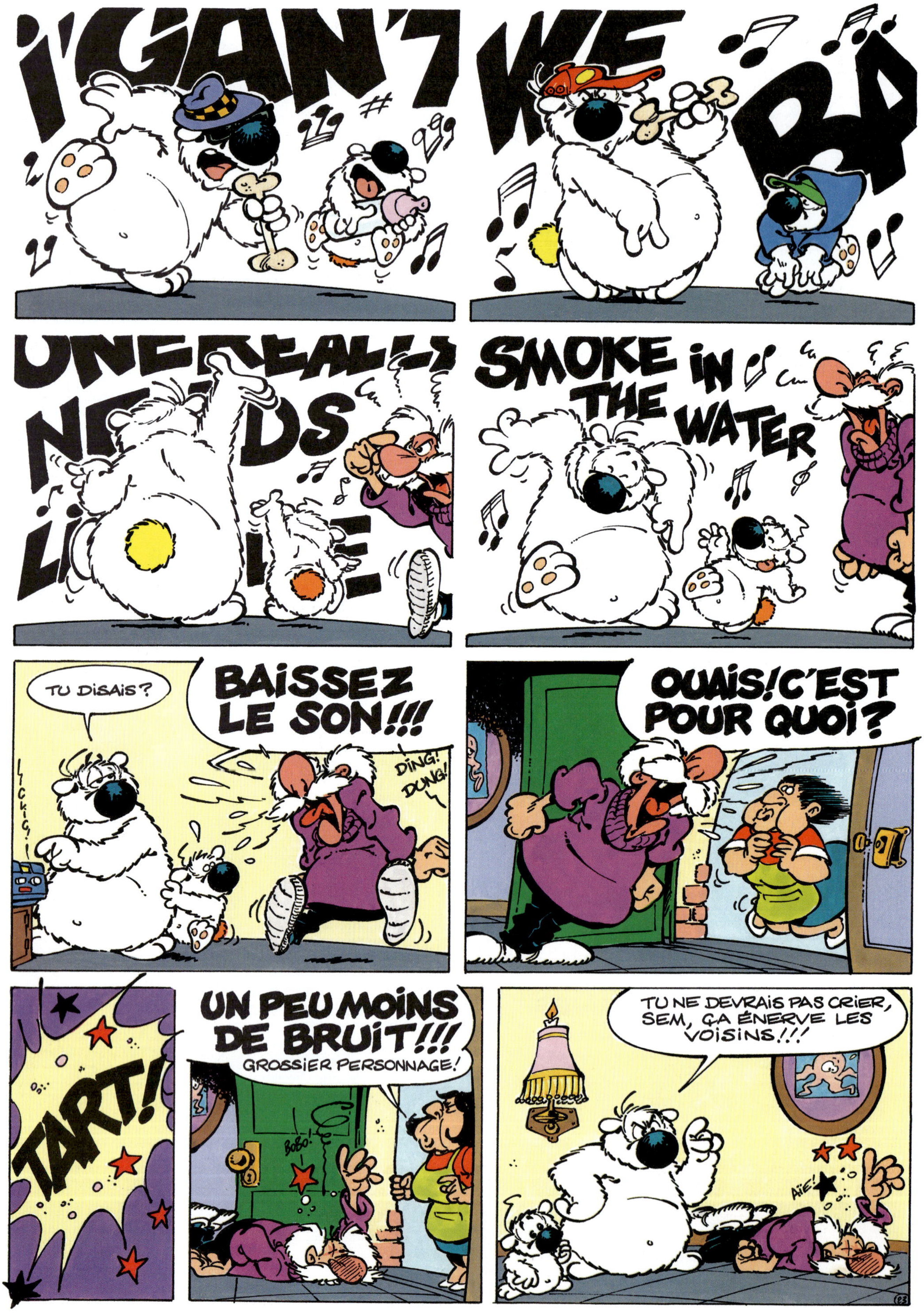

FAITES VOS JEUX, RIEN NE VA PLUS

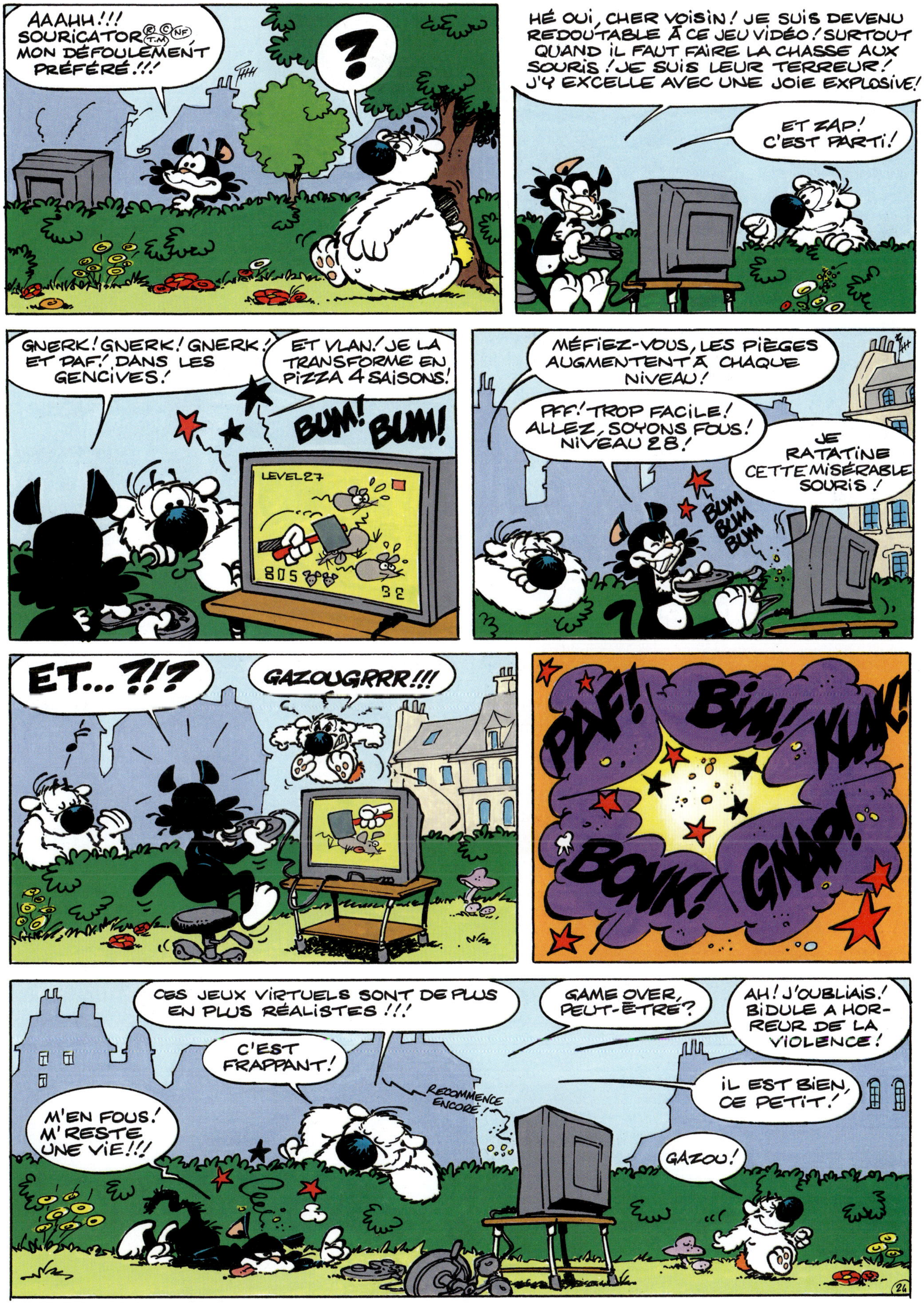

LOTO SATISFACTION

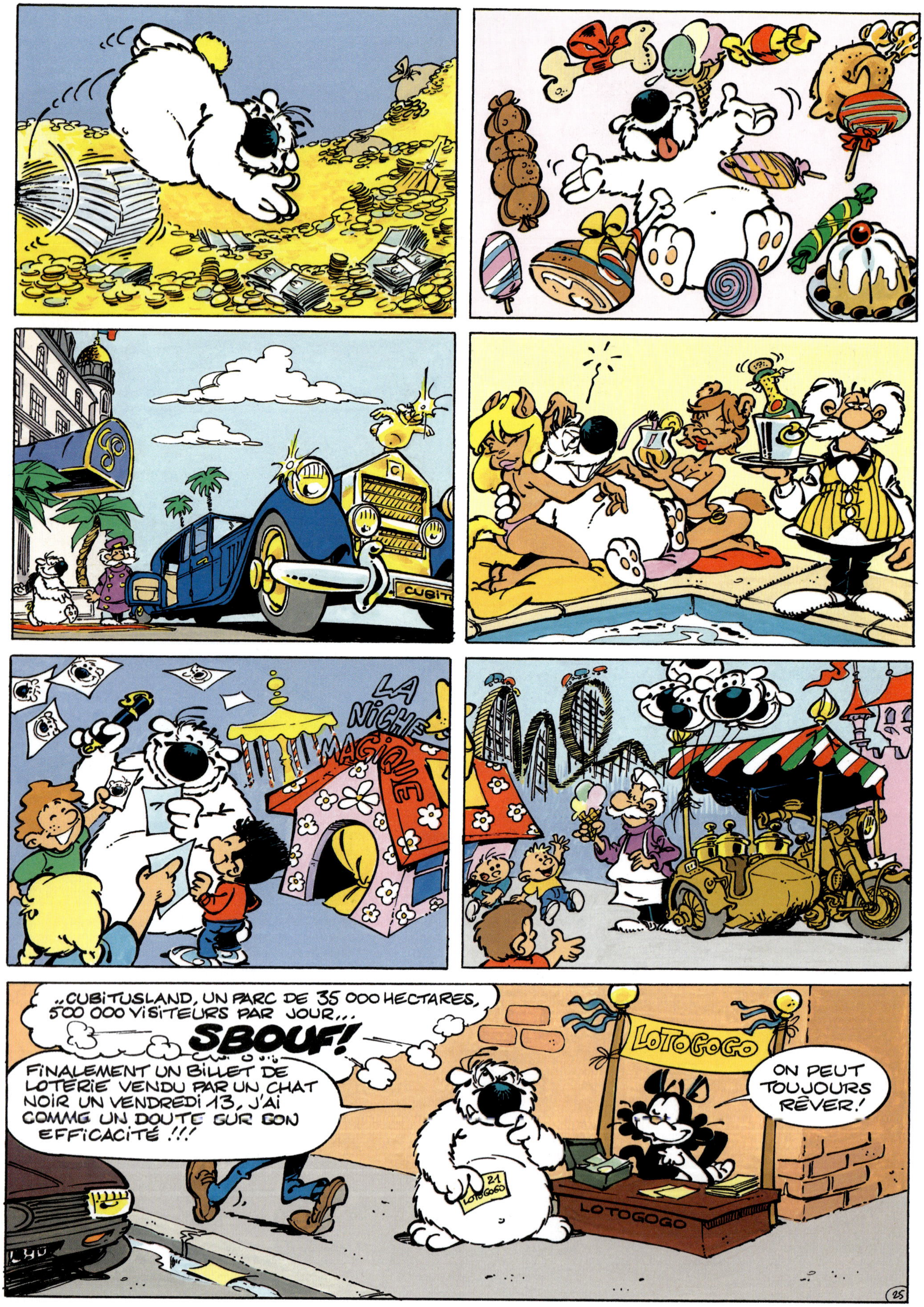

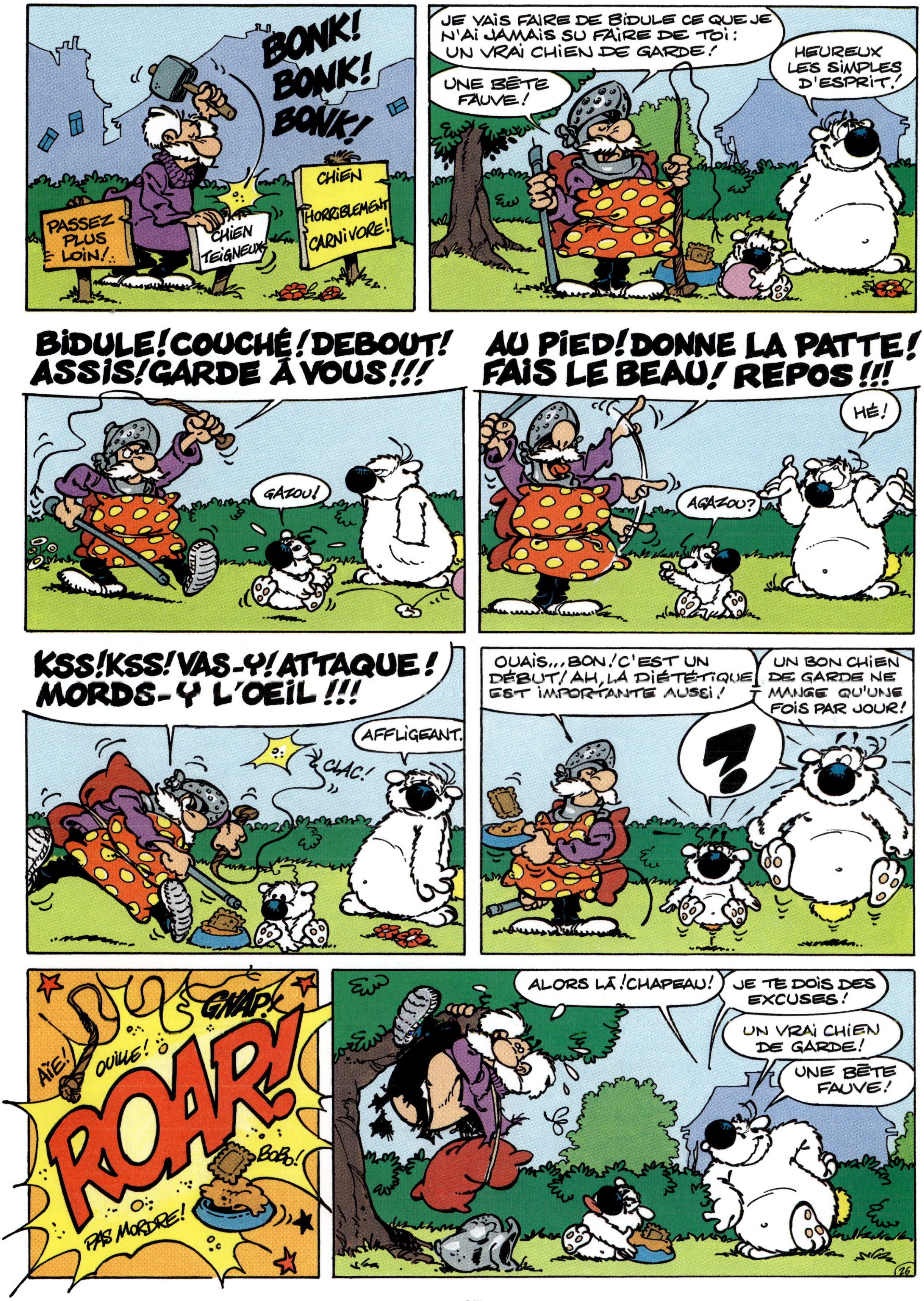
BONK! BONK! BONK!
PASSEZ PLUS LOIN!..
CHIEN TEIGNEUX
CHIEN HORRIBLEMENT CARNIVORE!
JE VAIS FAIRE DE BIDULE CE QUE JE N'AI JAMAIS SU FAIRE DE TOI : UN VRAI CHIEN DE GARDE!
UNE BÊTE FAUVE!
HEUREUX LES SIMPLES D'ESPRIT!
BIDULE! COUCHÉ! DEBOUT! ASSIS! GARDE À VOUS!!!
GAZOU!
AU PIED! DONNE LA PATTE! FAIS LE BEAU! REPOS!!!
HÉ!
AGAZOU?
KSS! KSS! VAS-Y! ATTAQUE! MORDS-Y L'OEIL!!!
AFFLIGEANT.
CLAC!
OUAIS... BON! C'EST UN DÉBUT! AH, LA DIÉTÉTIQUE EST IMPORTANTE AUSSI!
UN BON CHIEN DE GARDE NE MANGE QU'UNE FOIS PAR JOUR!
?
ROAR!
GNAP!
AÏE!
OUILLE!
BOBO!
PAS MORDRE!
ALORS LÀ! CHAPEAU!
JE TE DOIS DES EXCUSES!
UN VRAI CHIEN DE GARDE!
UNE BÊTE FAUVE!
26

L'EMBARRAS DU FROID

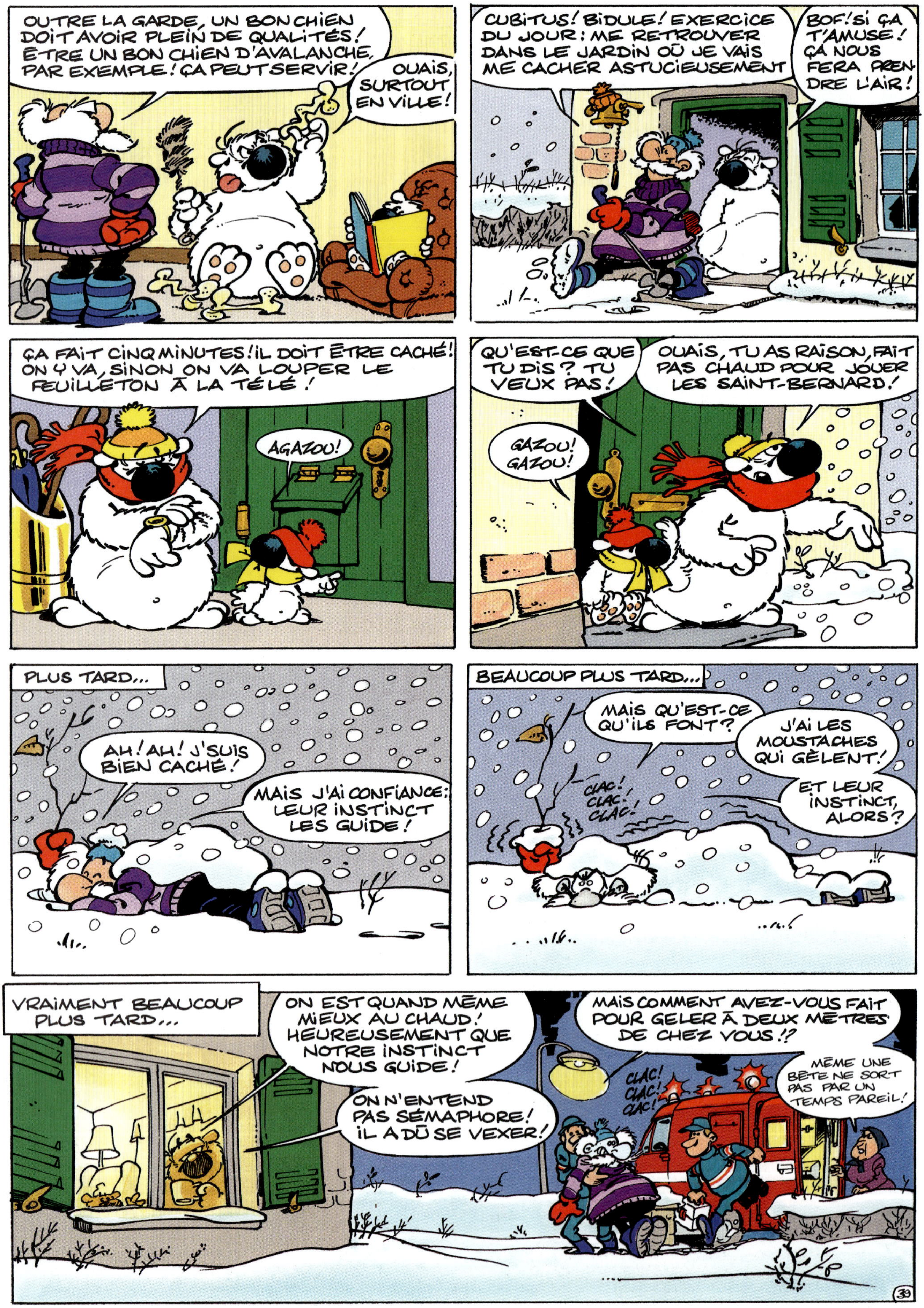

QUE SERAIS-JE SANS TOIT ?

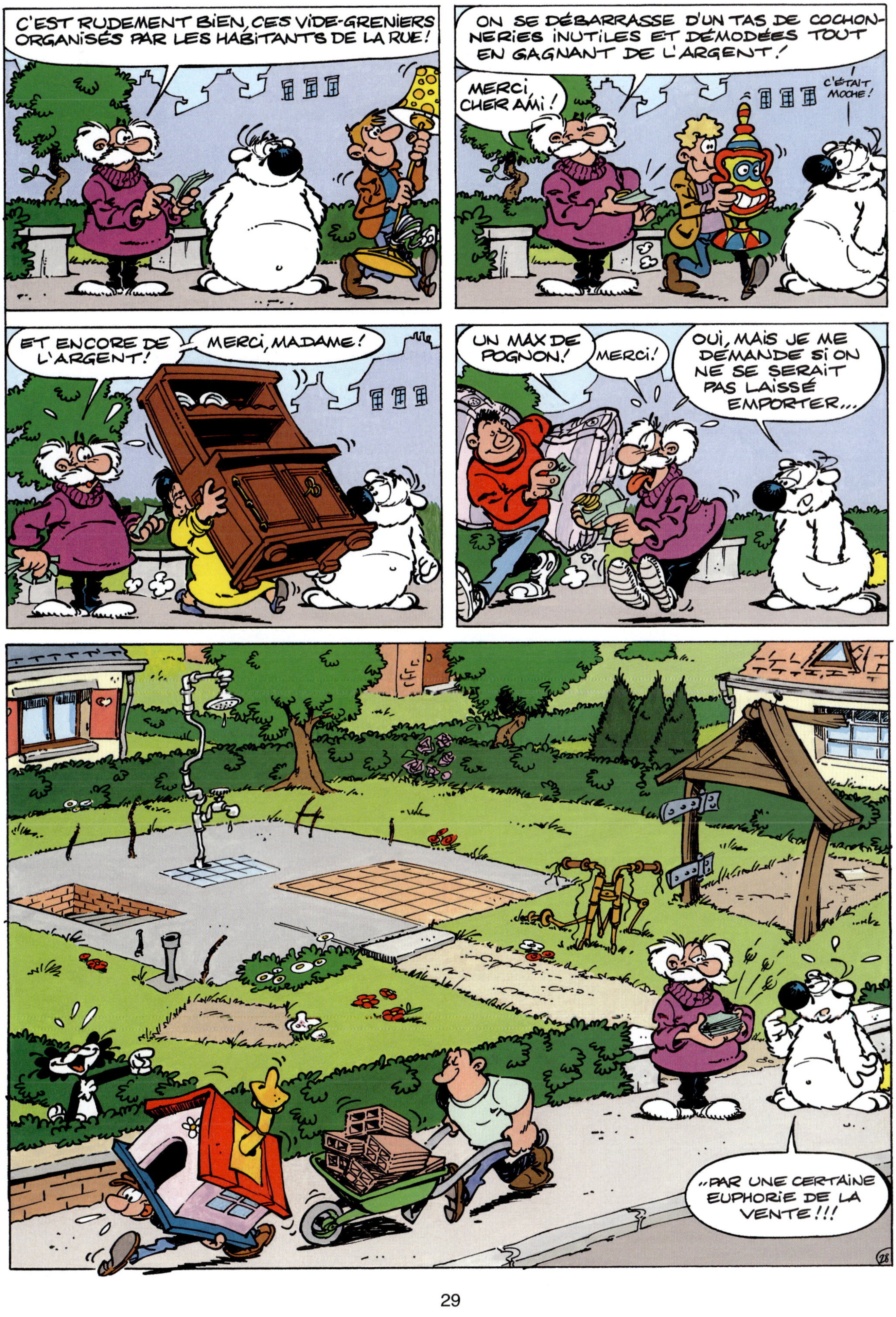

UN NOËL PAS COMME LES AUTRES

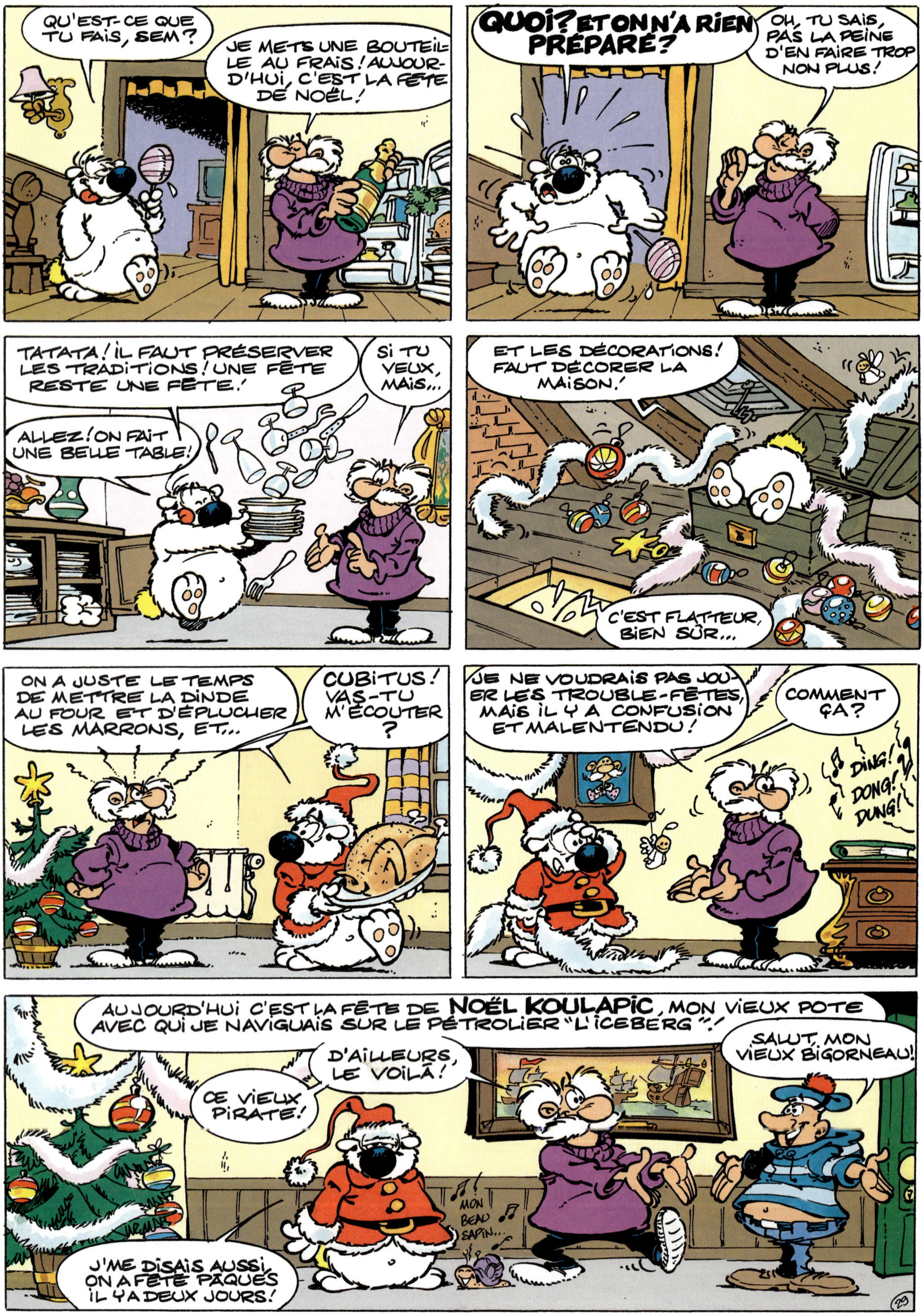

C'EST LE GROS QU'A LE SON

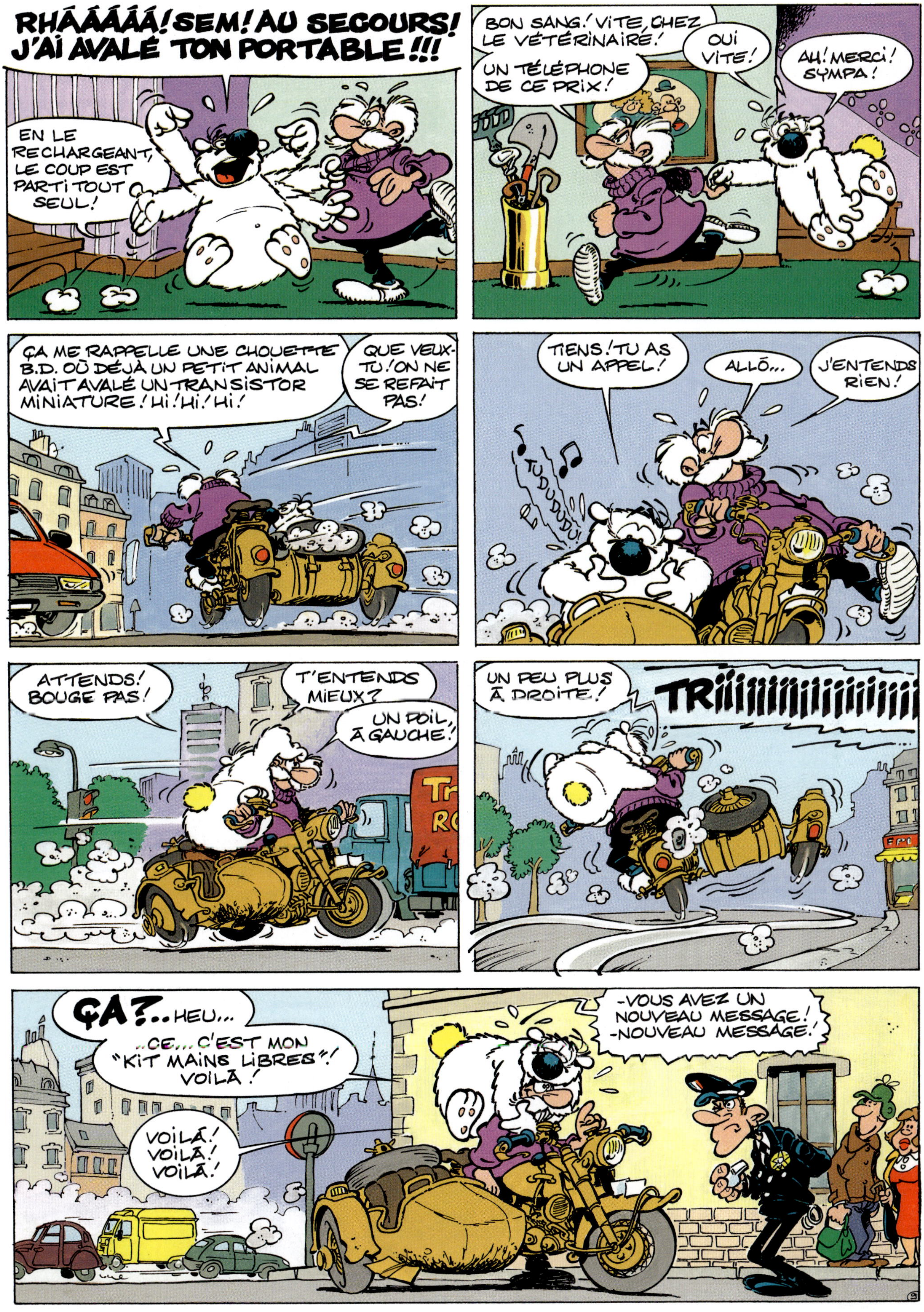

PILOTE DÉCHET

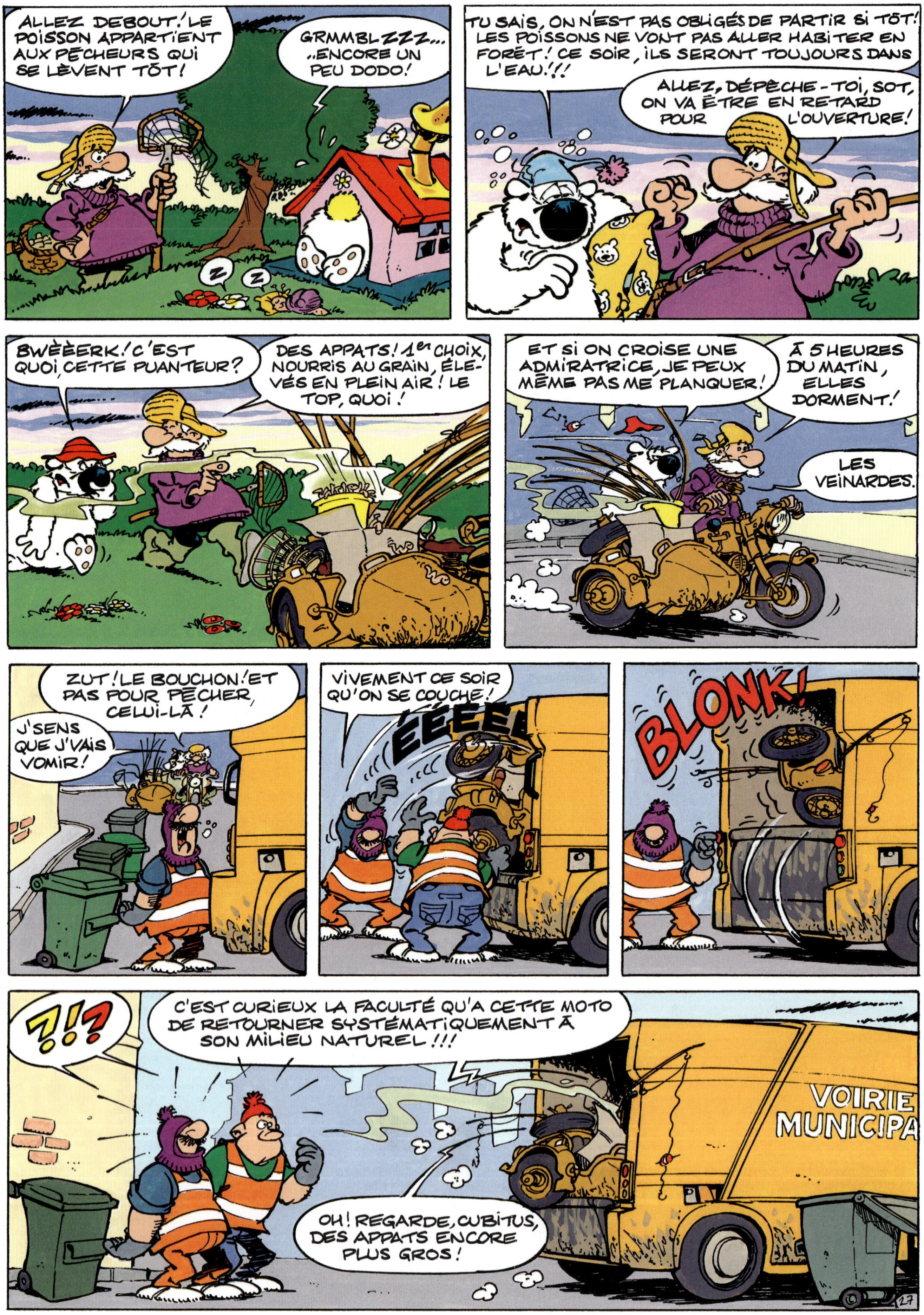

JE GROSSIS À VUE D'OEIL

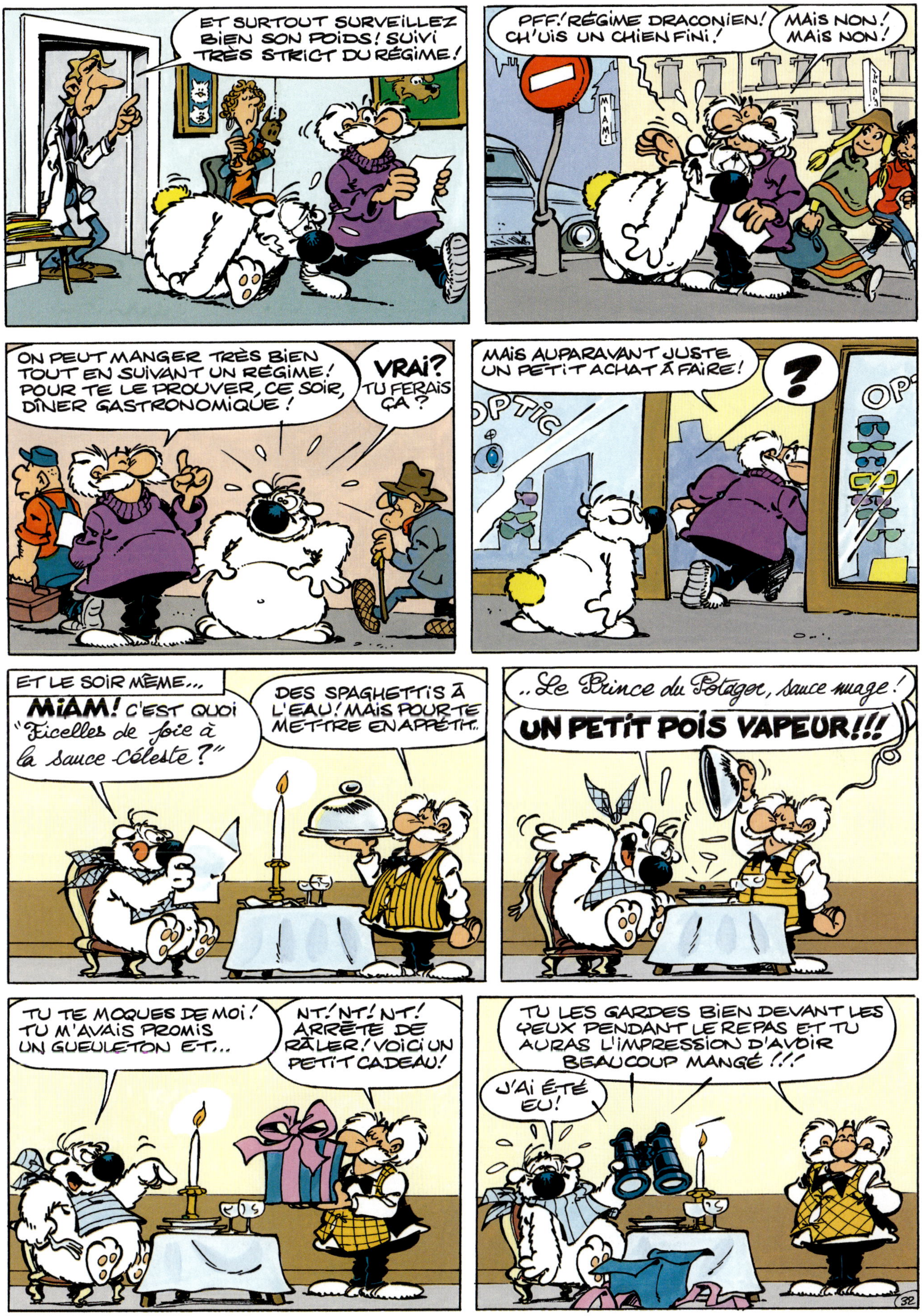

DE QUI SE MOQUETTE-T-ON ?

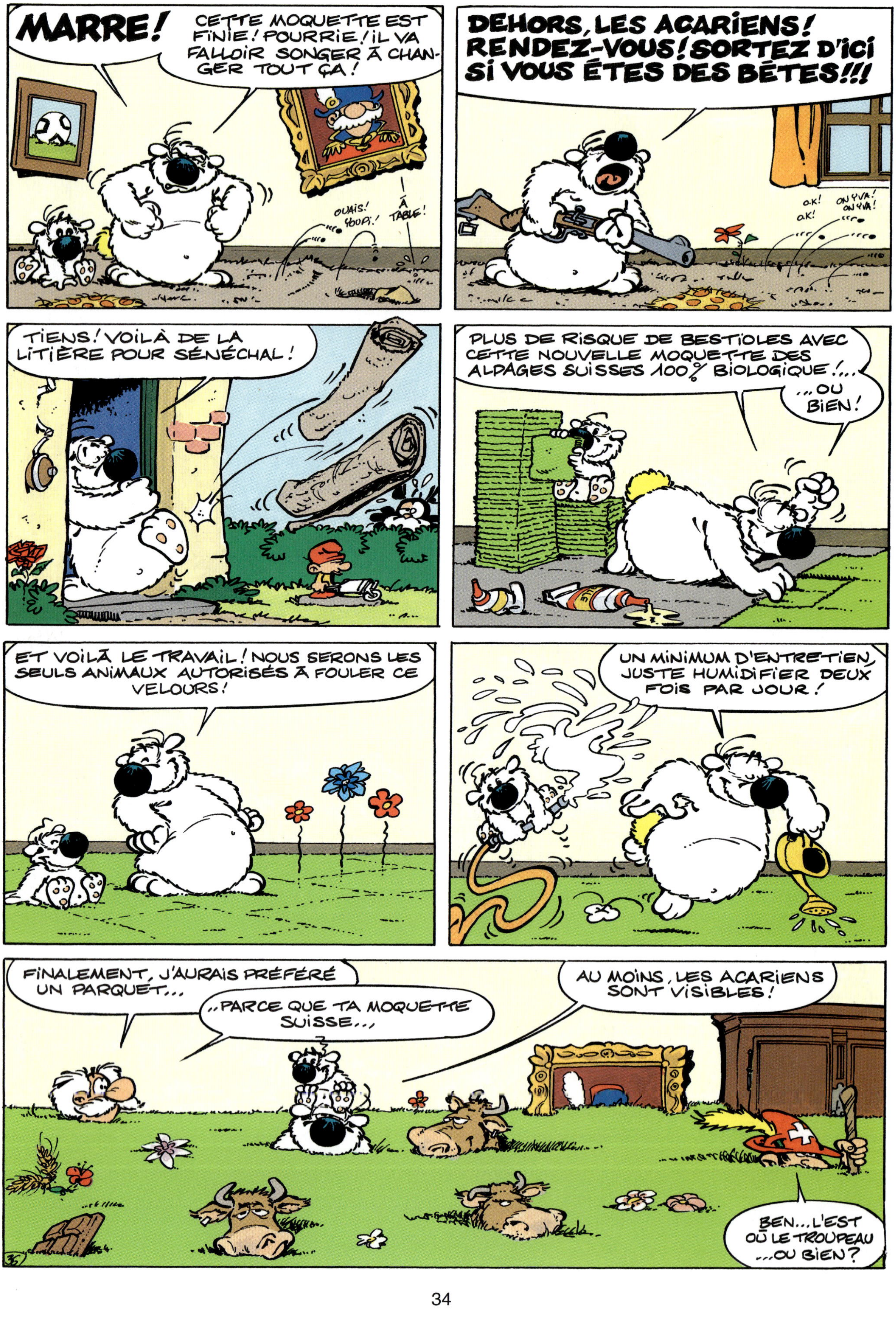

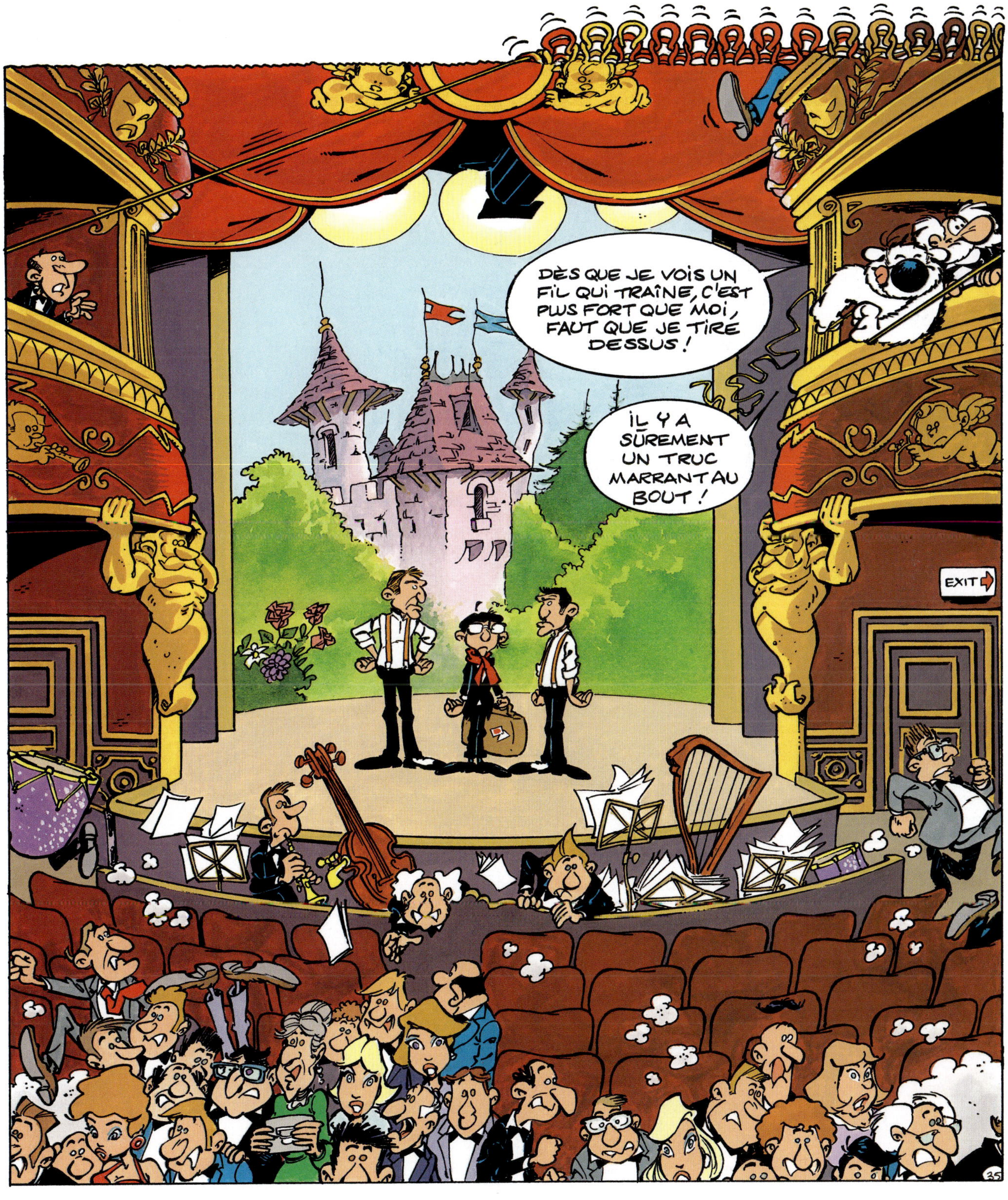
DÈS QUE JE VOIS UN FIL QUI TRAÎNE, C'EST PLUS FORT QUE MOI, FAUT QUE JE TIRE DESSUS !
IL Y A SÛREMENT UN TRUC MARRANT AU BOUT !
EXIT

FAITES PASSER LE MESSAGE

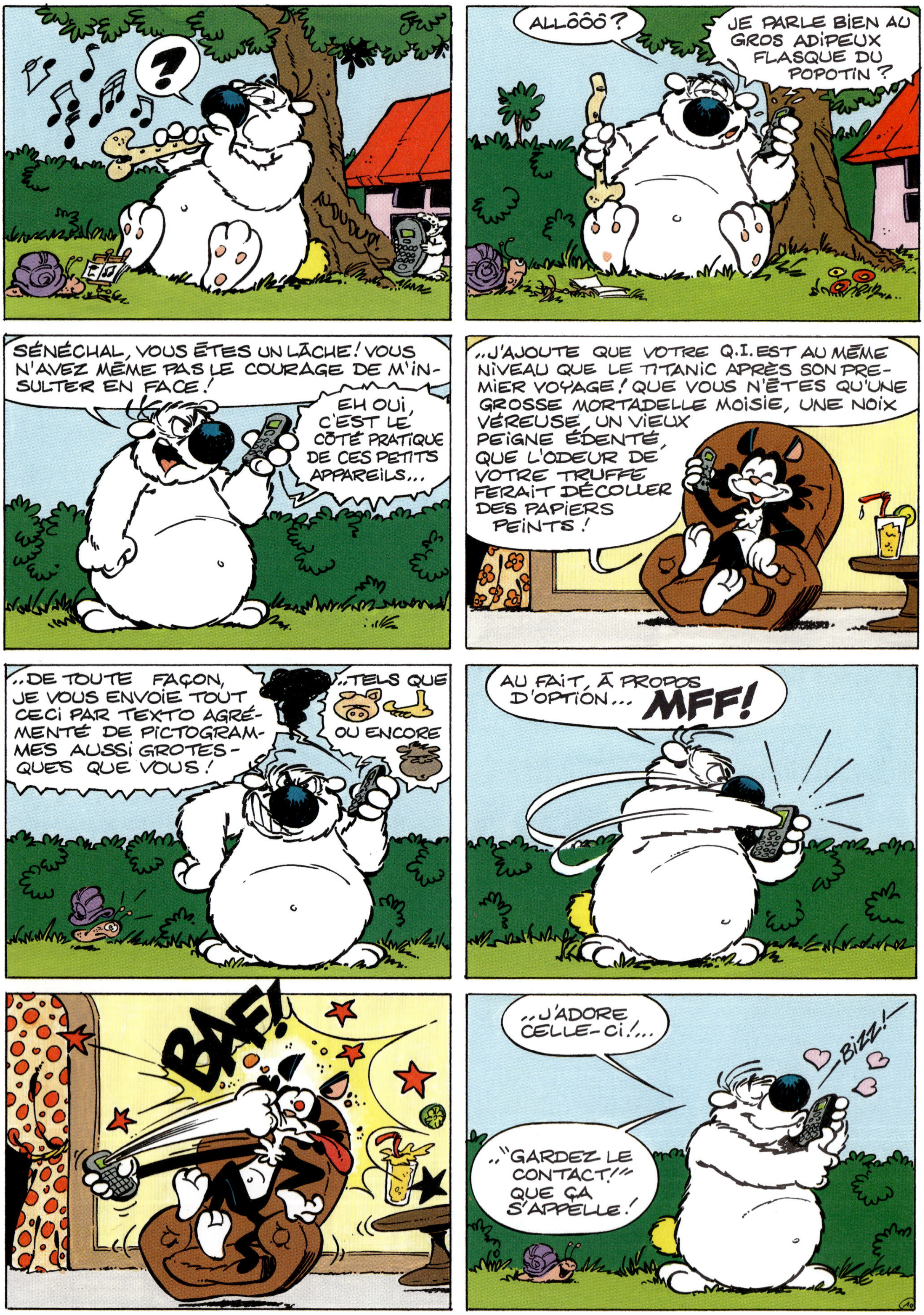

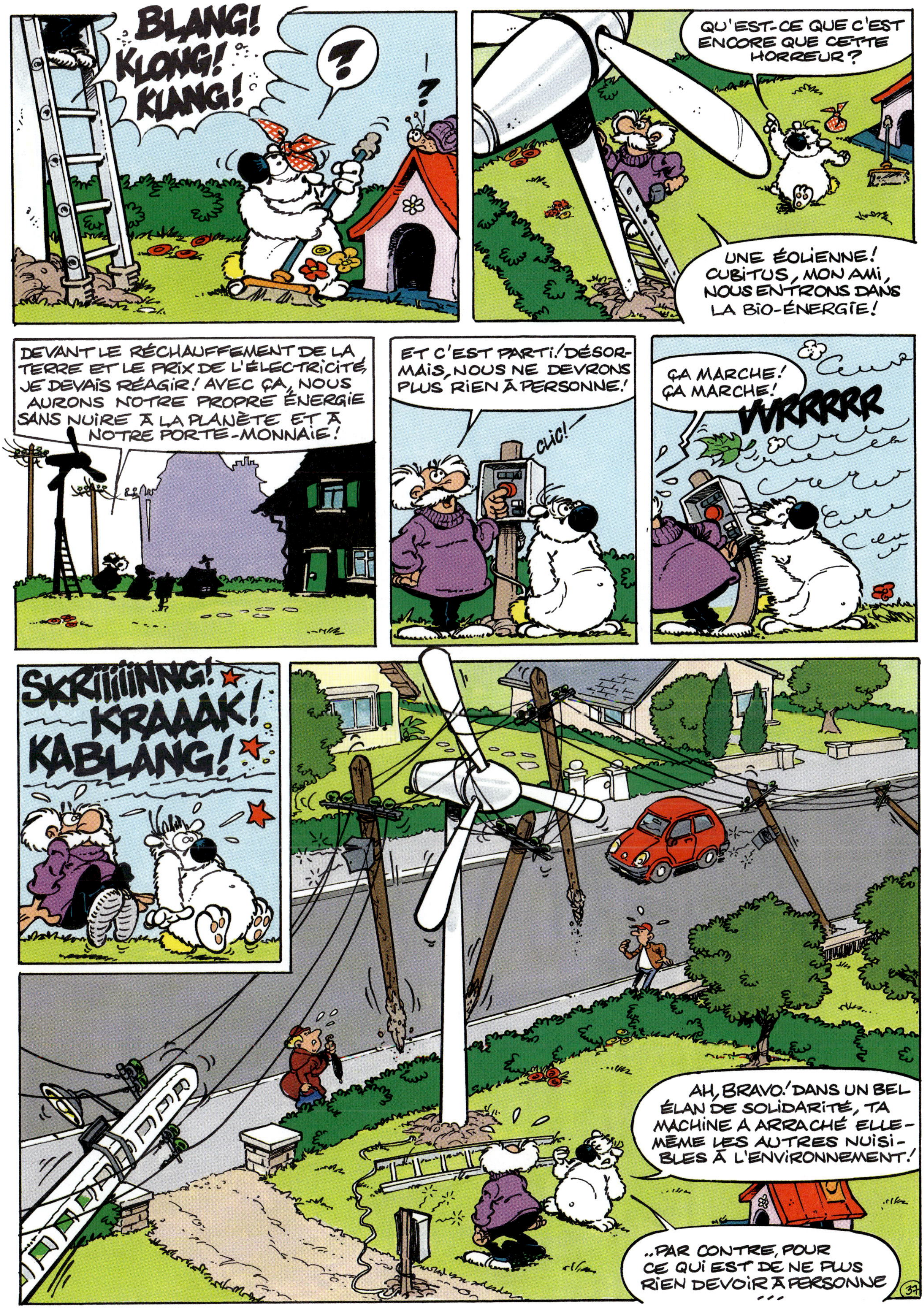
BLANG! KLONG! KLANG!
?
?
QU'EST-CE QUE C'EST ENCORE QUE CETTE HORREUR ?
UNE ÉOLIENNE! CUBITUS, MON AMI, NOUS ENTRONS DANS LA BIO-ÉNERGIE!
DEVANT LE RÉCHAUFFEMENT DE LA TERRE ET LE PRIX DE L'ÉLECTRICITÉ, JE DEVAIS RÉAGIR! AVEC ÇA, NOUS AURONS NOTRE PROPRE ÉNERGIE SANS NUIRE À LA PLANÈTE ET À NOTRE PORTE-MONNAIE!
ET C'EST PARTI! DÉSORMAIS, NOUS NE DEVRONS PLUS RIEN À PERSONNE!
CLIC!
ÇA MARCHE! ÇA MARCHE!
VVRRRRR
SKRIIIIINNG! KRAAAK! KABLANG!
AH, BRAVO! DANS UN BEL ÉLAN DE SOLIDARITÉ, TA MACHINE A ARRACHÉ ELLE-MÊME LES AUTRES NUISIBLES À L'ENVIRONNEMENT!
..PAR CONTRE, POUR CE QUI EST DE NE PLUS RIEN DEVOIR À PERSONNE ...
37

DIRECTION ASSISTÉE

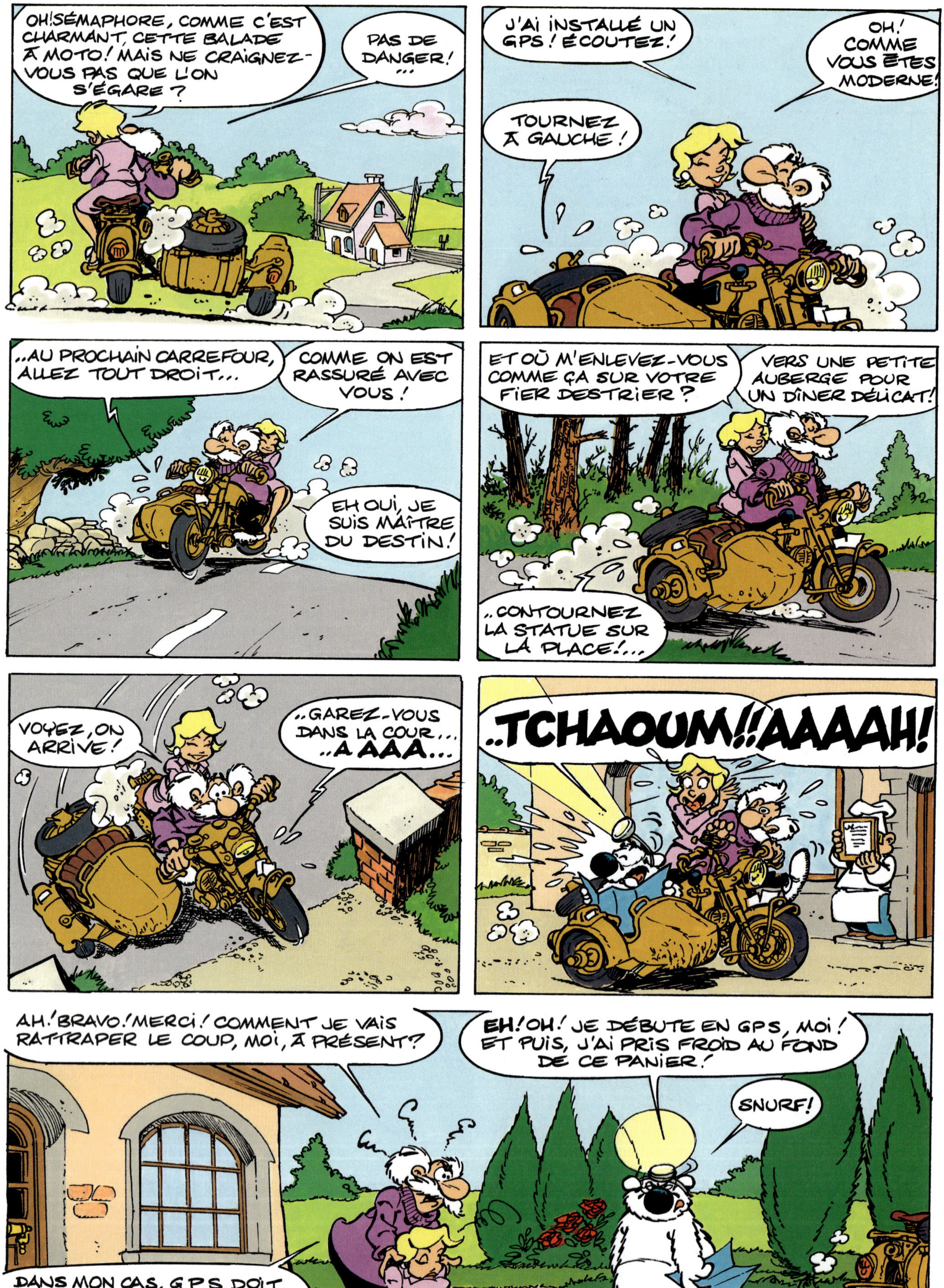

SI ON SE METTAIT AU COURANT

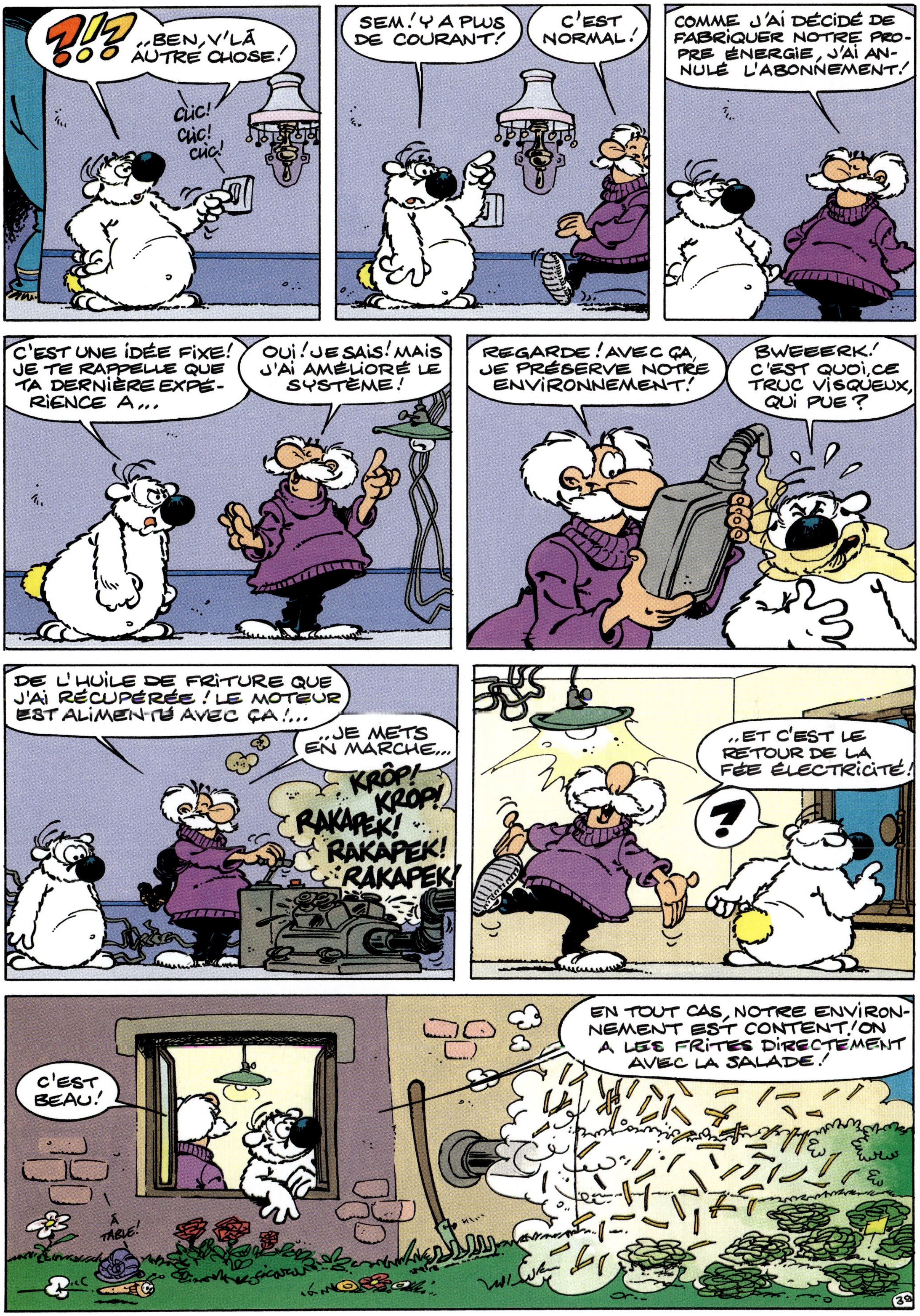

YOUPI, C'EST LA FÊTE !

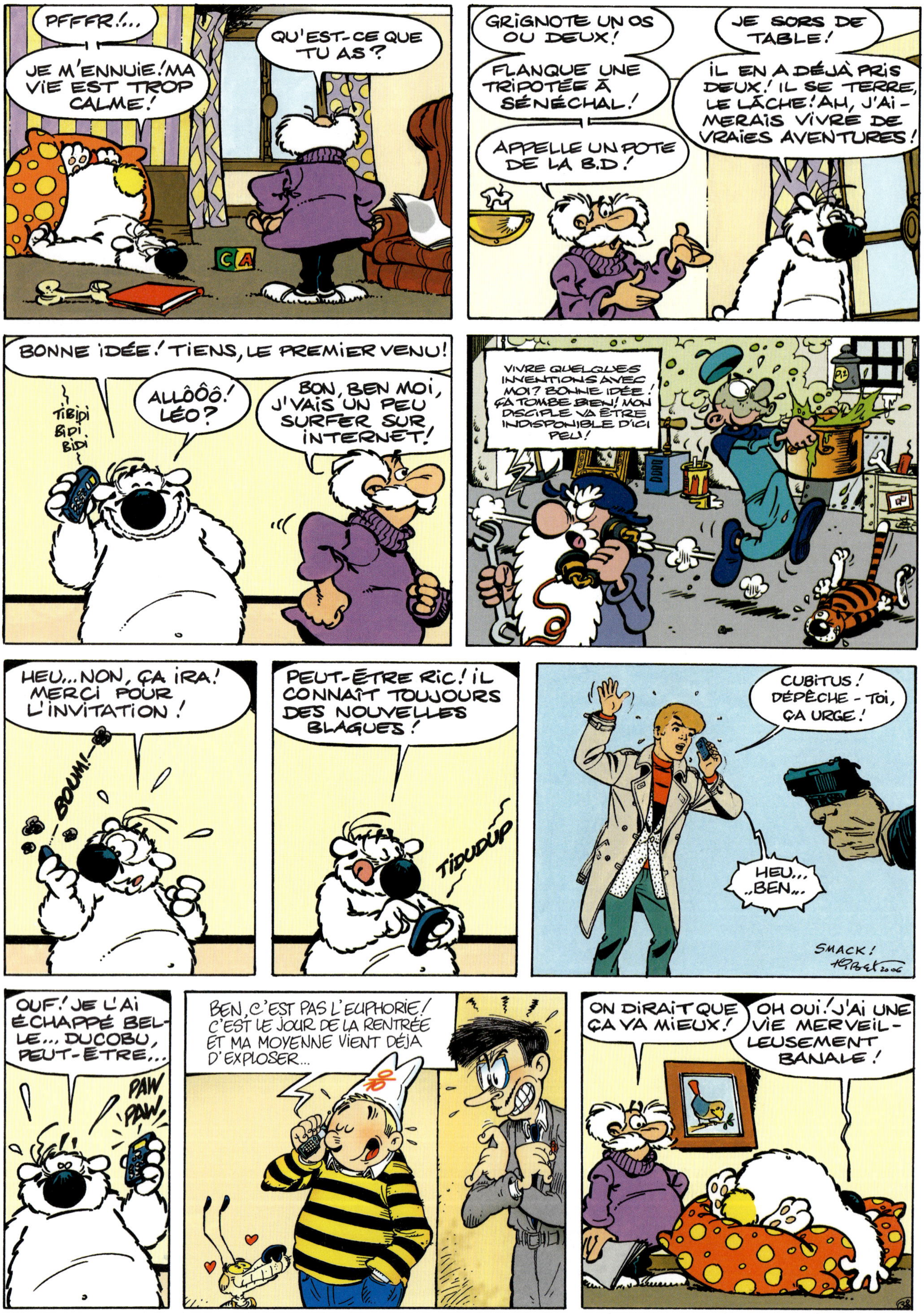

CHASSE GARDÉE

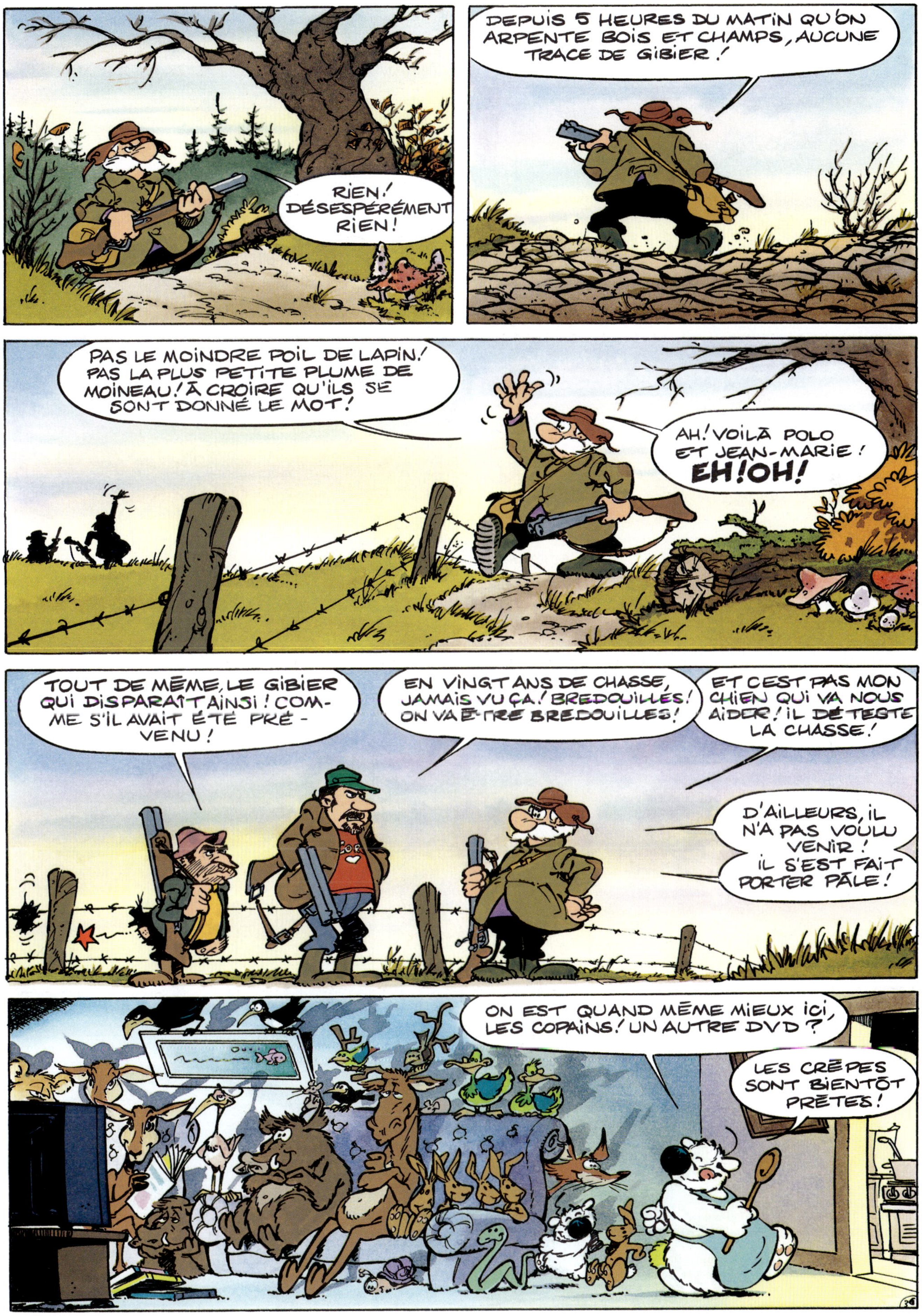

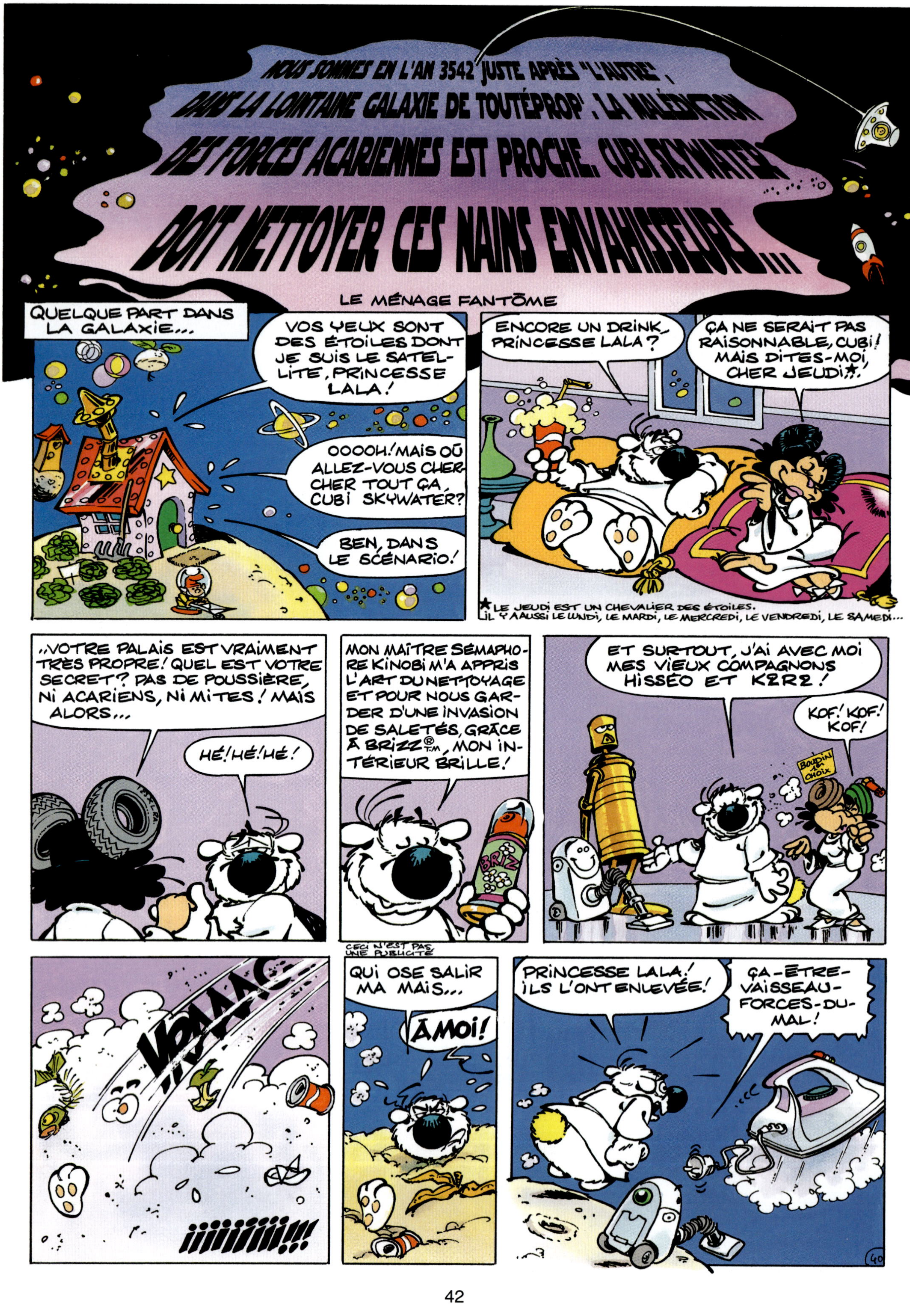
NOUS SOMMES EN L'AN 3542 JUSTE APRÈS "L'AUTRE", DANS LA LOINTAINE GALAXIE DE TOUTÉPROP'. LA MALÉDICTION DES FORCES ACARIENNES EST PROCHE. CUBI SKYWATER DOIT NETTOYER CES NAINS ENVAHISSEURS...!!
LE MÉNAGE FANTÔME
QUELQUE PART DANS LA GALAXIE...
VOS YEUX SONT DES ÉTOILES DONT JE SUIS LE SATELLITE, PRINCESSE LALA!
OOOOH! MAIS OÙ ALLEZ-VOUS CHERCHER TOUT ÇA, CUBI SKYWATER?
BEN, DANS LE SCÉNARIO!
ENCORE UN DRINK, PRINCESSE LALA?
ÇA NE SERAIT PAS RAISONNABLE, CUBI! MAIS DITES-MOI, CHER JEUDI*!
* LE JEUDI EST UN CHEVALIER DES ÉTOILES. IL Y A AUSSI LE LUNDI, LE MARDI, LE MERCREDI, LE VENDREDI, LE SAMEDI...
...VOTRE PALAIS EST VRAIMENT TRÈS PROPRE! QUEL EST VOTRE SECRET? PAS DE POUSSIÈRE, NI ACARIENS, NI MITES! MAIS ALORS...
HÉ! HÉ! HÉ!
MON MAÎTRE SÉMAPHORE KINOBI M'A APPRIS L'ART DU NETTOYAGE ET POUR NOUS GARDER D'UNE INVASION DE SALETÉS, GRÂCE À BRIZZ® T.M., MON INTÉRIEUR BRILLE!
BRIZ
CECI N'EST PAS UNE PUBLICITÉ
ET SURTOUT, J'AI AVEC MOI MES VIEUX COMPAGNONS HISSÉO ET K2R2!
KOF! KOF! KOF!
BOUDIN 1er CHOIX
VRAAAC
¡¡¡¡¡¡¡¡¡¡¡!!!
QUI OSE SALIR MA MAIS...
À MOI!
PRINCESSE LALA! ILS L'ONT ENLEVÉE!
ÇA-ÊTRE-VAISSEAU-FORCES-DU-MAL!
40

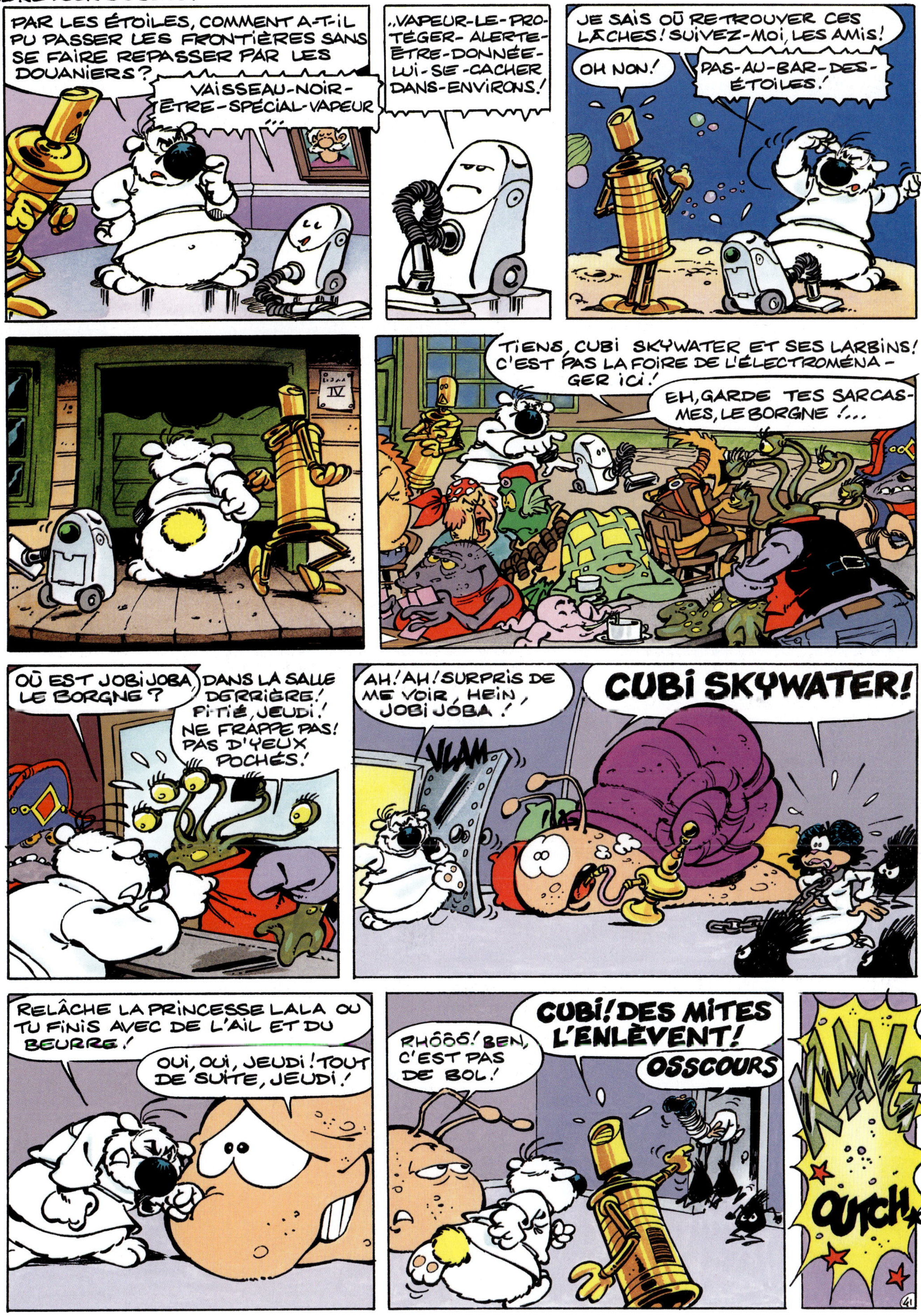
PAR LES ÉTOILES, COMMENT A-T-IL PU PASSER LES FRONTIÈRES SANS SE FAIRE REPASSER PAR LES DOUANIERS ?
VAISSEAU-NOIR-ÊTRE-SPÉCIAL-VAPEUR ...
..VAPEUR-LE-PROTÉGER-ALERTE-ÊTRE-DONNÉE-LUI-SE-CACHER DANS-ENVIRONS !
JE SAIS OÙ RETROUVER CES LÂCHES ! SUIVEZ-MOI, LES AMIS !
OH NON !
PAS-AU-BAR-DES-ÉTOILES !
IV
TIENS, CUBI SKYWATER ET SES LARBINS ! C'EST PAS LA FOIRE DE L'ÉLECTROMÉNAGER ICI !
EH, GARDE TES SARCASMES, LE BORGNE !...
OÙ EST JOBI JOBA LE BORGNE ?
DANS LA SALLE DERRIÈRE ! PITIÉ, JEUDI ! NE FRAPPE PAS ! PAS D'YEUX POCHÉS !
AH ! AH ! SURPRIS DE ME VOIR, HEIN, JOBI JOBA !
CUBI SKYWATER !
VLAM
RELÂCHE LA PRINCESSE LALA OU TU FINIS AVEC DE L'AIL ET DU BEURRE !
OUI, OUI, JEUDI ! TOUT DE SUITE, JEUDI !
RHÔÔÔ ! BEN, C'EST PAS DE BOL !
CUBI ! DES MITES L'ENLÈVENT !
OSSCOURS
KLANG
OUTCH
41

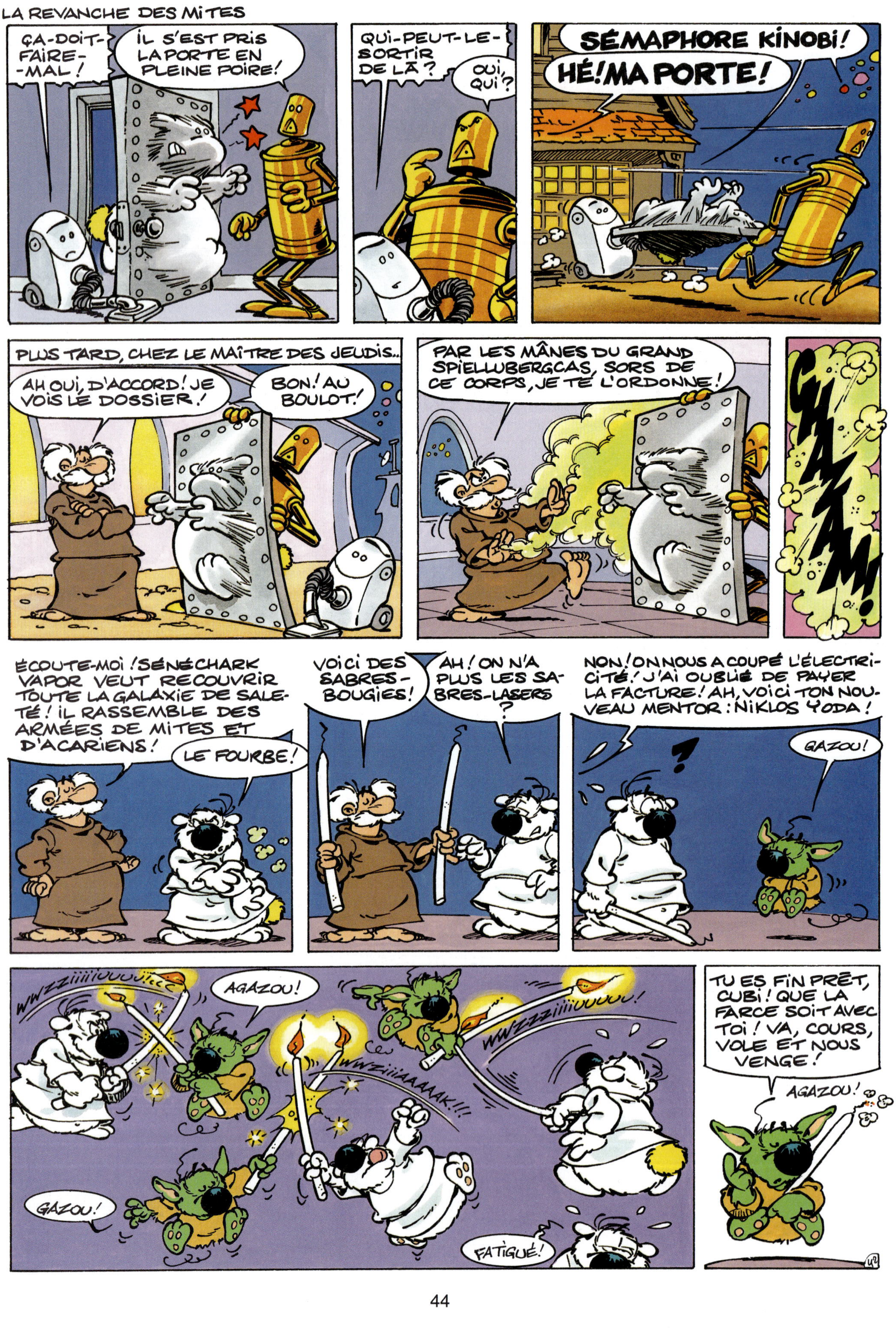

LA REVANCHE DES MITES
ÇA-DOIT-FAIRE--MAL !
IL S'EST PRIS LA PORTE EN PLEINE POIRE !
QUI-PEUT-LE-SORTIR DE LÀ ?
OUI, QUI ?
SÉMAPHORE KINOBI !
HÉ! MA PORTE !
PLUS TARD, CHEZ LE MAÎTRE DES JEUDIS...
AH OUI, D'ACCORD ! JE VOIS LE DOSSIER !
BON ! AU BOULOT !
PAR LES MÂNES DU GRAND SPIELLUBERGCAS, SORS DE CE CORPS, JE TE L'ORDONNE !
GHLAAM !
ÉCOUTE-MOI ! SÉNÉCHARK VAPOR VEUT RECOUVRIR TOUTE LA GALAXIE DE SALETÉ ! IL RASSEMBLE DES ARMÉES DE MITES ET D'ACARIENS !
LE FOURBE !
VOICI DES SABRES-BOUGIES !
AH ! ON N'A PLUS LES SABRES-LASERS ?
NON ! ON NOUS A COUPÉ L'ÉLECTRICITÉ ! J'AI OUBLIÉ DE PAYER LA FACTURE ! AH, VOICI TON NOUVEAU MENTOR : NIKLOS YODA !
GAZOU !
WWZZIIIIUUUII...
AGAZOU !
WWZZZIIIIUUUU !
WWZIIIAAAAAK !!!
GAZOU !
FATIGUÉ !
TU ES FIN PRÊT, CUBI ! QUE LA FARCE SOIT AVEC TOI ! VA, COURS, VOLE ET NOUS VENGE !
AGAZOU !

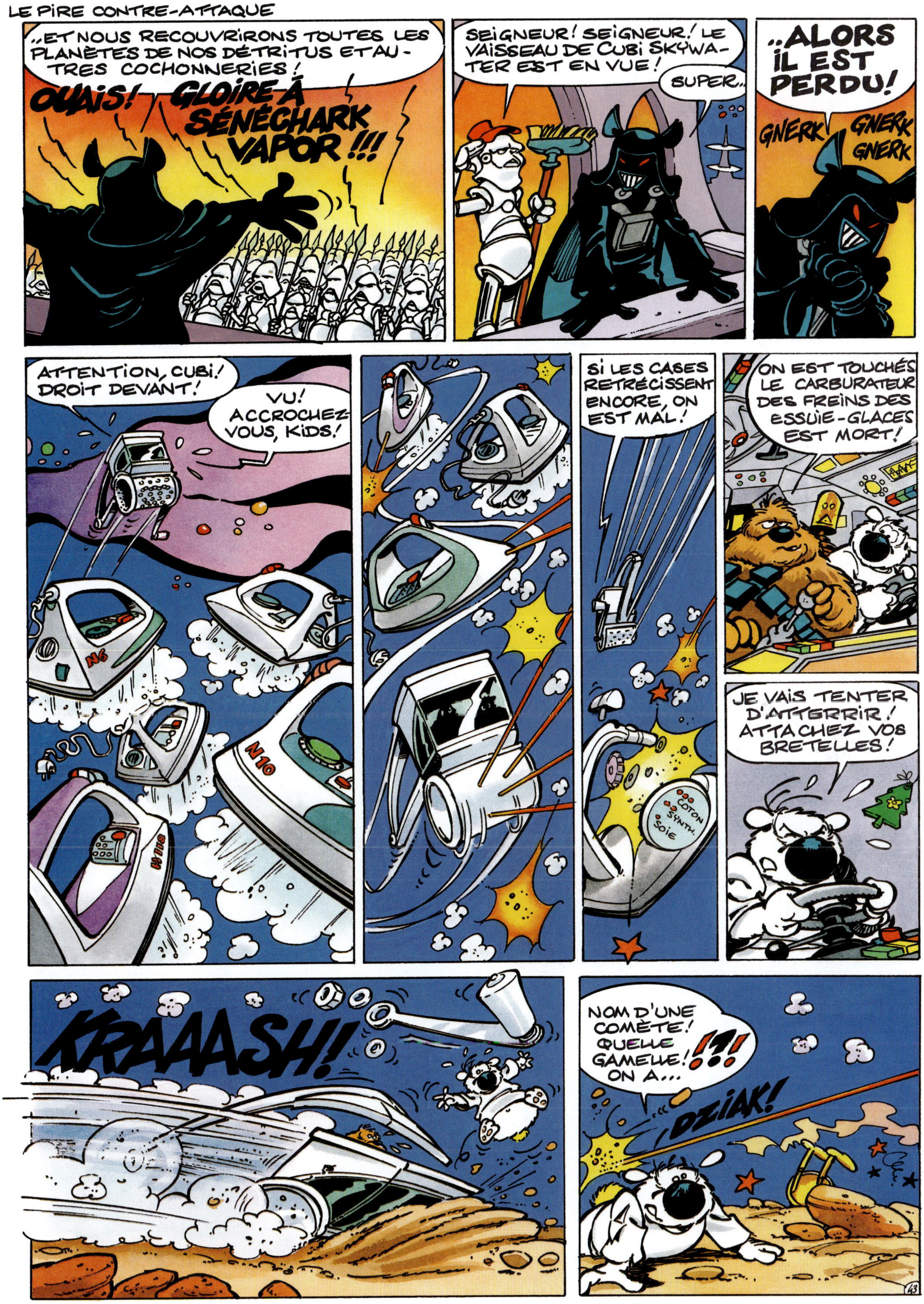
..ET NOUS RECOUVRIRONS TOUTES LES PLANÈTES DE NOS DÉTRITUS ET AUTRES COCHONNERIES !
OUAIS ! GLOIRE À SÉNÉCHARK VAPOR !!!
SEIGNEUR ! SEIGNEUR ! LE VAISSEAU DE CUBI SKYWATER EST EN VUE !
SUPER..
..ALORS IL EST PERDU !
GNERK GNERK GNERK
ATTENTION, CUBI ! DROIT DEVANT !
VU ! ACCROCHEZ-VOUS, KIDS !
N6
N10
SI LES CASES RETRÉCISSENT ENCORE, ON EST MAL !
COTON
SYNTH.
SOIE
ON EST TOUCHÉS ! LE CARBURATEUR DES FREINS DES ESSUIE-GLACES EST MORT !
JE VAIS TENTER D'ATTERRIR ! ATTACHEZ VOS BRETELLES !
KRAAASH !
NOM D'UNE COMÈTE ! QUELLE GAMELLE ! ON A...
!?!
DZIAK !
43

L'ATTAQUE DES CLOWNS

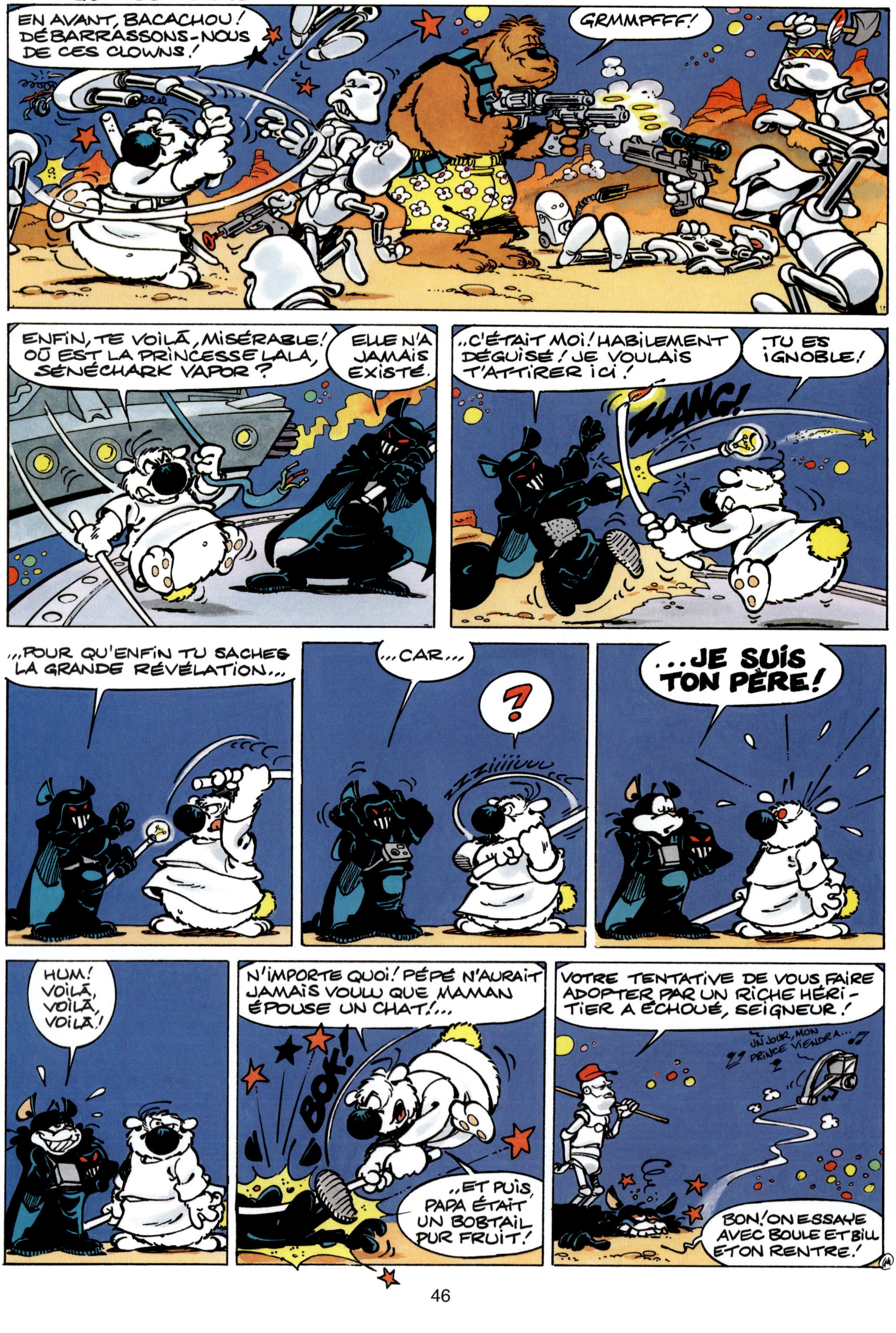